# An Edition of

# Luke Shepherd's Satires

# Medieval and Renaissance

# Texts and Studies

## Volume 240

Renaissance English Text Society

Seventh Series
Volume XXVI (for 2001)

# An Edition of

# Luke Shepherd's Satires

*by*

Janice Devereux

Arizona Center for Medieval and Renaissance Studies
*in conjunction with*
Renaissance English Text Society
Tempe, Arizona
2001

© Copyright 2001
Arizona Board of Regents for Arizona State University


**Library of Congress Cataloging-in-Publication Data**

Shepherd, Luke, fl. 1548.
    [Satires]
    An edition of Luke Shepherd's satires / [edited] by Janice Devereux.
      p. cm. — (Medieval and Renaissance texts and studies ; v. 240) (Renaissance
English Text Society ; 7th ser., v. 26)
    Includes bibliographical references (p. ).
    ISBN 0-86698-282-5 (alk. paper)
      1. Catholic Church—Poetry. 2. Religious satire, English. 3. Verse satire, English.
I. Devereux, Janice, 1946– II. Title. III. Medieval & Renaissance Texts & Studies
(Series) ; v. 240. IV. Renaissance English Text Society (Series) ; vol. 26.

PR2339.S52 S25 2001
821'.2—dc21

2001030817

This book is made to last.
It is set in Garamond,
smythe-sewn and printed on acid-free paper
to library specifications.


Printed in the United States of America

# Dedication

This edition is dedicated with special thanks to

SEYMOUR BAKER HOUSE

whose joyous scholarship is an inspiration and
whose encouragement, enthusiasm, guidance, and support
have been unfailing throughout this entire project.

# Contents

# INTRODUCTION

## Biography

Regrettably, we know very few biographical details about Luke Shepherd. He was a physician who lived in a reformist area of London in the 1540s. Strongly anti-Catholic in his religious beliefs, Shepherd voiced his criticism of the Roman Church in short, popular verse satires, most of which were printed by the Protestant printer, John Day. Apart from these general facts, we know little else about his life. His contemporary, John Bale, lists him under the Latinized version of his name, Lucas Opilio, details his birthplace as Colchester, in Essex, and describes him thus: "*poeta ualde facetus erat, qui in poematibus ac rhythmis Skeltono non inferior, in patrio sermone eleganter edidit, honestis iocis ac salibus plenos.*"[1] While no proof exists that Lucas Opilio and Luke Shepherd are one and the same person, the working assumption of this edition is that the person Bale describes is the same person whom Edward Underhill, a gentleman pensioner at the courts of Henry VIII, Mary I, and Elizabeth I, refers to as: "mr. Luke, my very frende, off Colemane strete visissyone [physician], who . . . wroote many proper bokes agaynst the papistes, for the wyche he was impresoned in the Flete; specially a boke called *John Boone and Mast Parsone* who resoned together off the naturalle presense in the sakermentt; wiche boke he wroote in the tyme off kynge Edwarde, wherewithe the papist[s] weare soore greved, specyally syr John Gresam, then beynge mayour."[2]

---

[1] John Bale, *Scriptorum Illustrium Maioris Brytanniae Catalogus*, 2 vols. (Basle: John Oporinus, 1557, 1559; Farnborough: Gregg International Publishers, 1971), 2: 109. "A most elegant poet, not at all inferior to Skelton in respect of his poems, especially in their rhythms. He published works full of suitable jests and exercises of wit in his native language." (Thanks to John Hale and Dorothy Knudson for this translation.)

[2] Edward Underhill, "Autobiographical Anecdotes," *Narratives of the Days of the Reformation, Chiefly from the Manuscripts of John Foxe the Martyrologist*, ed. John Gough Nichols (London, 1859), 171–172.

Because Underhill adds "John Daye dide pryntt the same boke,"[3] and because Bale also lists *Iohn Bon and Mast person* as Shepherd's work in his *Index*,[4] it seems certain that they are both referring to the same author.

Unfortunately, we know nothing else about Shepherd's life, and though bibliographers other than Bale, as well as later chroniclers, mention him and his work, he does not appear on any extant university roll or on any official list of physicians.[5] Raphael Holinshed refers to a "Lucas Shepherd borne in Colchester" and describes him as "an English poet" during Mary I's reign,[6] and Andrew Maunsell lists several of his works anonymously.[7] John Strype reprints Underhill's account of how the Lord Mayor of London, Sir John Gresham, sent for the printer of *Iohn Bon and Mast person* in order to ascertain and punish the writer of this satire, and how he relented from this course of action on learning that the poem was in circulation and much admired at the royal court. Strype records Shepherd's imprisonment, inferring that it occurred at the close of Henry VIII's reign but offers neither evidence nor details of this internment.[8] Thomas Warton later writes him off as "a petty pamphleteer in the cause of Calvinism" but also suggests that Bishop Tanner owned more than one prose work of Shepherd's.[9] Both Bale and Warton refer

---

[3] Underhill, "Anecdotes," 172.

[4] John Bale, *Index Britanniae Scriptorum*, ed. Reginald L. Poole and Mary Bateson (Oxford: Clarendon Press, 1902), 283.

[5] Arthur F. Kinney hypothesizes that Shepherd's name may be a pseudonym based on the name of the evangelist, Luke, and the image of Christ as the Good Shepherd. See John N. King, *English Reformation Literature: The Tudor Origins of the Protestant Tradition* (Princeton: Princeton University Press, 1982), 253 n. 49.

[6] Raphael Holinshed, *Chronicles of England, Scotland, and Ireland*, ed. Henry Ellis et al., 6 vols. (London: J. Johnson, F. C. and J. Rivington, T. Payne, et al., 1808), 4: 153.

[7] Andrew Maunsell, *The First Part of the Catalogue of English printed Bookes: Which concerneth such matters of Diuinitie, as haue bin either written in our owne Tongue, or translated out of anie other language: And haue bin published, to the glory of God, and edification of the Church of Christ in England* (London, 1595, STC 17669), pt. 1, passim.

[8] John Strype, *Ecclesiastical Memorials, Relating Chiefly to Religion, and the Reformation of It, and the Emergencies of the Church of England, under King Henry VIII. King Edward VI. and Queen Mary I*, 3 vols. (Oxford: Clarendon Press, 1822), 2: pt. 1, 181–182.

[9] Thomas Warton, *History of English Poetry*, 4 vols. (1774–90; New York: Johnson Reprint, 1968), 3: 316. Warton's remark is unsubstantiated. The entry on Shepherd (Lucas Opilio) in Thomas Tanner's *Bibliotheca Britannico-Hibernica*, ed. David Wilkins (London: Bowyer, 1748), 562, is a paraphrase of Bale and reads as follows: "Colcestriae in agro Essex.

to Shepherd's now lost translation of the Psalms,[10] and a later bibliographer, Joseph Ritson, adds that Shepherd: "wrote, in elegant Engleish, certain jocular and wity pamphlets, against the hateers [sic] of truth; versify'd certain psalms; and did many other little things, none of which are now to be met with."[11] Unfortunately, Ritson does not list his sources or give any other indication of what these "many other" works might be. It is quite possible that Shepherd was both a political and a popular writer, recruited to write anti-Catholic satires by a Protestant patron. However, no evidence of such patronage or of any other political connections has been found. Extensive research has not uncovered any new information about Shepherd's life or the circumstances of his death. Nor is there any evidence of his will having been proved.[12]

## Historical Background

Shepherd's works were probably printed during the first two years of Edward VI's reign, a time when the change in political power resulted in a huge upsurge in the number of religious and polemical works printed in London.[13] This literature affirmed the destruction of sacramentals, images, and chantries, but above all else it attacked and derided the Catholic Mass. In

---

natus; poëta valde facetus, in poëmatibus et rhythmis Skeltono non inferior. Scripsit Anglice *Adversus veritatis osores libellos aliquot.* Transtulit in metra Anglicana *Psalmos aliquot.* Claruit A. MDLIV." Shepherd's individual works are not listed in the bibliography. I am grateful to Shef Rogers for kindly providing this information.

[10] Bale, *Catalogus*, 2: 109; Warton, *History*, 3: 316.

[11] Joseph Ritson, *Bibliographia Poetica:A Catalogue of Engleish* [sic] *Poets, of the Twelfth, Thirteenth, Fourteenth, Fifteenth, and Sixteenth Centurys,* [sic] *with a Short Account of Their Works* (London: C. Roworth, 1802), 330–331.

[12] Searches of the Public Records Office, the Prerogative Court of Canterbury Wills, and the Essex County Council Archives have not revealed any evidence of Shepherd's birth, life, or death. The parish registers of the Archdeaconry of Colchester did not commence until 1538, and Shepherd's name does not appear in the Personal Name Indexes or in the Index of Essex Wills. Nor is his name recorded in the names of the men of Colchester sworn in the tithing of the king in January 1521, or in a list of inhabitants swearing fealty in November 1534, or in the Borough Court Rolls 1327–1564. Shepherd is not listed in the Coleman Street Ward subsidy roll (1542).

[13] John N. King, "Freedom of the Press, Protestant Propaganda, and Protector Somerset," *The Huntington Library Quarterly*, 40 (1976): 1–9.

1548 two hundred and twenty-five works were published in London, more than twice the number printed in the previous year.[14] Of these, thirty-one were tracts against the Mass or the celebration of the feast of Corpus Christi.[15] Given the extent of the religious revision which had already taken place, it is notable that such a copious number of works were produced at this time. By mid-year, many traditional Catholic devotional practices had been changed or modified: numerous feast days were abrogated, images abolished, the doctrine of the Real Presence relinquished, communion in both kinds reinstated for the laity, processions outlawed, most sacramentals banned, Evensong and Matins no longer celebrated in Latin, and the way cleared for the Mass to be said in English. Despite the introduction of these reforms, the rectification of conservative practices and abuses was still the most important element in the writings of many Protestants. Indeed, arguments in the debate over the Reformation continued in print and tapered off somewhat only when the first Prayer Book of 1549 established an official (if not uniform) doctrine regarding the central question of the Eucharist.[16]

The tradition of literature employed for political reasons was already well-established in the early Tudor era. Henry VII found it extremely useful to secure literary artists to create a legitimate political background for a house new to the monarchy in England, and his court attracted historians and moral philosophers, as well as poets, all expected to celebrate and consolidate the new Tudor sovereignty. Along with individual patrons, the Crown and its agents also engaged in the system of literary patronage, and during the regime of Henry VIII the need to employ authors to defend, explain, or justify official policy was far greater than it had been under Henry VII. Moreover, Henry VIII's battle with the papacy over his divorce from Catherine of Aragon, and his clash with the Continental Protestants, necessitated the Crown hiring skillful propagandists.[17] Besides the traditionally political tools of the court masque, drama, public spectacle, and pageantry, there came into

[14] King, *English Reformation Literature*, 88; Susan Brigden, *London and the Reformation* (Oxford: Clarendon Press, 1989), 438.

[15] King, *English Reformation Literature*, 89; Brigden, *London and the Reformation*, 436.

[16] See Diarmaid MacCulloch, *Thomas Cranmer: A Life* (New Haven: Yale University Press, 1996), 398–416.

[17] See A. G. Fox, *Politics and Literature in the Reigns of Henry VII and Henry VIII* (Oxford: Basil Blackwell, 1989), passim.

being a stream of humanist dialogues and serious religious rebuttals, including Henry VIII's work, *Assertio Septem Sacramentorum* (12 July 1521), and presently Thomas Cromwell's ministry would attain a hitherto unknown level of brilliance in propaganda.

During the 1530s, Cromwell commissioned Protestant authors to write propaganda that attacked conservatives opposed to religious change. The writers in his service produced ballads, dramas, pamphlets, translations, and sermons for a variety of needs and for different occasions. Cromwell thus manipulated and influenced a wide audience, which broadened when he sponsored his own dramatic company to tour the neighboring countryside, as well as to perform for his personal guests. From 1537, John Bale led Cromwell's troupe of players, and his plays, with their reforming messages, were part of the company's repertoire. Frequently, the dramas presented arguments that underpinned the king's position, especially the royal supremacy, and suggested an allegorical relationship between the king and various Old Testament figures, but they also afforded Cromwell a chance to argue against sacramentals and other practices that he planned to abolish as soon as it was expedient to do so. Bale facilitated his patron's strategy by revising and updating his plays. In *King Johan*, for instance, he incorporates a scathing commentary on various false images discovered during Cromwell's visitation of the monasteries (see lines 1215–1230).[18] The success of this political propaganda is attested to by the fact that the number of recorded dramatic performances nationally increased greatly up until the time of Cromwell's demise in 1540 and fell just as precipitously after his execution.[19]

In addition to encouraging religious change by using Protestant propaganda in dramatic form, Cromwell also set about making the Scriptures available to the people in English. In August 1537 he licensed the printing of a Bible translated by one Thomas Matthew, although in fact this name was a fiction and the translation was almost certainly William Tyndale's.[20] That

---

[18] See John Bale, *The Complete Plays of John Bale*, ed. Peter Happé, 2 vols. (Woodbridge: D. S. Brewer, 1985).

[19] For this and much of what follows regarding Cromwell's use of propaganda, I am indebted to Seymour Baker House, "Literature, Drama, and Politics," *The Reign of Henry VIII: Politics, Policy, and Piety*, ed. Diarmaid MacCulloch (London: Macmillan, 1995), 181–201.

[20] Tyndale's Bible in turn was based heavily upon Luther's version.

a new English Bible was to be printed for use in the churches was an encouraging sign to non-conservatives, since Cardinal Wolsey had banned Tyndale's Bible (opposed by church officials from its inception) in 1526. Furthermore, in September *The Bishops' Book* (otherwise known as *The Institution of a Christian Man*) was printed, and later in the same year Cromwell gained the king's approval to commission Miles Coverdale to produce a new translation of the Bible. These events appeared to reflect a new and radical attitude towards traditional religious practices, and the English reformers saw them as a catalyst which would proclaim the beginning of a Protestant age. However, the king refused to approve *The Institution of a Christian Man* and at once set about making emendations (some two hundred and fifty in all) to it. Most of these corrections concerned the doctrine of justification by faith alone, although Henry also questioned the document's attitude towards the saints and the sacrament of marriage. Despite the king's opposition to much of the content of *The Bishops' Book*, Cromwell was able to continue with his reforms, especially the exposure and destruction of fraudulent images. A year later, he published the Royal Injunctions which, though mainly extensions of the Injunctions of 1536, now also condemned the practice of candles before images and images themselves to which offerings or pilgrimages had been made. Moreover, the new Injunctions required each parish church to acquire a copy of the Bible in English by Easter 1539.[21] This instruction was augmented a year later when a Royal Proclamation appointed Cromwell to approve any new translation of the Bible.

Conceivably, if Cromwell had not fallen from the king's favor in 1539–40 much of the reversal of the reformation of 1530–38 would not have occurred. As it happened, Cromwell was executed on 28 July 1540, and his protégé, Robert Barnes, with two other reformers, Thomas Garrett and William Jerome, was burned for heresy at Smithfield two days later. While their deaths were for political reasons rather than as a result of the Act of the Six Articles (June 1539), which made denial of transubstantiation a heretical offense now punishable not by recantation but by death by burning, their Protestant contemporaries must have believed that the old religion was now

---

[21] Richard Grafton and Edward Whitchurch printed the officially authorized Great Bible in April 1539.

back in place and that persecution of heresy was taken up again.[22] The king had underlined his orthodox position when he personally debated with John Lambert at his hearing on 16 November 1538. Condemned as a sacramentarian, Lambert was burnt to death six days later. The king was determined that religious reformation had gone far enough; on the same day that he disputed with Lambert, Henry also issued his Proclamation *Prohibiting Unlicensed Printing of Scripture, Exiling Anabaptists, Depriving Married Clergy, Removing St. Thomas á Becket from Calendar.*[23] Cromwell, rather than the king, probably engineered this last prohibition. It would have been simple enough for him to convince Henry that Becket was an example of successful political rebellion against the Crown and that his cult was a threat to the Royal Supremacy. At the same time, removing him from the calendar of saints complemented Cromwell's ambition to demolish image veneration throughout England.

Despite persecution and exile, the reformers remained active during the next few years. Preachers like John Willock, Dr. Edward Crome, and John Porter preached in London, regardless of Richard Smith's opposition and Bishop Bonner's unexpected attempt to inhibit all unlicensed preaching. On the part of the Gospellers, there was an optimism that if they had patience the world would turn again: an optimism bolstered when Bonner set up six copies of the English Bible in St Paul's. However, the reformers' confidence was short-lived. The Act of the Six Articles, which reinstated conservative doctrine (including transubstantiation, auricular confession, communion under one kind only, and private Masses), was held in check to a large extent while Cromwell was alive. His execution altered the situation in favor of the conservatives. During the remainder of 1540 and in 1541, the search for heretics continued, and the erstwhile liberal Bonner now turned persecutor. The Protestant bishops, Hugh Latimer and Nicholas Shaxton, resigned their sees and gave up preaching. Bale fled to the Continent, Crome recanted, and Porter was imprisoned for expounding the Gospel in St Paul's (and later died

---

[22] Three conservative priests, Thomas Abell, Richard Featherstone, and Edward Powell, were executed for treason (denying the king's supremacy) at the same time, day, and place as Barnes, Garrett, and Jerome (Brigden, *London and the Reformation*, 315).

[23] Philip Hughes and James F. Larkin, eds., *Tudor Royal Proclamations*, 3 vols. (New Haven: Yale University Press, 1964–69), 1.186.

in Newgate). Robert Wisdom was tried for heresy and recanted, and Bonner was attacked over the execution of the youth Richard Mekins, who, despite conflicting evidence against him, went to the stake as a sacramentarian and a follower of Barnes. Moreover, John Foxe details some two hundred parishioners in London alone who were presented to the authorities that year for questioning. Though some accusations were trivial, many were serious and had dire repercussions for those involved. For example, Robert Ward, shoemaker, of St Andrew's parish in Holborn, was presented for holding against the sacrament of the altar and "died in prison in Bread-street."[24] While these numerous presentations were not repeated, Bonner was still determined against the reformers. William Turner withdrew to Basel in 1543, and Thomas Becon and Robert Wisdom recanted the same year. They retreated to the Midlands and later to Staffordshire. Robert Singleton was not so fortunate. Despite recantation alongside Becon and Wisdom, he was charged with treason and executed at Tyburn the following March.

By 1539, the king not only restored most conservative doctrines to the English Church, but he also initiated a course of action to tighten up official restraints on the printed word. Censorship of books and printing was not unfamiliar to Londoners under Tudor government, but in the early part of Henry VIII's reign the process by which a check was kept on the printing and importing of English books was haphazard to say the least. Generally, books that the authorities considered to be heretical were banned, and all books printed had to receive an episcopal license. However, the banning of books by official declaration does not seem to have been very successful. Between 1529 and 1536, four Royal Proclamations were issued against the reading, owning, importing, publishing, or printing of unsuitable books before the more extensive Proclamation of 16 November 1538, which gave the responsibility of licensing the printing of books to the Privy Council (or to others appointed by the monarch), and forbade, on pain of imprisonment and the confiscation of goods, the importation of books in English without a specific license from the king himself.[25] Thus the duty of investigation and control in regard to the licensing of books was taken away from the Church and assumed

---

[24] John Foxe, *The Acts and Monuments*, ed. Stephen Reed Cattley, 8 vols. (London: R. B. Seeley and W. Burnside, 1839), 5: 447.
[25] Hughes and Larkin, *Tudor Royal Proclamations*, 1.186.

by the Crown. In 1543 the king took the process one step further and forbade all books of the Old and New Testament in English, as well as books comprising or teaching religious material contrary to his command. Owning, retaining, printing, or publishing "any Englishe bokes or wrytings concerning matier againste the holye and blessed Sacrament of the Aultare . . . or other Englishe bokes or wrytings whiche heretofore have been abolisshed and condempned by the Kings Proclamacions" now became unlawful by Statute.[26] That the Privy Council took its new duties seriously regarding the control of the printed word is shown by the fact that the Statute was passed on 22 January and on 8 April eight printers (Whitchurch, Bedyll, Grafton, Lant, Keyle, Mayler, Petit, and Middleton) were accused of the "printing off suche bokes as wer thowght to be unlawfull, contrary to the proclamation made on that behalff," and were imprisoned in the Fleet. They were released some two weeks later only after the payment of several fines.[27] Subsequently, twenty-five booksellers appeared before the Council and were also subjected to financial penalties.[28]

However, the king was determined to address more than just the problem of English books. Censorship, intended to prevent widespread individual interpretation of the Scriptures, was written into the Act for the Advancement of True Religion and for the Abolishment of the Contrary (1543), which went a lot further than the Proclamation of 1538. As well as forbidding either clergy or laity to preach, teach, or defend any matters contrary to the determination set forth by the king, this Statute was to establish "a certaine forme of pure and sincere teaching, agreable with Godds woorde and the true doctryne of the catholicke and apostolicall Churche." It also reinforced the Act of the Six Articles, insisting that they remain and continue as they did before this new Act. Furthermore, the Statute severely restricted the reading of the Bible in English. Henceforth, only the aristocracy and merchants would legally have access to the Scriptures. Under threat of a month's imprisonment, "no woomen nor artificers prentises journeymen serving men

---

[26] 34/35 Henry VIII c. 1.

[27] John Roche Dasent, ed., *Acts of the Privy Council of England*, 4 vols. (London: Eyre and Spottiswoode, 1890), 1: 107, 117. I have followed Brigden's standardization of the printers' names here (Brigden, *London and the Reformation*, 345).

[28] Dasent, *APC*, 1: 120.

of the degrees of yeomen or undre, husbandemen nor laborers shall reade . . . the Byble or Newe Testament in Englishe, to himselfe or any other pryvatelie or openlie." Provision was made for noblemen, gentlemen, and merchants to study the Bible, and even to read it to their families in their own houses or gardens, while noblewomen and gentlewomen "maie reade to themselves alone and not to others any [Textes] of the Byble or Newe Testament."[29]

By 1543 the new formulary of religion was complete. Archbishop Cranmer finally conceded his fight to include justification by faith alone and the current prescription emphasized transubstantiation, the Mass, confession, and rituals. Convocation passed *The King's Book* on 30 April. It was read before the nobility in the Council Chamber at Westminster on 5 May, and it was published shortly afterwards under the title *A Necessary Doctrine and Erudition for any Christian Man*. With its publication, Catholic doctrinal orthodoxy seemed firmly back in place. *The King's Book*, enforced by law, was now the official standard in religion.

Henry VIII's later parliaments dealt with very little of a religious nature, but the bills discussed by both Houses suggest a change in the climate of London, where the reforming party seemed set to prevail. Within months of the Act for the Advancement of True Religion, the king backed Cranmer against the Catholic faction at Court, Dr. London was imprisoned for making untrue accusations against the Protestants at Windsor (he later died in the Fleet), and Bishop Gardiner's nephew and secretary, Germain Gardiner, was executed for denying the Royal Supremacy. The session of 1544 saw a bill introduced to the Commons which attempted to curtail overzealous or false witnesses. This new legislation required special commissioners or a Justice of the Peace to present a person arraigned under the Act of the Six Articles to a jury of twelve men. No longer could a parishioner be convicted of heresy simply on the word of two other people (the person to whom the accused spoke the alleged heresy and a witness) as was the case up until then. The new law did not nullify the Act of the Six Articles, but it did act as a kind of restraint, and it was passed only after fierce opposition from Gardiner and the Duke of Norfolk. The next parliament, that of 1545, finally passed

---

[29] 34/35 Henry VIII c. 1. The square brackets indicate an editorial emendation in the 1810–22 edition from their source which read "Text."

an act granting to the king all chantries and similar institutions which had been dissolved since 1536 through unlawful personal arrangements and also giving to the king the power to appoint commissioners to dissolve all remaining chantries, colleges of priests, hospitals, and guilds. However, the chantry bill conferred this right only on Henry VIII specifically, which accounts for the new act, the Dissolution of the Chantries Act, passed at the beginning of Edward VI's reign. Henry VIII's last parliament concerned itself almost exclusively with a bill for the attainder of Norfolk and the Earl of Surrey. The death of the king cut short the session some fourteen days after its opening meeting. It seemed perhaps the time had come for the world to turn again.

With Henry VIII's death, London was inundated with controversial literature. Why this upsurge happened is not a simple question to answer. Many of the reasons which initially appear obvious become less so as we examine them further. For example, one suggested reason for the increase in Protestant writing at this point is that it was a reaction to the tightening of censorship from 1538 onwards. Henry's death, therefore, was probably the signal to the reformers to write and print whatever they wanted. However, Statutes of the Realm (unlike Royal Proclamations, which have the force of law but lapse when the king dies) continue to be the law until they are repealed, and Edward VI's first parliament did not meet until 4 November 1547, when the Repeal of Statutes Act repealed the Act for the Advancement of True Religion.[30] The increase in the publishing of printed matter, directly after the old king's death, attests to the fact that the Statute in itself was not a deterrent to the reformers. The powerful personality of Henry VIII himself (reinforced by the Statute of 1543) had doubtless been enough of a threat to ensure erstwhile silence; thus, when his personage was removed from the political scene, so was the constraint on the authors.

## Shepherd's Works in Context

Henry VIII's death allowed Reformation literature to flourish; the accession of Edward VI (1547–53), reared and educated by Protestant tutors, further facilitated this flowering. Henry had intended a Council of Regency during Edward's minority, but his plans were negated when the new king's

---

[30] 1 Edward VI c. 12.

uncle, Edward Seymour, the Earl of Hertford, created the office of Protector-
ship, then seized it for himself and replaced the legitimate council with a
Privy Council he personally selected. This body excluded the most conserva-
tive of the old king's Council, Bishops Bonner and Gardiner. Hertford was a
known Protestant, a man of ideals and of letters, who corresponded with
John Calvin and who employed a Protestant household, including the
reformer, William Turner, as his chaplain and physician. Furthermore, most
of those who comprised the Council (with the possible exception of Thomas
Wriothesley) were known to have reformist leanings, or at least were not
openly Catholic, and in theory the Lord Protector had their support. For the
first time in its history, England had a government which was officially
Protestant.[31]

In the months which followed the setting up of this new government there
was unprecedented freedom from persecution, especially with regard to the
reading and printing of English books. However, engaging in almost any
literary activity was still officially unlawful and, therefore, dangerous: a good
enough reason to encourage anonymity among writers and printers. Another
reason why many writers chose anonymity at this time was that Hertford's
position was in some ways tenuous. The Lord Protector had not established
his authority without opposition or challenge, and it was by no means certain
that he would remain in power or be able to continue steering the Privy
Councillors in the direction of doctrinal change. Indeed, some of the Coun-
cillors at this time were probably more interested in their own personal
ambitions than in furthering the Protestant cause or in supporting Hertford
(now the Duke of Somerset).[32] Consequently, many reformers felt that the
safest course to take was an anonymous one.

The aim of these determined Protestant writers was the public reformation
of the English church, especially those areas concerned with rites, and the
abolition and annihilation of Catholic practices, especially that of the Mass.
Scathing criticism and extreme opposition to this rite was illustrated in all
literary genres, although there were more prose tracts against the Mass than

---

[31] However, it is interesting to note Cranmer's disclosure that in the months before his
death Henry was beginning to renew his earlier commitment to the evangelical cause and had
specific plans to revise the Mass (MacCulloch, *Cranmer*, 357–360).

[32] Christopher Haigh, *English Reformations: Religion, Politics, and Society under the Tudors*
(Oxford: Clarendon Press, 1993), 169.

there were verse satires or plays. While most writers drew on late medieval devotional literature for their themes, they also expanded the conventions of the traditional writings. In addition to translating the Scriptures or composing complaints, they applied various literary techniques to polemical works, frequently producing narratives or fictionalized dialogues in which characters dramatically argue the reformers' point of view. This is in marked contrast to the very traditional style of the Catholic texts from the same, or slightly later, period. Many saw the relaxation of crown censorship, under Somerset's government, as a means towards furthering the reformation. It paved the way for the publication of a huge body of vernacular printed material that was both popular and intelligible.

The overwhelming majority of mid-sixteenth-century extant English polemical texts are Protestant ones, which suggests that Protestant texts outnumbered contemporary Catholic texts and that popular evangelical works received more editions than Catholic ones.[33] Moreover, it was still treasonous to possess, retain, publish, or write Catholic texts, although, as we have seen with Protestant authors, laws are not necessarily a deterrent to committed writers. Nevertheless, even as late as 1550, little John Nobody, in the anonymous ballad of the same name, laments that he "durst not speake" but declares, "The fashion of these new fellows [the Protestants is] . . . so vile and fell," and claims censorship as the reason for the lack of a conservative voice.[34] In addition, the two principal contemporary Catholic writers who gained popular fame, Miles Hogarde and Richard Smith, were mercilessly ridiculed by Protestant authors.[35]

---

[33] The only significant extant conservative compositions from this period are Richard Smith's *A brief treatyse settynge forth diuers truthes necessary both to be beleued of chrysten people, & kepte also, whiche are not expressed in the scripture* [sic] *but left to y̍ church by the apostles tradition* (London, 1547, *STC* 22818), and Miles Hogarde's *The Abuse of y̍ blessed sacrament of the aultare* [1547?] quoted in Robert Crowley's *The Confutation of the mishapen Aunswer to the misnamed, wicked Ballade, called the Abuse of y̍ blessed sacrament of the aultare. Wherin, thou haste (gentele Reader) the ryghte vnderstandynge of al the places of scripture that Myles Hoggard, (wyth his learned counsail) hath wrested to make for the transubstanciacion of the bread and wyne* (London, 1548, *STC* 6082).

[34] Thomas Percy, *Reliques of Ancient English Poetry Consisting of Old Heroic Ballads, Songs, and Other Pieces of Our Earlier Poets, Together with Some Few of Later Date,* ed. Henry B. Wheatley, 3 vols. (London: Swan Sonnenschein, 1910), 2: 133–137.

[35] See King, "Protestant Propaganda," passim.

Both the diversity of style and the content of the printed religious debates suggest that originally there were many more examples which are no longer extant. We know of some of these works only because they, or extracts from them, survive in other authors' tracts. For example, Ponce Pantolabus's [John Huntington's] verse, *The genealogye of heresye*, is no longer extant per se, but John Bale reprints it with a rebuttal in his 1545 work, *A mysterye of inyquyte contayned within the heretycall Genealogye of Ponce Pantolabus*.[36] Similarly, Shepherd prints and refutes John Mason's poem, *Antigraphium*,[37] in *The comparison betwene the Antipus and the Antigraphe or answere thereunto, with An apologie or defence of the same Antipus And reprehence of the Antigraphe*.[38] Likewise, Hogarde's *The Abuse of yᵉ blessed sacrament of the aultare* exists only in the version quoted in Robert Crowley's *The Confutation of the mishapen Aunswer to the misnamed, wicked Ballade, called the Abuse of yᵉ blessed sacrament of the aultare. Wherin, thou haste (gentele Reader) the ryghte vnderstandynge of al the places of scripture that Myles Hoggard, (wyth his learned counsail) hath wrested to make for the transubstanciacion of the bread and wyne*.[39] Contemporary bibliographies also record disputative works no longer extant; of these Bale's various catalogues provide the most comprehensive and trustworthy lists.

As one of the main writers of popular polemical works published in London during the late 1540s, Luke Shepherd composed works that widen our appreciation of popular genres. His nine extant anti-Catholic works include eight verse satires: *A pore helpe; The vpcheryng of the messe; Pathose, or an inward passion of the pope for the losse of hys daughter the Masse; Iohn Bon and Mast person; Antipus; The comparison betwene the Antipus and the Antigraphe or answere thereunto, with An apologie or defence of the same Antipus And reprehence of the Antigraphe; Phylogamus; Doctour doubble ale*, and one short satiric prose work, *Cauteles preseruatory concerning the preseruation of the*

---

[36] *STC* 1303. Reprinted in Seymour Baker House, "An Unknown Tudor Propaganda Poem," *Notes and Queries* n.s. 39 (1992): 282–285.

[37] Shepherd attributes the authorship of this work to Mason in *Phylogamus* (25–29; 51–54).

[38] *STC* 5605a.

[39] *STC* 6082. Hereafter referred to as *The Confutation of the mishapen Aunswer to the misnamed, wicked Ballade, called the Abuse of yᵉ blessed sacrament of the aultare*.

*Gods which are kept in the pixe.*[40] Shepherd presents a Protestant perspective by criticizing the Roman Church and its clergy, rather than by employing persuasive arguments for reform. For example, in the poem, *A pore helpe*, he does not argue the case for clerical marriage, but instead mocks and censures Catholic priests for their lecherous behavior:

> . . . ye leade euyll lyues
> With other mennes wyues
> And wyll none of your owne
> And so your sede is sowne
> In other mennes grounde
> True wedlocke to confounde
> (*A pore helpe* 84–89)

Similarly, in *The vpcheringe of the messe*, Shepherd does not argue the efficacy of the Scriptures or expound the Protestant tenet of Christ's once-and-forever redemption of humanity but rather mocks the sacrificial aspect of the rite and derides the notion of the Mass as a popular source of benefits and a cure for all ills.

Despite the fact that Shepherd turned to writing for only a very brief time, his clever, witty poems illustrate that he was widely read and well educated. His texts are full of religious, literary, and classical allusions. He frequently writes in Latin or pseudo-Latin, and doubtless he expects his audience to know the difference. He also makes use of his medical background, employing scientific vocabulary and references. In addition, he sometimes takes a character from classical literary tradition and adopts the figure for his own satiric purpose. For example, in *Pathose, or an inward passion of the pope for the losse of hys daughter the Masse*, Shepherd draws on both classical and contemporary representations of a minor dramatic character, Dromo, to attack the Roman church and its pontiff. Such usage suggests an unusually keen sense of audience on Shepherd's part. He intends his satires to entertain as well as to instruct and enlighten, and although his texts do not rely on

---

[40] See King, *English Reformation Literature*, 252–270. For new evidence of Shepherd's prose work, see Janice Devereux, "An Addition to Luke Shepherd's Canon," *Notes and Queries* n.s. 42 (1995): 279–281.

references to other writers' works for their success, the allusions and their connotations add to the reader's enjoyment of the poems.

While Shepherd's satires treat some of the general issues of the Reformation, mostly those related to the Mass and the Eucharist, he also engages in personal vituperation, making biting, acrimonious attacks on contemporary figures, especially conservative writers and churchmen. For instance, he criticizes the traditional religious beliefs, ambition, and accretion of titles, positions, and monetary rewards of the statesman, Sir John Mason, and treats his writing with contempt:

> O Poete so impudent
> Whyche neuer yet was studente
> To thee, the Goddes prudente
> Minerua is illudente
> Thou wrytest thynges dyffuse
> Incongrue, and confuse
> Obfuscate and obtuse
> . . . . . . . . . . . . . . . .
> O Poet rare and Recent
> Dedecorate / and endecent
> Insolent and insensate
> Contendyng and condensate
> Obtused and obturate
> Obumbylate, obdurate
> (*Phylogamus* 230–236, 255–260)

Local clergy also come in for criticism. Shepherd thus depicts a London curate as a dissolute drunkard who neglects his clerical duties in favor of ale-drinking:

> . . . this good felow stout
> . . . . . . . . . . . . . . . . .
> He leaueth nought therin
> He careth not a pyn
> How much ther be wythin
> So he the pot may wyn
> He wyll it make full thyn
> And wher the drinke doth please
> Ther wyll he take his ease

And drinke ther of his fyll
Tyll ruddy be his byll
. . . . . . . . . . . . . . . .
. . . he is redy and prest
Where good ale is to rest
And drinke tyll he be drest
When he his boke shulde study
He sitteth there full ruddy
Tyll halfe the day be gone
. . . . . . . . . . . . . . . . . .
I neuer herde him preach God wot
But it were in the good ale pot
            (*Doctour doubble ale* 58, 71–79, 123–128, 161–162)

Likewise, Stephen Gardiner, Bishop of Winchester, is frequently the target of Shepherd's derision. As well as making sardonic remarks about his episcopal estate in Southwark (a location infamous for its brothels), he ridicules Gardiner's variety of career interests and ironically mocks his intelligence:

He hath ben a pardoner
And also a garddener
He hath ben a vytailer
A lordly hospytelar
A noble teacher
And also a preacher
. . . . . . . . . . . . . . .
. . . this famous clarke
He is learned beyond the marke
            (*A pore helpe* 295–300, 309–310)

One of Shepherd's strengths as a writer lies in his witty approach to what are potentially dry or abstruse religious subjects and themes. For example, *Iohn Bon and Mast person* is a dialogue in which a humble character, in the tradition of Piers Plowman, and a cleric conduct a debate that centers around the Mass and, in particular, the sacrament of the Eucharist. The plowman, Iohn Bon, is depicted as rough and uneducated, but his beliefs are based on common sense. His seemingly naive questions and responses utterly confound the priest, who appears both ignorant and gullible. While

Iohn Bon seems simple and artless, his witty punning on Corpus Christi, with its overtones of subservience, and his pretended shock at the priest's ability to "make his maker," reveal a cleverness which highlights the incompetence of the priest to explain or defend, in any meaningful way, the doctrine of transubstantiation. Although this poem appears to follow the tradition of earlier English anti-clerical writers, Shepherd, unlike William Langland, for example, offers no practical solutions to the abuses he decries. His purpose is not to convert his audience through argument. His aim here is to ridicule the Catholic doctrine of the Real Presence, which he does through the plowman's absurd questions regarding the gender of Corpus Christi, whom he misunderstands as a saint:

#### Iohn
They aer the more to blame I swere by saynt Steuen
But tell me mast parson one thinge and you can
What saynt is copsi cursty a man or a woman?
#### Parson
Why Iohn knoweste not that? I tel the it was a man,
It is Christe his owne selfe and to morowe is hys daye
We beare hym in prosession and thereby knowe it ye maye
#### Iohn
I knowe mast parson? and na by my faye
But methinke it is a mad thinge that ye saye
That it shoulde be a man howe can it come to passe
Because ye maye hym beare with in so smal a glasse
(*Iohn Bon and Mast person* 9–18)

Ridicule is also Shepherd's main purpose in his ingenious prose work, *Cauteles preseruatory concerning the preseruation of the Gods which are kept in the pixe*, which details instructions to the clergy on how to preserve unconsumed communion hosts. Shepherd marvels at the incongruity which allows the priests to be clever enough to "make" their God in the Eucharist but not learned enough to protect the consecrated hosts from going moldy, being "eaten of a mouse, ratte or munkay," or being "borne away" by "robin redbrest or philip Sparowe." Consequently, he proffers itemized instructions on how to store and protect the communion hosts and what procedures to adopt if, despite all their precautions, the hosts turn moldy and decay. Most of these instructions are patently absurd: for example, the suggestion that the priests should turn the hosts frequently to prevent them going rotten, or the suggestion that the priests should carry the moldy hosts onto the roof of the church and lay them out singly on a net of silk to dry in the sun, making sure they watch them carefully so that birds do not steal them. Alternatively, Shepherd suggests that the priests wipe the hosts and lay them on a clothed frame over a chafing dish in which brimstone burns so that they turn white again. Equally ridiculous is the suggestion that hosts should be stored in a box in the chimney to keep them dry, that they should be consecrated only on clear, sunny days and never when a south wind is blowing. The writer's final advice exhorts the priests to cover the host with the chalice during Mass to prevent it being blown away suddenly by the wind. Shepherd concludes by promising that he will compose more clerical tracts for instruction in the future and ends the treatise seriously with an affirmation that all those who are true believers in God ultimately shall be rewarded with "eternal ioye."

## *Literary Aspects of the Satires*

Shepherd's satires are a direct, personal, and Protestant response to the day-to-day situation which he observed around him in London. The old Catholic ways had legally been abolished, but Shepherd knew that in practical terms this, in fact, was not the case. In various local churches adherence to Catholic practices and rites still prevailed. While many London parishes made the transition from the established Catholic praxis to the newer, more Protestant service, some parish clergy were known for their steadfast adherence to the old ways. Many wills were Catholic in their format and tone, and some vicars and curates, who were not overtly Protestant, still managed to retain their church offices. These conservative clerics are part of Shepherd's London landscape, and his aim is to ridicule those who will not conform to the new way. This technique is particularly evident in *Doctour doubble ale*, where Shepherd mounts a scathing assault on the Catholic Church by means of a derisive attack on a specific London cleric.

Clever, cogent, and witty, Shepherd's propaganda depends upon the literary and rhetorical devices of invective, puns, colloquial language, and sarcasm, as well as hyperbole, apostrophe, invocation, sexual innuendo, and Latin parodies. Shepherd personifies the Mass in several poems, but his use of figurative language to achieve satiric ends is often confined to stylized Protestant images (for example, the Mass is imaged as the enemy of the Gospel; the pope is depicted as Simon Magus; the Tower of Babel represents the Roman Church) or to idiosyncratic images which typify the specific characters who are the objects of his invective (these images often involve puns on the names or occupations of the characters). The verse satires also rely heavily on rhyme, rhythm, and alliterative language for effect, and several of them illustrate his Skeltonic fondness for lines of iambic tetrameter.[41]

Shepherd's energetic and easily accessible language, his exaggerations and his scornful irreverence as well as his sense of humor, give his works an appealing sense of drama. Shepherd's avoidance of overt doctrinal theology or persuasion may suggest an intended audience which already agrees with his point of view and therefore does not need to be converted. However, it may also suggest that Shepherd relies on humor to influence a traditionally conservative audience. That Shepherd's satires were popular is evidenced by the fact that at least two of his poems, *A pore helpe* and *Antipus*, were printed in a second edition, and by Edward Underhill's contemporary reference to the circulation of *Iohn Bon and Mast person* at court.[42]

### *A pore helpe*

Ostensibly, the purpose of the satire *A pore helpe* is to act as a shield of faith to protect the Mass from those who seek to expel the Roman Church and all her practices and rites. Dramatically beginning with a rhetorical request for help against the Protestants, the poem quickly turns into a complaint about the cowardice of the Church's allies. The narrator praises the few stalwarts who defend the Mass and Christ's physical presence in the Eucharist in their writing, and then curses those who deny the validity of the sacrifice of the Mass or the efficacy of sacramentals. In the next part of the poem, however, the narrator curiously defends the Mass, by ridiculing the reformers' arguments against transubstantiation rather than justifying the Mass

---

[41] *A pore helpe, The vpcheringe of the messe, Pathose, or an inward passion of the pope for the losse of hys daughter the Masse*, and *Phylogamus*.

[42] Underhill recalls his conversation with John Gresham, Mayor of London: "As we weare att dynner, he [Gresham] sayde ther was a boke putt forthe called *John Boone*, the maker wheroff he wolde also searche for. 'Wy so? (sayde I,) thatt boke is a goode boke; I have one off them here, and ther is many off them in the courte'," Underhill, "Anecdotes," 172.

and the Eucharist, ending the defense with a prayer to the "Blessed sacrament," requesting Christ's support against the Gospellers.

The seemingly Catholic narrative voice ironically presents opposing Protestant ideas, thus compelling the reader to question the veracity of the narrator. For instance, the stylized Protestant image in the prefatory verse emphasizes the shield and buckler of faithfulness cited in the ninety-first Psalm but takes on a different meaning when interpreted ironically as the kind of faith necessary for the acceptance of the Catholic doctrine of the Mass. Likewise, the reminder that the Mass is "Not grounded on scripture" may reflect a self-satisfied Catholic view, but it may equally reflect a disdainful Protestant one. However, in the next lines, the crudely scathing tone of the complaint about the lecherous behavior of the priests suggests a distinctly Protestant voice raised in criticism of clerical celibacy.

At line 81, Shepherd's narrator forgets the pretense of a Catholic viewpoint and reverts back to a Protestant voice when describing the priests and their practices. The dramatic irony already achieved by the ambivalent point of view is now further highlighted when the narrator literally forgets which side of the dichotomy needs to be supported. As a result, the narrator is increasingly distanced from the text as the poem focuses on the central issue of this part of the work, the satirizing of the doctrine of the Eucharist.

The unconventional arguments reinforce the notion that Shepherd employs his narrator not to offer a Catholic point of view, but unwittingly to advance an ironic argument against the sacrament of the altar. The arguments state that Christ is not materially present in the Eucharist, as his body cannot be seen in the host; that those who teach Christ's corporeal presence are heretics; and that the host, locked up in a pyx, subjected to the vagaries of the weather, eaten by animals, or destroyed by fire, cannot contain the body of Christ. Subsequently, the recital assumes an irreverent tone because the reserved hosts are often subject to just the kind of predicaments as those the narrator describes.[43] Moreover, Shepherd presents the lines in the form of a mock litany, as a parody of prayer, where the constantly repeated first word is the negative "Nor" rather than a traditional religious invocation. Since a considerable distance exists between what the narrator says and what those words signify to the reformers, the juxtaposition of the two interpretations

---

[43] For misfortunes of the host, see Miri Rubin, *Corpus Christi: The Eucharist in Late Medieval Culture* (Cambridge: Cambridge University Press, 1991), passim.

adds to the overall irony. In addition, the misfortunes which can befall the consecrated hosts constitute a Protestant proof that Christ does not exist in any material way in the Eucharist. The narrator's final argument against Christ's bodily presence in the Eucharist is theologically more important than the others, but ironically this argument is flung at us in four small words, "Nor offered vp agayne." Inherent in these simple words is the whole Protestant teaching that Christ's redemption represents a once-and-forever atonement, not an act which can be repeated, and that, therefore, the Mass cannot be a sacrifice but only a ceremony of remembrance. By cleverly understating this significant argument, Shepherd underlines further the absurdity of his Catholic narrator's position, and the fact that his narrator does not elaborate on the argument or attempt to explain it in any way suggests once more an intended audience whose viewpoint is known.

At this point in the satire, the narrator shifts from the doctrine of the Eucharist to the figure of Stephen Gardiner, Bishop of Winchester and staunch supporter of Catholicism. Gardiner is described as an unwavering protector of the Mass, and we are encouraged to believe that if anyone in England can reverse the recent religious reformation, then he is the person to do it. References to Gardiner appear in four of Shepherd's poems,[44] and though Shepherd is scathing to the point of invective, he acknowledges the bishop's ability and treats him as a worthy antagonist.[45] Almost half of this satire is devoted to indirect attack on Gardiner. Although he is not actually named in the text, positive identification is possible because Germain Gardiner, Gardiner's nephew and secretary is specifically named.[46] In addition, Shepherd puns on Gardiner's name "And also a garddener" and records various official positions which he held. Also, like William Turner and John Bale, he refers to Gardiner as the "fox," lying in hiding, waiting to pounce on its next victim, an image which doubles as a pun as well, referring to Christ hiding in the host and to Gardiner's imprisonment for refusing to accept the Injunctions and the *Book of Homilies*.[47]

---

[44] A *pore helpe* and *The vpcheringe of the messe*, passim; *Pathose* (479) and *The comparison betwene the Antipus and the Antigraphe or answere thereunto, with An apologie or defence of the same Antipus And reprehence of the Antigraphe* (217).

[45] Shepherd does not extend such deference to other contemporary conservatives.

[46] *A pore helpe* (301–302).

[47] See Commentary on *A pore helpe* (182, 183).

In *A pore helpe*, Shepherd concentrates on both Gardiner's steadfast defense of the Catholic Church and on his physical appearance. We are reminded of his wisdom and his intractable upholding of the Roman Church. However, Shepherd's list of Gardiner's praises invites ironic interpretation. Phrases like "a noble clarke," "what a man is this," and "this learned man" cry out for such interpretation, and while "stout" undoubtedly refers to Gardiner's loyalty to Rome, we cannot help be aware of its other meaning, "corpulent," especially when we are reminded of a contemporary's remark about the bishop's unprepossessing physical appearance.[48] Shepherd's satirical pièce de résistance is the title itself: for all that Gardiner is the Church's champion, he is still but "A pore helpe" to Catholicism against "these felowes newe," the Gospellers and reformers.

Shepherd makes several oblique references to Gardiner's now lost verses against the Protestants.[49] His comments are obscure enough for us to wonder about the precise content of Gardiner's works, although the scornful tone of these lines leaves us in no doubt as to what Shepherd thought of his writing style. Extending his scorn for Gardiner to include "All the whole broode" of Catholic priests, Shepherd describes them as "Skuruy, skabed, and skalde / Shauen, shorne, and balde." He accurately depicts the shaven tonsures of the Roman clergy, but the combination of the alliteration and the colloquial language add another dimension, suggesting a portrait that illustrates the physical results of a debauched lifestyle. Shepherd concludes with a comment about Gardiner's talent for elusiveness and also his ability to control adverse situations and turn them to his own advantage.

The last part of the poem sees the satire come full circle. The narrator lists liturgical changes, laments the loss of traditional rites, and concludes with a rousing affirmation of a local curate who adamantly refuses to change to the new ways and who adheres to the old Catholic practices that by now have been officially abolished. The poem's ironic commendation thus draws public attention to this priest. Shepherd names the curate (Henry George) and his church (St Sepulchre's) and later devotes an entire poem (*Doctour doubble ale*) to him. By including Henry George in this satire, Shepherd reminds his

---

[48] See Commentary on *A pore helpe* (275).

[49] Gardiner's only extant poem is *Theyr dedes in effecte, my lyfe wolde haue* (London, 1548, *STC* 11593.5).

audience that despite recent religious reforms some local conservative clerics still retain church offices and maintain Catholic rites and practices.

### The vpcheringe of the messe

The title of this satire suggests that, despite her established history and the countless benefits she can bestow, the Mass needs "vpcheringe" to remain in England at this time of Protestant reform. Like *A pore helpe*, this poem also pretends a Catholic viewpoint: the narrator assumes the persona of a cleric who laments the demise of the Mass and the current prevalence of the Scriptures. Nevertheless, he argues, the Mass will outlast her opponent, the Gospel, over whom she has many advantages. These include preventing or curing diseases, expelling epilepsy, fever, and plague, and controlling the weather. The target of Shepherd's propaganda is the continuing celebration of the Mass "in many holy places" and her continuing residence in London, where she still has an influential following.

Despite its seeming simplicity and accessibility, *The vpcheringe of the messe* is a more complex text than appears on first reading. For example, although the narrator passionately bemoans the Mass's demise, he unexpectedly explains that it is not "grounded" in the Scriptures, thus reiterating a common Protestant argument that the sacrament of the altar is "made bi men." He proffers this doctrine as a series of rhetorical questions, attempting to persuade us rather than tell us. His ridicule of the Scriptures ironically constitutes the truth according to the reformers:

> Ye thinke nothing but scripture
> Is only clene and pure . . .
> The scripture hath nothing
> Wher by profyte to bryng
> But a lytyll preaching
> With tattling and teaching
> (43–51)

While the narrator's purpose is to ridicule the Scriptures, the emphasis on the preaching and teaching of the Gospel, in fact, reflects the basic tenet of Protestantism. Despite the narrator's obvious Catholic point of view, he sometimes leaves us with very sound Protestant advice: "But must your ears applie / To learnyng inwardlye." Thus the ironic ridicule forces the reader to question the validity of any defense of the Mass.

Having made us doubt the Mass's integrity, the narrator now praises her and declares that through the efforts of her powerful allies she will eventually regain her position of pre-eminence. Consequently, the last part of the poem focuses on one of her most steadfast defenders, Stephen Gardiner. Here Shepherd cleverly combines fiction and fact, setting his propaganda within a historical framework. He mentions Bishops Bonner and Gardiner as champions of the Mass, but only Gardiner is discussed at any length. Shepherd acknowledges Gardiner's ability, his eloquence in preaching, and his steadfast loyalty to Catholicism.

Despite the many references to Gardiner, the primary concern of this text is the downfall of the Mass in England. Shepherd personifies the Mass as Mistress Missa, imaged as a beautifully arrayed woman, the Gospel's adversary, the pope's strumpet daughter, a quack doctor, the controller of the weather, a "swete flowre," and, finally, Eve's companion in hell. While the Mass is always portrayed as a woman in this text, at no point does she become a character in a narrative. Shepherd heaps up the images in order to illustrate Catholicism's duplicity and corruption. The conventional images, which include the Gospel and the Mass as antagonists, the Mass as the whore of Babylon, and the association of the sacrificial Mass with Cain, are familiar to Shepherd's readers. His readers are also familiar with contemporary texts that detail benefits of the Mass and satires that link the Bishop of Winchester's name with local brothels, many of which were located in rental property owned by his diocese on the south bank of the Thames.[50] Although Shepherd's satire lists ostensible benefits of the Mass, such as solicitude and charity or cures from ghastly diseases, the narrator also displays the Mass as a sham, a false ritual which opposes the Scriptures and claims to re-enact Christ's sacrifice on the Cross for the redemption of humanity. Likewise, the narrator ironically extols Gardiner's loyalty to the Mass, "He loueth hir wel, god wot," but with a wonderfully

---

[50] See Jerome Barlowe and William Roye, *Rede me and be nott wrothe* (London, 1528, *STC* 21427); William Turner, *The huntyng & fyndyng out of the Romishe fox whiche more then seuen yeares hath bene hyd among the bisshoppes of Englong after that the Kynges Hyghnes had commanded hym to be dryuen out of hys realme* (London, 1543, *STC* 24353) and William Punt, *A new Dialoge Called The Endightment agaynste mother Messe* (London, 1548, *STC* 20499).

incongruous image he undercuts the prelate's devotion, comparing his ardor for the Mass to that of a drunkard's for his "good ale pot."

In the last part of the poem, the narrator openly adopts a Protestant voice and flagrantly satirizes the Mass: "And if she chaunce to dye / I can not helpe it I." He insists that she must now return to "hir natiue contrie" and, treating her as though she were already dead, intones a mock requiem for her. He misquotes the opening prayers of the Mass for the Dead, wishing her everlasting pain rather than eternal rest, and the narrator makes it clear that he believes she is more suited to reside in hell than in heaven. Beneath the bantering tone, however, lies a much more serious implication. The comforting words, "Eternal rest grant unto them, O Lord, and let perpetual light shine upon them,"[51] are an affirmation of religious belief, a plea to God for mercy on behalf of the person who has died, and also an assumption of hope for salvation on the part of the person praying. By denying the Mass these specific words, the narrator banishes her beyond the pale and reinforces the Protestant opposition to the doctrine of purgatory and to the efficacy of prayers for the dead.

Shepherd satirizes the language of the Mass in the final section of the poem, using a mixture of Latin and English words and endings to mock the Latin rite. By employing macaronic verse (see lines 347–381), Shepherd underlines the foolishness of those who believe in such things. Creating pseudo-Latin words for his end-rhymes, the narrator tells the Mass's supporters:

> Full smale maye be your gloria
> When ye shal heare thys storia
> Then wil ye crie and roria
> (369–371)

Not only does Shepherd expect his audience to recognize Latin references, but he also counts on his readers to understand when he is playing games with them as well. What appears on the surface to be an unsophisticated rendition of Latin vocabulary is, in fact, a satirical denunciation of those who obstinately cling to the old Roman ways and an unequivocal Protestant

---

[51] See Commentary on *The vpcheringe of the messe* (360–361).

farewell to the Mass as a form of worship: "We shal se hir no moria." This farewell anticipates her permanent departure in the final lines of the poem, when she is packed off back to Rome.

### *Pathose, or an inward passion of the pope for the losse of hys daughter the Masse*

In *Pathose, or an inward passion of the pope for the losse of hys daughter the Masse,* a sequel which is the longest and most complex of his works, Shepherd extends the image of the Mass as the whore of Babylon returning to her father, the pope. In the form of a loosely structured but dramatic narrative, the satire attacks the doctrine of transubstantiation and condemns Catholic insistence that the Mass is a daily re-enactment of Christ's redemptive sacrifice for the sins of humanity.

Shepherd personifies the Mass as the dying daughter of the pope. Paradoxically, her father appeals to the pagan gods and goddesses to restore his beloved daughter to health because he has concluded that the Christian God is powerless to aid her. In exchange for their help, the pope offers these deities his devotion and loyalty. Despite repeated appeals, however, the pope fails to obtain a cure for his daughter and, in an abrupt reversal that symbolizes the alleged deviousness of the Roman Church, banishes the Mass and all her retinue to hell to reside for ever with "the prince infernal / In derknes eternal." The satire concludes with an affirmation that the devil originated both the pope and the Mass. The closing epigram thus reflects the popular contemporary Protestant accusation that the pope holds his authority not from God, but from Satan.

Shepherd's propaganda centers on the pope's dissatisfaction with Christ and with his subsequent resolve to change his allegiance to the pagan deities, Bacchus and Ceres. Narrative interruptions invite retrospective assessment of the pontiff's character as a dogmatic, foolish, and illogical leader unable to see the inappropriateness of his promise to offer the Mass as a grateful sacrifice to the pagan gods. Similarly, the metaphor of the Mass as the pope's daughter and the use of satiric genealogy to indicate their relationship to Mohammed (which implies that the Catholic Church is as heathen as Islam) are typical Protestant rhetorical devices. Equally typical is the parody of the Mass when the pope petitions Bacchus and Ceres, proffering sacrifices "To mytygate your moode." Profanely, he reminds them that his daily offering of bread and wine should ensure his request is granted. In addition, Shepherd satirizes alleged

Catholic belief in the clergy's power to control Christ's presence in the
Eucharist, for the priest to "make his maker," when the pope ridicules the
sacrament of the altar:

> Though I do him forsake
> Yet dare I vndertake
> (At pleasure) him to make
> (175–177)

The papal narrator functions as a ludicrous vehicle for Protestant propaganda.
Shepherd sets up a powerful contrast between the previously simple, foolish
pope and this abusive, impious pontiff who mocks and rails at Christ.
Audaciously re-defining his relationship with Christ, "I get no thing hym by
/ I Recke not of him I," the pontiff declares his blatant contempt for the
authority of God.

Alongside this satiric determination to be superior to God is an extraordi-
nary violence aptly illustrated by the earlier lines: "And vse him as me listis /
Betwene my holy fistis." Shepherd presents us with the grotesque image of
the pope spitefully trying to beat his God into submission. Outrageously, the
pope turns Christ's commission of St. Peter (Matthew 16:19) back on
himself, boasting "and *he* shall not chose / But what *I* bynde and lose"
(emphasis added). Moreover, the pope berates "this beggerly Christ" for his
lowly appearance and his lack of ostentation. In a deeply ironical passage, the
pope criticizes Christ for his Christian virtues of humility and modesty. The
ceremony, pomp, and splendor associated with the papacy affords an ironic
contrast to the gospel image of Christ entering Jerusalem, "Vpon a pore asse,"
a text that Shepherd's narrator quotes scornfully. A parallel between Aescula-
pius's raising Androgeos from the dead and Christ raising Lazarus further
emphasizes the pope's alleged lack of spirituality. Christ brought Lazarus back
to life, and the pope trusts that Aesculapius can likewise save his dying
daughter. In a final sacrilegious outburst, the pope declares that Venus will be
pleased when his daughter is cured. Discussion of her cure in terms of a
sexual pun makes it clear what her specific illness is and why the goddess of
love is eager to have her whole again.

By contrast to his hostile language to God, the tone of the pope's lament
for his dying daughter appears affectionate and loving. However, his lament
is a parody that exploits the traditional image of the tormented, emaciated,

lovesick lover. Furthermore, it becomes apparent that the true reason for the pope's desire to save the Mass is not paternal love but fear of the loss of power due to her demise. While the last part of the satire depicts the pope as a distraught parent grieving over his "childe so sycke," the subsequent description of the Mass in terms of a whore dying from syphilis makes it harder to view this as a portrait engendered by paternal love. Yet the pope continues to describe the Mass in loving terms and his poem to her (appropriately offered in Latin) affectionately begins "O beautiful offspring."[52] The opening is deceptive, as the poem does not extol her virtues but portrays her as a diseased impostor sensibly abandoned by the people who previously worshipped her. Employing the image of the Mass as a woman being stripped naked, Shepherd describes her loss of popularity and power. The double meanings in the Latin poem emphasize the dissolute pope's grief at the physical loss of his daughter and contrast with the ironically Protestant message he delivers in the final lines, "The Scriptures are being preached purely."[53]

Repeatedly, much of what the pope says about the Mass can be interpreted in more than one way, which frequently results in a lewd undertone in the passages about her. The pope constantly declares his love for her, but the sexual innuendoes, including the pun on "inward" in the title (which is repeated at line 316), leave us in little doubt about the incestuous nature of the relationship. The illicit relationship is further highlighted by the image of the Mass as a beautiful, but ailing young woman, ultimately transformed into a pox-ridden, dying harlot. When the Mass ceases to be of use to him, the pope ruthlessly discards her, sending her off with "A careful kysse" to avoid catching the pox from her.

In a sardonic dismissal, the pope blesses the Mass and sends her to the devil, who will make her "his heire." In an unexpected outcome, the pope repudiates the Mass, thus acquiring the chance to proffer "obedience" to the ruler of hell and reserve a future place for himself in Satan's domain. The final irony is that when the pope banishes the Mass, he unwittingly divests himself of all outward trappings of Catholicism. The last nine lines of the

---

[52] For translation, see Commentary on *Pathose* (683–718). Seymour Baker House very generously advised on Shepherd's Latin and contributed most of the translations.

[53] "Ecce scripture / Predicantur pure," *Pathose* (715–716).

satire exhibit a marked change in point of view, when a resolute Protestant voice finally concludes that both "Pope and messe" are "deuelishnes."

### Iohn Bon and Mast person

Shepherd's only verse satire written in dialogue form, *Iohn Bon and Mast person* is a polemical work against the Eucharist and the feast of Corpus Christi. A unique feature of this poem is the woodcut illustration that precedes it. The illustration, depicting a Corpus Christi procession, had originally been used in various Catholic works. A contemporary reader encountering the title page of Shepherd's satire would therefore immediately be aware of the ironic antithesis of this particular picture and text. The prefatory verse which encapsulates the whole poem is directed to the "poore fooles," the priests in the illustration. It points out to them that, as Christ is not physically present in the "wafar cake," their devoted veneration of the communion host is nothing short of idolatrous.

Various distinct features, including this example of a woodcut illustration, make Shepherd's *Iohn Bon and Mast person* different from his other texts.[54] Apart from *Antipus*, which is a single sheet folio poem, *Iohn Bon and Mast person* is the shortest of his works. Also Shepherd's only satire located in a specific time and place, the poem is set on the eve of the feast of Corpus Christi in the country, outside London but close enough for its characters to be aware of what is going on in the city. Unlike Shepherd's other verse satires, *Iohn Bon and Mast person* is remarkably uncomplicated and accessible. For example, the poem contains no enigmatic personal attacks on Catholic figures nor any Latin or pseudo-Latin passages. The satire is straightforward and the contemporary references and allusions are mostly obvious. Apart from the prefatory verse, which comprises a rhyme-royal stanza and a repeated half-line admonition, the dialogue is written, without discernible pattern, in couplets, tercets, and quatrains with a single rhyme.

The satire uses Iohn Bon, a plowman, to attack the doctrine of transubstantiation and the feast of Corpus Christi by mocking and deriding the character of Mast Person, the priest. The priest's arrogant and foolish manner

---

[54] While it is possible that the woodcut illustration was inserted at the instigation of the Protestant printer, John Day, the apparent composition of an introductory verse suggests collusion on the part of the author and the publisher.

puts him at a disadvantage compared to the cheerful, inquiring, and humorous Iohn Bon. Iohn Bon manipulates the cleric throughout the entire poem, from his first ridiculous question about the gender of Corpus Christi to his incisive parting shot: "But praye not so for me for I am well Inoughe."

Shepherd marginalizes the priest by not allowing him to contribute actively to the argument. He answers the plowman's questions in a cursory way, but he does not expand or comment on any of his points. Relying on emotional outburst rather than on rational discussion, he rails at the plowman, accuses him of being mad, and calls him a heretic. Iohn Bon's seemingly deferential apology highlights the cleric's gullibility and increases the irony of the situation for the audience because the priest is completely unaware of the plowman's raillery. The cleric corrects none of the basic mistakes that his rustic parishioner makes in regard to religious rites. For example, when Iohn Bon remarks, "But as for cropsy cursty to be a man or no / I knewe not tyll thys day," the cleric does not seem surprised that the plowman should confuse the feast-day as a person, nor does he criticize him for doing so. Likewise, he makes no remark about the plowman's mockingly erroneous words for Corpus Christi. Similarly, when the priest ironically informs us that the Mass is as good as the "Pistell or Gospel," he completely ignores the plowman's blasphemous response: "The fowle euyll it is, whoe woulde thynke so muche." Furthermore, he fails to recognize the significance of the puns when, near the end of the poem, Iohn Bon declares: "But masse me no more messinges. The right way wil I walke."

In *Iohn Bon and Mast person*, Shepherd adapts the dialogue format for his own purpose of casting scorn and derision on the Roman Church. Rather than presenting two characters who debate a central issue and arrive at a conclusion, he portrays a rationalistic layman who asks awkward questions and an inept cleric incapable of providing logical answers or explanations. By contrast to much of the dogmatic writing of this period, which is seriously moralistic in tone, the facetiousness of Shepherd's dialogue is refreshingly witty, entertaining, and enjoyable. For example, the insistence by the priest that Christ is created in the Eucharist and resides physically in the communion host elicits the witty retort from the plowman that indeed Christ must be "an elfe" in order to fit into it. Furthermore, the combination of the dialogue format, the elementary rhyme scheme, and the unsophisticated, colloquial language of both characters belie the cleverness and the underlying comic tone of Shepherd's satirical arguments. While Iohn Bon appears to be a simple countryman eager to learn about the doctrine of transubstantiation, his ingenious punning on Corpus Christi and the seeming guilelessness of his mockery and derision of the priest demonstrate a shrewdness (well above the level of a mere rustic) that emphasizes the cleric's inadequacy to explain or justify Catholic doctrine.

The comedy in Shepherd's dialogue hinges on how his characters talk at cross purposes. For instance, Iohn Bon continually asks ridiculous questions or makes ludicrous statements which the priest misinterprets as examples of naivety, a misperception that underlines the cleric's ignorance and simple-mindedness. Shepherd sets the priest up as a target for ridicule when he cannot contend with Iohn Bon's queries. Although the cleric is concerned about the plowman's apparent ignorance of the significance of Corpus Christi, he is unable to explain the mystery of the Eucharist to the plowman, an inability that further emphasizes the priest's incapacity to carry out his Christian ministry.

Iohn Bon's outwitting of the priest is highly entertaining. Furious at the plowman's logical conclusion that the communion host is physically too small to contain Christ, the priest accuses him of heresy. Confused by Iohn Bon's ingenious retaliation, the priest is unaware of critical overtones in the plowman's skeptical replies to subsequent descriptions of the various parts of the Mass. Thus, Shepherd ridicules the Roman Church by the derisive vocabulary he assigns Iohn Bon to comment on the ritual and by portraying the priest as foolish and oblivious. When the plowman satirically commends the priest on being "morenly well learned," we are aware that the priest does not comprehend the ambiguity of the remark and thinks this a compliment.

The next part of the poem focuses on the act of consecration itself. The plowman professes astonishment that in the Eucharist the priest can "turne the breade to fleshe" but swears his amazement by "the deuell" rather than by God. Iohn Bon feigns wonder at the priest's insistence that he can also "tourne the wyne to bloude," and Shepherd produces a comic effect as the priest hastens to reassure the plowman that the blood "be wine in taste."

Iohn Bon seemingly asks the priest to present a logical explanation for the Eucharist, but, in fact, he manipulates the cleric into a risible situation. Despite Iohn Bon's apparent simplicity, he knows the priest cannot explain transubstantiation, which is a mystery to be taken on faith alone. He also knows that any attempt at explanation will make the priest look foolish. Therefore, by demanding such a rationalization he forces him into an impossible position. The priest cannot defend the doctrine of the Eucharist on the grounds of reason; he can only attempt to justify it as an article of faith, a response which empowers Iohn Bon to dispute it. The plowman argues against transubstantiation, logically claiming that priestly assertion does not prove doctrinal "truth." Surprisingly, the priest does not refute Iohn Bon's argument, but instead bewails the implementation of recent liturgical changes.

Shepherd's contrived conclusion highlights his satire's purpose. Although many religious reforms have already been accomplished, old practices nevertheless remain. Shepherd attacks the Mass in *Iohn Bon and Mast person* because conservative clerics, willing to risk exposure to the authorities, still celebrate the newly abrogated Mass. Despite the Protestant vantage point, propaganda is necessary if the liturgical and doctrinal changes already wrought are to be permanently achieved.

### Antipus

*Antipus* is a compact poem that also primarily satirizes the Roman Church's doctrine of transubstantiation. Beginning with a two-line heading that summarizes the text with a Latin tag about truth, the poem's body consists of eleven couplets that present topsy-turvy biblical allusions as though they were true and build up to ironic paradoxes regarding the doctrine of transubstantiation. Punning on the word "verily" at the beginning of each line of each couplet, Shepherd plays with the idea of truth and falsehood throughout the whole poem. He does this by reversing the action of well-known biblical stories, creating absurd outcomes ("So verily dyd Goliad distroye Dauid the Kynge") which he pretends are true, ironically insisting that equally true are the claims of the conservatives who state that a priest can create Christ in the Eucharist ("So verily these thefes the prestes can make their maker"). In addition, Shepherd uses other contrary assertions ("As verily as the deuyll hath perfecte loue and hope / As verily as Isesicles wythin be hote and holowe / As verily as bread doeth make and bake the baker") to ridicule traditional Catholic tenets, such as the belief that the pope holds his power directly from God and that the Roman clergy are the true successors of Christ and his apostles.

The satire attacks both the doctrine of transubstantiation and the alleged corruption and deception of the Roman Church. Shepherd's assault on simony draws on contemporary allusions to the pope and Simon Magus as idol-worshipers and exploiters of the laity. Shepherd extends this image of corruption, citing the Church's widespread procedure of exacting fines from dissenters and of frequently imprisoning people for not paying their tithes. Further developing this image, Shepherd ends the poem with a brief *ad hominem* attack against a local ecclesiastic, William Layton (Leighton), drawing a parallel between this dishonest "thefe" and "robber" and the simony of the Catholic Church.

A well-known preacher at St. Paul's, Layton was an outspoken defender of the Mass. Rather than refuting Layton's Catholic arguments, however, Shepherd launches into a personal attack on him and uses him as a specific example of Catholic hypocrisy. He accurately points out that Layton's creditors were pressing him for payment of his debts,[55] derides him openly, mocks his preaching, and concludes that Layton's belief in the sacrament of the altar allies him to the "falshed" of popish idolatry.

Shepherd's attack on Layton is an eight-line appendix printed in small type, centered underneath the couplets which comprise the larger part of the poem. The printed marginal pointer hand at the beginning of this octave, the difference in the type size, the centering of lines on the page, and the presentation of the stanza as a riddle (an impression the quickening, sing-song pace of the lines reinforces) all focus attention on Shepherd's rhetorical habit of attacking a specific contemporary as a means of ridiculing Catholicism in its entirety. As a result, the format of the *ad hominem* attack against Layton diminishes Shepherd's antagonist by reducing him to a textual appendage.

## The comparison betwene the Antipus and the Antigraphe or answere thereunto, with An apologie or defence of the same Antipus And reprehence of the Antigraphe

*The comparison betwene the Antipus and the Antigraphe or answere thereunto, with An apologie or defence of the same Antipus And reprehence of the Antigraphe* is a composite satire that contains a reprint of *Antipus* followed by John Mason's *Antigraphium*, a work which sets out to refute Shepherd's piece

---

[55] See also Cathleen Hayhurst Wheat, "Luke Shepherd's *Antipi Amicus*," *Philological Quarterly* 30 (1951): 58–68.

line by line. Predictably, Mason's work mimics *Antipus* in form, structure, and content, although its rhythm is frequently uneven and at times it appears somewhat clumsy in contrast to the original. The heading of the *Antigraphium* cleverly distorts and extends Shepherd's Latin tag. The ensuing twelve couplets invert Shepherd's pairings, with the following minor changes: Mason denies the falsity of the pope and modifies Shepherd's acerbic "proude prelates" to "meke" ones. A further couplet contends that the Eucharist is created not by the power of the priest, as Shepherd distorts Catholic belief, but is consecrated by God himself through the priest's words. Additionally appended couplets unexpectedly deny Layton's allegiance to the Roman Church while asserting his righteousness. Mason concludes with a defense of Layton that comprises six additional couplets under the sub-heading "The Writer," and a further five couplets under the sub-heading "The Sacrament." These doggerel couplets revile the reformers, denounce the heretical writer of *Antipus*, and reinforce the Catholic doctrines of the mystery of faith, transubstantiation, and Christ's redemption.

*Apologia Antipi*, Shepherd's much longer reply to Mason's refutation, is a polemical tract against transubstantiation, as well as a personal attack on Mason and contemporary defenders of the sacrament of the altar. Unlike his more sophisticated assaults on Stephen Gardiner, the *Apologia Antipi* treats Mason with disdain, condemning him for his traditional religious beliefs, worldly ambition, and lack of literary originality. Shepherd predicts that Mason's work will not endure and patronizingly explains that "A boy of twelue yere olde" could write a better defense of the Eucharist. Although Shepherd attacks Catholic practices that survive proscription, his forceful assault is primarily directed at those individuals who still publicly oppose these changes in their writings. Mason bears the brunt of this assault, as he does in *Phylogamus*, but Shepherd also assails well-known Catholics like Richard Smith, Miles Hogarde, and William Bell.

In contrast to the *Antigraphium* which (apart from its heading) is written entirely in couplets, the first part of *Apologia Antipi* consists of a two-line heading followed by fourteen rhyme-royal stanzas, the first seven of which criticize and refute Mason's work, while the remaining stanzas set forth a Protestant argument against the sacrament of the altar. In order to engage Mason immediately in this text, Shepherd reworks his original two-line heading from *Antipus* to lodge a punning attack on Mason for Catholic "deception." In effusive Skeltonics, Shepherd denounces Mason's intelligence and puns on his name, pretending he is a bad "cowcher of stones" who neglects to use his mason's tools in the craft of writing. Even more insulting is Shepherd's claim that Mason's unconvincing arguments were composed with the covert aid of a famous defender of the Mass, Richard Smith.

Although the two sets of rhyme-royal stanzas are not separated from each other on the page, the tone changes after the seventh stanza as Shepherd begins his serious argument against Christ's physical presence in the Eucharist. He claims that the belief in transubstantiation lacks scriptural authority. Citing Saint Augustine as his authority, he affirms the spiritual presence of Christ in the communion service, "To eate the breade worthely the Lordes death to betoken," and his text emphasizes the commemorative aspect of this ceremony by recalling Christ's words at the Last Supper, "when ye shall, [sic] do this do it rememberinge me."[56] Finally, Shepherd brings his disputation back to Mason, expressing the hope that this papist will eventually be enlightened by the very scriptures he rejects.

The remainder of the satire directs an *ad hominem* attack at specific individuals as a means of assaulting Catholicism in general. The structure of the lines mirrors Shepherd's denunciation of William Layton in *Antipus* by setting out his objections in four couplets that culminate in the half-line in which "Amonge Papistes" becomes "With papistes." The imitation of Mason suggests rhetorical disdain grounded in literary and religious contempt. Shepherd matches the Catholic writer's six couplets with five epigrams of his own, but the concluding six-line stanza replaces five couplets by his adversary. The familiar tone and colloquial language (see lines 192–207) contrast sharply with the seriousness of the preceding religious debate. Shepherd affirms Mason as an idolatrous fool by addressing him informally as "shepe-biter," "dawe," and "hoddy doddy" and reinforces his criticism by the sentence construction he now employs. Although his use of caesura initially suggests that the latter half-lines represent mere afterthoughts, the device accentuates the most important ideas. "Nothinge haue you written," Shepherd charges Mason, "but ye be answered there to." The word "Finis" suggests a conclusive defeat of Mason, but, conversely, this short segment is the preamble to a final assault on specific contemporaries. The concluding

---

[56] *The comparison betwene the Antipus and the Antigraphe* (150; 161); Luke 22:19–20.

rhyme-royal stanzas employ boisterous rhyme, mock riddles, and punning allusions to rail against Mason, Smith, and other Catholic "idolaters." The sing-song rhythm denounces these conservatives as "fooes to Antipus" who unsuccessfully attempt to silence Protestant opposition.

Shepherd exploits scriptural typology to ridicule Mason for building the Tower of Babel (a contemptuous Protestant figure for the Roman Church) and Smith (punningly named for the first smith, Tubalcain) for forging his tools. An absurd extension of the image associates the confusion and chaos that followed the building of the Tower of Babel by the descendants of Noah with the rise and fall of the papacy. Shepherd's punning analogies vilify Hogarde, Smith, Bell, and three "papists" who are otherwise unidentified: Paynter, Perkins, and Gray. Despite the obscure details of some of the references, the vivid descriptions leave the reader with a keen sense of Shepherd's vigorous opposition to these Catholic figures.

At the end of the satire, Shepherd returns to a general criticism of Catholicism. The very last lines of the poem are a parody of a litany whose lines highlight the evils of the old religion, mimicking intoned prayers with their constantly-repeated first word and their repetitive pattern of stress. Shepherd's litany is contemptuously dismissive, presenting the invocations as a mindless string of words that could presumably continue forever:

> In knauery.
> In heresy
> In baudry.
> In popery.
> Etcetera
> (236–240)

## Phylogamus

*Phylogamus* begins with a different kind of litany, one that feigns a recital of the talents and virtues of the author of the *Antigraphium*. Written in irregular iambic tetrameter, *Phylogamus* is a derisive satire against clerical celibacy. It attacks writers like Mason and Smith who defend Catholic ideology, and it denounces the Roman Church for refusing to allow its priests to marry. *Phylogamus* replies to a lost work in which Mason defended clerical celibacy in a classical, poetic style. No official record of Mason's title exists, but an anonymous pamphlet, *The wyll of the Deuyll. And last Testament*, refers to "our sweete Mazon" (Mason) as a papist and "the Authour of *Heresyes Wylle and Testament*." Almost certainly it is the work to which Shepherd is responding.[57]

Indicating that Mason employed Latin for part, if not all, of his defense, Shepherd contemptuously mocks his arguments executed "in suche fyne latyn." Lines 112–131 of *Phylogamus* contain thirteen Latin lines which may quote from Mason's work. Unlike the other Latin lines in *Phylogamus*, these thirteen lines appear to have been originally written in couplets in the manner of Mason's *Antigraphium*. Printed in smaller type, the Latin verses are interspersed with Shepherd's verse translation or commentary on Mason's text. Irregular line-lengths and the occasionally forced rhyme scheme indicate that Shepherd omits or alters some of Mason's lines and inserts some of his own both in English and in Latin. For instance, a line which refers to the fate of deceased married clergy, "In sempiterna supplicia" ("in everlasting torture"), is a witty transposition of the words from the Mass for the Dead: "requiem sempiternam" ("everlasting rest") and "remedium sempiternum" ("everlasting help").[58] Shepherd thus puns that clerics who marry in order to avoid the "torture" of celibacy will subsequently suffer everlasting torture in hell.

Shepherd mocks Mason by composing appalling Latin verse for his derisive reply. This satirizes the Roman Church's insistence on priestly celibacy, despite the absence of scriptural prohibition.[59] It also censures clerics who, having sworn a vow of celibacy, are unable or unwilling to keep it. Furthermore, it attacks Mason for deriding Protestant clerics who enter into marriage. Employing hyperbolic flattery, a satirical exhortation enjoins "Poetes fine" to defer to this new writer's superior craft, but it quickly turns into an invective attack on Mason. Ironic passages entitled "The Prayse of the Meter" and "The Prayse of the Poete" exploit excessive alliteration, invocations, and rhetorical questions and acclaim the new poet's high-flown style. Shepherd links Mason to other defenders of Catholicism and satirically applauds Richard Smith whom he claims has shaped the "new Poetes Tooles."

---

[57] *The wyll of the Deuyll. And last Testament* (London, 1548, *STC* 6793.6), Civ[v].

[58] Shepherd may intend this as a double pun as "supplicia" can mean "entreaty" as well as "torture."

[59] See 1 Timothy 3:2.

Charging Mason with "insensate ... Obtused and obturate" falsification, Shepherd nevertheless pretends that his arguments are so persuasive that he now denounces those clerics "That be alredy marryed."

The initial lines of Shepherd's refutation sub-titled "A Latten Clubbe, or Hurle Batte" can apply either to married priests or to celibate clergy who break their vow of celibacy. However, ambiguity soon gives way to a diatribe on the lewd behavior of unmarried clerics who will not lead chaste lives. In another jarring shift in perspective, Shepherd vilifies unmarried priests, who are "Given to unchastity," "Not having wives / Conquering others," "Serving Priapus," who "ravish everywhere." Obscene language corresponds to the behavior of clerics who are "Wanton goats," "Living as wolves," "Seeking out pudenda," and their behavior is shocking because of the crude nature of the allegations.

Imitating Mason, Shepherd composes his refutation in Latin, but he constructs it not out of couplets, but in consecutive rhyming lines of irregular number with no obviously discernible pattern.[60] Set apart from the other lines, the last line of the Latin text, "Ecquid Uos Beo?" is ambivalent and it does not rhyme with any of the previous Latin lines. It most probably should be read as the heading of the next part of the poem, but it can also be interpreted as a summation of "A Latten Clubbe." Likewise, the Latin words can be translated in more than one way, and the subsequent line of the poem ("Lo now how like you thys?") is, in fact, one translation of this Latin line. Also a taunt ("Is this enough for you?"), the line introduces the last part of the satire. Initially confusing to the reader, kaleidoscopic shifts in perspective allow Shepherd to condemn unmarried priests who are unchaste as well as priests who marry because they cannot otherwise lead chaste lives. The wholly negative thrust of the satire indicates that the text addresses a Protestant readership that accepts clerical marriage.

In yet another shift, the last section of the satire begins with an antithetical attack on Protestant clerics who take wives. Sardonically playing devil's advocate, Shepherd mocks clerics opposed to the rosary and the Eucharist in language reminiscent of the papal lament in *Pathose* (lines 328–329). Shepherd ridicules celibacy by dramatizing the kind of cleric whom he satirizes

---

[60] For translation, see Commentary on *Phylogamus* (303–362).

throughout this poem, Catholic priests who cannot live without sexual relationships, despite their vow of celibacy.

The rest of the poem is fairly obscure. Shepherd appears to champion Protestantism against Mason and Smith but confounds the reader by referring to himself in the third person and speaking about his conservative opponents using the possessive pronoun "our" rather than "their." Shepherd furthers this confusion about point of view by re-entering the text in the first person (lines 462–465), offering his services as a propagandist "To fyght thus in your quarrell." Shepherd offers assistance to Mason "Either wyth boke or word / Soone wyl I be the thyrd." This apparently straightforward reference to the number of refutations inspired by Mason's work may actually constitute a sarcastic offer to succeed Smith and Mason as defender of clerical celibacy: "Wel wel ye knowe my mynde."

The *a*-rhymed lines in the concluding octave wittily personify divergent attitudes towards marriage. Thus "Philogamus" (lover of marriage) helps "Misogamus" (hater of marriage) and comforts him against "Monogamus" (single marriage), who concludes that "Apogamus" (outside of marriage) and his fellow priests are finally forsaken. In the penultimate line, Shepherd allies himself with "Phylogamus" but leaves us still wondering with an unsolved riddle in the final line: "What call Ye Hym."

### Doctour doubble ale

Shepherd's anti-clerical poem, *Doctour doubble ale*, attacks the Roman Church by satirizing an appallingly ignorant, drunken, and dissolute local London curate whose fondness for strong ale earns him the name of Doctour Doubble Ale. Drinking has so clouded this cleric's intellect that he now ignores both his daily prayers and pastoral care for the pleasures of the alehouse. Shepherd juxtaposes the Protestant narrator's scornful comments about clerical ignorance with the drunkard priest's justification of his corrupt practices and thus exposes the curate as a man who cannot tell the difference between "Gods worde" and "the Deuels," who refuses to contemplate change, and who justifies himself as a man "ernest in the cause / Of piuish popish lawes."

Doctour Doubble Ale typifies the worst of the abuses that the reformers were determined to correct. Despite recent changes in church practices, he adheres to the old Catholic ways. He still reads his bede rolls (thus encouraging prayers for the dead), he persists in his advocacy for the souls in purgatory, and he watches out for heresy in his parish. The poem initially centers on the curate's love of the ale pot, his habit of seeking out ale-houses where the drink is served in large rather than small measures, and his custom of persuading other idle fellows to join him in his carousing. The closest this curate comes to fulfilling his preaching duty is the drunken advice he gives his drinking companions in the taverns. The narrator mocks Doctour Doubble Ale's conservative persistence, pointing out that in spite of his high opinion of his own cleverness, the curate is not learned at all because the breviary he reads cannot teach him the truth whereas the Scriptures could. However, unlike the young "cobblers boy" who now appears in the poem, Doctour Doubble Ale cannot interpret the Gospel correctly. In contrast to the cleric, this uneducated youth personifies the Protestant belief in the priesthood of all believers and in the universal accessibility of the Scriptures.

The intrusion of a markedly Protestant voice here signals an actual historical event, the apprehension and presentation before the authorities of a young lad on a heresy charge. Five short onomatopoeic lines reflect the commotion and uproar that surround the boy's capture and his imprisonment in the Counter, the London Guildhall prison. This account probably refers to Richard Mekins, a fifteen-year-old youth, who went to the stake (30 July 1541) as a sacramentarian despite extremely contradictory evidence. The execution of one so young horrified London's populace and contributed to the cruel reputation of its bishop, Edmund Bonner.[61] Shepherd's inclusion of the story presents us with a local Protestant martyr and provides Doctour Doubble Ale with an antagonist to rail against. Contrasting the untrained youth who can read and is sober with the drunken, conservative cleric, Shepherd draws the conclusion that the "cobblers boy" is more suited to be a curate than the papist who now holds that position.

Half-way through the poem, Doctour Doubble Ale assumes the role of narrator and continues the tale in the first person. Unexpectedly, we hear not the cleric's life story but a hodgepodge of seemingly unconnected bits and pieces, which echoes the "hubble shubble" of the lines concerning the capture of the "cobblers boy." In a masterpiece of ironic self-confession, the curate

---

[61] Foxe, *Acts*, 5: 440–442.

describes his enthusiasm for ale and his contempt for the reformers who he hopes will burn at the stake in Smithfield. Lamenting the passing of the old ways and the introduction of new-fangled ideas, he reiterates his refusal to allow the sacraments to be administered in English in his church. Affirming his belief in the efficacy of the Mass, moreover, he vows that he will never "forsake / That I of a cake / my maker may make."

Doctour Doubble Ale contemptuously dismisses the reformers of his parish: "And let these heretikes preach / And teach what they can teach." Ironically, he does not comprehend that, despite his repudiation, the reformers *will* preach and teach and no doubt convert at least some of his parishioners. Conversely, his earnest insistence, "My parish I know well / Agaynst them wyll rebell," contradicts the curate's woeful neglect of his parishioners. By drawing attention to the distance between what Doctour Doubble Ale says and what his words signify, Shepherd emphasizes, by contrary example, the very essence of Protestantism, preaching and teaching. The satire's effect here is twofold because it requires the reader to interpret the words literally and to understand that Doctour Doubble Ale himself treats them as an absurdity.

At line 331, the original narrator replaces Doctour Doubble Ale in the text and lists recent church reforms not as the curate does, in a litany of laments, but as a catalogue of positive improvements. The narrator illustrates the curate's skill at deceiving his parishioners with an old story traditionally used to discredit the clergy. The narrator further emphasizes the priest's incompetence by inventing mock Latin rhymes, a contrivance which implies that Doctour Doubble Ale does not know the correct Latin words and can only say his prayers because he has learned them (sometimes wrongly) by rote. Doctour Doubble Ale's bad Latin dramatizes the Reformation attack on semi-illiterate clerics who were unable to read the Gospel correctly. The curate's corrupt Latin mimics the act of changing bread and wine into the Eucharist in the Mass. "You cannot do as much as I can,"[62] the curate tells us, meaning that he can do what his audience cannot, that is, transmute bread and wine into the body and blood of Christ. Doubtless, Doctour Doubble Ale confuses the celebration of the Mass with drinking the communion wine. The poem's irony deepens when we remember the curate praising ale as a

---

[62] "Tu non potes facio / Tot quam ego," *Doctour doubble ale* (407–408).

drink better than wine,[63] and Shepherd subsequently extends the irony even further. Instead of the words of consecration of the host, "Hoc est enim corpus meum" ("For this is my body"), Doctour Doubble Ale misquotes, "Hoc est lifum meum" ("This is my life," line 413).

In accord with his habit of discrediting specific opponents of religious reforms, Shepherd models Doctour Doubble Ale on Henry George, the curate of St Sepulchre's, who continued to celebrate the Mass in Latin, despite recent changes in the practice of the liturgy.[64] Like Henry George, Doctour Doubble Ale maintains his allegiance to Rome because of his personal belief in Catholic doctrine, but also because he has no intention of abandoning what he perceives as his perquisites of office. Adhering to the old ways allows Doctour Doubble Ale to enjoy a secular life. Certainly, he has no desire to give up his familiar pleasures, privileges, and drinking in order to accept the new Protestant way, which would require a life of moral rectitude and involve him in the very things that he avoids most assiduously, reading the Bible and preaching God's word to his flock.

Shepherd focuses *Doctour doubble ale* not on a well-known contemporary figure like Bishop Gardiner, but on a less-known nonconformist cleric like Henry George, who otherwise escapes the notice of the authorities. Clearly, Shepherd sees such clerics as hypocritical and dangerous. His colorful and realistic satire thus illustrates his concerns and also helps to explain why reformist propaganda flourished at a time when most Catholic practices and rituals had been abolished.

### *Cauteles preseruatory concerning the preseruation of the Gods which are kept in the pixe*

In contrast to Shepherd's verse satires, his sole surviving prose work, *Cauteles preseruatory concerning the preseruation of the Gods which are kept in the pixe*, is surprisingly straightforward. Traditionally, a cautels sets out in a written form the rubric for correctly implementing the sacraments. *Cauteles*

---

[63] "This alum finum / Is bonus then vinum," *Doctour doubble ale* (400–401).

[64] Shepherd also identifies Harry George as the curate of St Sepulchre's in *A pore helpe* (382–385). See also Commentary on *A pore helpe* (382–385) and *Doctour doubble ale* (280–285). Henry George's conservatism is evidenced in the predominantly Catholic wills he witnessed, even during Edward VI's reign (Brigden, *London and the Reformation*, 440).

*preseruatory* parodies this prescription, concerning itself with ironic directions regarding the preservation of the unconsumed communion hosts rather than with the proper procedures for administering the sacrament of the altar. Ostensibly written as a handbook for parish clergy, *Cauteles preseruatory* provides seemingly useful instructions to Catholic priests on how to protect communion hosts from the ravages of both the weather and various kinds of pestilence as well as how to preserve them against attacks from birds and small animals such as mice, rats, and monkeys.

The unnamed narrator begins by criticizing priests who allow their host-made-God to be corrupted, go moldy, or breed worms, be eaten by small animals, or be carried away by birds. If priests truly change bread and wine into the body and blood of Christ, then surely the preservation of the consecrated hosts should be their prime concern. For the edification of these priests, therefore, the narrator will compose a "lytell worke" of instruction on how to preserve communion hosts. If the priests follow its advice, both they and their "god" will avoid the condemnation to which they are at present daily subjected. The narrator offers instructions concerning the manufacture of communion hosts and a catalogue of directions for their preservation as well as advice regarding the hosts which have gone moldy, despite the care taken to preserve them from decay. The tract concludes with a marked change in voice as the narrator now plainly espouses Protestant doctrine, trusting that all those who believe truly in God shall experience eternal life and that all idol "worshippers and makers" shall be confounded. The discourse concludes formally, with a prayer of praise to the Trinity.

As readers, we find it easy, at first, to accept this tract at its face value as an instructional text on how best to preserve communion hosts from contamination and decay. Shepherd presents the work in such a matter-of-fact way that we may forget the piece is entirely satirical; that the advice, which pretends to be so thoughtful, is essentially absurd. Initially, Shepherd deceives us by the complex sentence structure, formal expression, and solemn tone in which he compares judicious men of scholarship and talented artisans with Catholic priests who cleverly create their God from the accidentals of bread and wine. The narrator's subsequent suggestion of a "munkay" as a potential threat to the Eucharist, however, undermines the gravity of the text.

The satire becomes more evident when the narrator suggests that priests store the unconsecrated hosts in dry conditions. But to suggest that in

England the hosts should be stored away during the winter or whenever the weather is foggy or rainy would render them unavailable for religious use. Given that the reason for reserving the Eucharist is so the sick and dying of the parish may receive the viaticum, curtailing the supply of communion hosts completely defeats its purpose. Similarly, advice that priests check the hosts frequently to make sure that they are not in a state of decomposition is entirely sensible but is completely undercut by the following sentence: "Prouided alway that ye do it in cleare whether."

Likewise, the narrator's cure for hosts that have gone moldy and soggy is wonderfully ridiculous and conjures up a comical picture of the village priest climbing onto the church roof to lay out the communion hosts "one by one vpon a fayre cloth to take the sun." This piece of nonsense is followed by instructions that appear to be perfectly reasonable, like making sure that the hosts are not blown away by the wind or eaten by birds, except when we bear in mind that exposing the hosts to the weather and birds in the first place is a ludicrous thing to do. In the same way, the narrator's advice that hosts should be carefully protected from animal scavengers does not appear to be outlandish at first, but we sense mockery when a spaniel is described as "vermyne" and when we learn that a "robin redbrest" is likely to swoop down during the celebration of the Mass and "flie away" with the communion host while the priest is praying with his eyes closed.

In addition to trite advice and biased theological arguments, however, the narrator also delivers some low-key, but effective, anti-Catholic propaganda. Throughout the entire tract the priests are made to look foolish and implausible, not only because they need advice on how to preserve unconsumed communion hosts but because the advice the narrator gives them is nonsensical. Nevertheless, the advice is presented to the priests as if it were scientifically reasonable, albeit slightly unconventional, and this pseudo-seriousness serves to camouflage much of the underlying anti-Catholic tone of the work so that even while the narrator is bombarding them with absurdities, we have to keep reminding ourselves of Shepherd's particular polemical bias. This point is cleverly illustrated in the text when the narrator explains how to restore the discolored communion hosts to their original white brilliance. The suggestion concerning bleaching and purifying the hosts by placing them over burning brimstone appears quaint, until we recall the biblical reference to the destruction of Babylon and the punishment of the false prophets and idolaters in the lake of burning fire and brimstone (Revelation 19:20; 20:10; 21:8), and the fact that, for the reformers, Babylon, false prophets, and idolaters represent the Roman Church.

Despite the triteness of the advice, many of the ideas proposed in this tract have some basis in traditional theological debate. For instance, the narrator insists that the wafer maker must be a virtuous man if the hosts he produces are to be long lasting. By pretending to believe that the tradesman's character influences the product he makes and by interpreting "wafer maker" as the priest who makes his God, as well as the person who makes the actual host, the narrator ridicules the medieval debate over whether or not a celebrant needs to be in the state of grace in order to consecrate the host. Conversely, the narrator also reminds the reader of the popular belief among early reformers that the unworthiness of the minister vitiated the sacrament.[65] Similarly, the reference to choosing "the fairest roundest and whighteste" hosts for consecration or trimming them if they are not perfectly shaped parodies the traditional instructions for the proper manufacture of communion hosts.[66]

Moreover, the narrator satirizes the religious regulations of the Roman Church governing the reception of the Eucharist. Usually, the laity received the Eucharist at Easter and, possibly, once or twice more during the year, but the practice had grown up of allowing the servers at Mass to consume left-over fragments of the celebrant's host. The narrator suggests that the unconsecrated scraps, trimmed from the hosts to make them look perfect, will bestow the same benefits as the consecrated fragments. Likewise, the narrator warns the priests against administering spoiled communion hosts to healthy people who may detect their corruption and spit them out. Shepherd's audience knows that in such cases the priest is expected to dispose of the defiled host by swallowing it himself.[67] Far better, then, to reserve any contaminated host for the sick because the rotten host will act as a purgative and, although the sick person may vomit it up, the illness will be expelled at the same time. Furthermore, the narrator advises, the laity will react to such a miraculous cure by giving praise and "much glory" to the priests' God.

---

[65] See Brigden, *London and the Reformation*, 67; 406.

[66] See Rubin, *Corpus Christi*, 39–43.

[67] See Commentary on *Cauteles preseruatory* (Aviᵛ).

# INTRODUCTION

By trivializing traditional conservative belief in miracles effected by the communion host, while at the same time mocking such superstitious behavior by "the comon people," Shepherd suggests to his audience the relationship between the miraculous powers of the Eucharist and the miraculous faith necessary to believe in Christ's physical presence in it. He thus reminds readers of the Protestant arguments against the doctrine of transubstantiation. As well, his description of the pyx suspended "betwene the altare and the roffe" recalls derisive references to the reserved host (Jack of the Box and Round Robin), thus presenting a Protestant point of view. In yet another shift in perspective, the conclusion negates the narrator's previous, conservative advice. In the last page of the work, the narrator's voice becomes openly Protestant, and the tract ends abruptly with an appeal to Christ to apportion true justice on the Day of Judgment.

# The

# Texts

## I

## *A pore helpe,*

**The bukler and defence**
**Of mother holy kyrke,**
**And weapen to driue hence**
**Al that against her wircke**

WYll none in all this lande     
Step forth and take in hande
These felowes to withstande
In nombre lyke the sande
5    That with the Gospell melles
And wyll do nothynge elles
But tratlynge tales telles
Agaynst our holy prelacie
And holy churches dygnitie
10    Sayinge it is but papistrie
Yea fayned and Hipocrisy
Erronious and heresye
And taketh theyr aucthoritie
Out of the holy Euangelie
15    All customes ceremoniall
And rytes ecclesiasticall
Not grounded on scripture
No longer to endure
And thus ye maye be sure
20    The people they alure
And drawe them from your lore
The whiche wyll greue you sore
Take hede I saye therfore
Your nede was neuer more
25    But sens ye be so slacke
It greueth me a lacke
To heare behynde your backe
Howe they wyll carpe and cracke     
And none of you that dare
30    Whiche one of them compare
Yet some there be that are

So bolde to shewe theyr ware
And is no priest nor deacon
And yet wyll fyre his becone
35 Agaynst such felowes frayle
Make out with tothe and nayle
And hoyste vp meyne sayle
And manfully to fyght
In holy prelates ryght
40 With penne and ynke and paper
And lyke no triflynge Iaper
To touche these felowes in dede
With all expedient spede
And not before it nede
45 And I in dede am he
That wayteth for to se
Who dare so hardy be
To encounter here with me
I stande here in defence
50 Of some that be far hence
And can both blysse and sence
And also vndertake
Ryght holy thynges to make
Yea God within a cake
55 And who so that forsake                    [Sig Aii$^v$]
His breade shall be dowe bake
I openly professe
The holy blyssed masse
Of strength to be no lesse
60 Then it was at the fyrst
But I wolde se who durst
Set that amonge the worst
For he shulde be acurst
With boke, bell and candell
65 And so I wolde hym handell
That he shulde ryght well knowe
Howe to escape I trowe
So hardy on his heade

4

Depraue our holy breade
70 Or els to prate or patter
Agaynst our holy watter
This is a playne matter
It nedeth not to flatter
They be suche holy thynges
75 As hath bene vsed with kynges
And yet these lewde loselles
That bragge vpon theyr Gospelles
At ceremonies swelles
And at our christined belles
80 And at our longe gownes
And at your shauen crownes
And at your typettes[1] fyne         Aiii
The Iauelles wyll repyne
They saye ye leade euyll lyues
85 With other mennes wyues
And wyll none of your owne
And so your sede is sowne
In other mennes grounde
True wedlocke to confounde
90 Thus do they rayle and raue
Callynge euery priest knaue
That loueth messe to saye
And after ydle all daye
They wolde not haue you playe
95 To dryue the tyme awaye
But brabble on the Byble
Whiche is but vnpossible
To be learned in all your lyfe
Yet therin be they ryfe
100 Whiche maketh all this stryfe
And also the Paraphrasies
Moche dyfferyng from your portaises

---

[1] typettes] typttes 1548.

5

They wolde haue dayly vsed
And portaise cleane refused
105 But they shall be accused
That haue so farre abused
Theyr tongues agaynst suche holynes
And holy churches busynes [Sig Aiiiᵛ]
Made hundred yeares ago
110 Great clearkes affyrmeth so
And other many mo
That searched to and fro.
In scripture for to fynde
What they myght leaue behynde
115 For to be kept in mynde
Amonge the people blynde
As wauerynge as the wynde
And wrote therof suche bokes
That who so on them lokes
120 Shall fynde them to be clarkes
As proueth by theyr warkes
And yet there be that barcke
And saye they be but darcke
But harke ye loulars harke
125 So well we shal you marcke
That yf the worlde shall turne
A sorte of you shall burne
Ye durst as well I saye
Within this two yeares daye
130 As soone to runne awaye
As suche partes to playe
When some dyd rule and reygne
And auncient thynges mayntayne
Whiche nowe be counted vayne Aiiii
135 And brought into dysdayne
Suche men I saye they were
As loued not this geare
And kept you styll in feare

To burne or faggottes bere
140 Then durst ye not be bolde
(Agaynst our learnynges olde
Or images of golde
Whiche nowe be bought and solde
And were the laye mannes boke
145 Wheron they ought to loke)
One worde to speake a mysse
Can ye saye nay to this?
No no ye foles I wysse
A thynge to playne it is.
150 Then dyd these clarkes diuyne
Dayly them selues enclyne
To proue and to defyne
That Christes body aboue
Whiche suffered for our loue
155 And dyed for our behoue
Is in the sacrament
Fleshe bloude and bone present
And breade and wyne awaye
As sone as they shall saye
160 The wordes of consecracion                    [Sig Aiiii$^v$]
In tyme of celebracion
So muste it be in dede
Thoughe it be not in the crede
And yet these felowes newe
165 Wyll saye it is not true
Christes body for to vewe
With any bodyly eye
That do they playne deny
And stifly stande therby
170 And enterpryse to wryght
And also to endyght
Bokes both great and small
Agaynst these fathers all
And heresy it call

7

175   That any man shulde teache
Or to the people preache
Suche thynges without theyr reache
And some there be that saye
That Christ cannot all day
180   Be kept within a box
Nor yet set in the stockes
Nor hydden lyke a fox
Nor presoner vnder lockes
Nor clothed with powdred armyne
185   Nor bredeth stynkynge vermyne
Nor dweleth in an howse
Nor eatyn of a mouse            Av
Nor rotten is nor rustye
Nor moth eaten nor mustye
190   Nor lyght as is a fether
Nor blowne awaye with wether
Nor moulde or he be spent
Nor yet with fyre be brente
Nor can no more be slayne
195   Nor offered vp agayne
Blessed sacrament for thy passion
Here and se our exclamacion
Agaynst these men of newe facion
That stryue agaynst the holy nacion
200   And Iest of them in playes
In tauerns and hye wayes
And theyr good actes dysprayse
And martyrs wolde them make
That brent were at a stake
205   And synge pype mery annot
And play of wyll not cannot
And as for cannot and wyll not
Thoughe they speake not of it it skyll not
For a noble clarke of late
210   And worthy in estate

Hath played with them chekmate
Theyr courage to abate
And telles them suche a tale          [Sig Av<sup>v</sup>]
As makes theyr bonettes vale
215     And marreth cleane the sale.
Of all theyr whole pastyme
And all is done in ryme
Oh, what a man is this
That yf he coulde I wysse
220     Wolde mende that is amysse
His meanynge is in dede
That yf he myght well spede
And beare some rule agayne
It shulde be to theyr payne
225     I thynke they were but worthye
Because they be so sturdye
To rayle agaynst the wyrcke
Of our mother holy kyrke
Yet some there be in fume
230     And proudly do presume
Unto this learned man
To answere and they can
And wene they had the grace
His balad to deface
235     And trowe ye that wyll be?
Nay nay beleue ye me
I take my marke amys
If once he dyd not mys
A very narowe his
240     Well yf you come agayne          [Sig Avi]
Maye happen twelue men
Shall do as they dyd then
Haue you forgote the bar
That euer there you war
245     And stode to make and mar
By god and by the countrey

You had a narowe entrey
Take hede of coram nobis
We wyll reken with vobis
250 If you come agayne
We wyll knowe who pulled the henne
For all your bolde courage
You maye paye for the porage[2]
And are you nowe so bragge
255 You maye come to lagge
Your happe may be to wagge
Upon a wodden nagge
Or els a fayre fyre
May happe to be your hyer
260 Take hede least you tyer
And lye downe in the myer
Holde fast by the mane
By the masse it is no game
If my Lorde waxe not lame
265 You wyl all be tame
When you heare hym next
Marke well his texte                    [Sig Aviᵛ]
He hath ben curstly vext
I feare me he be wext
270 A popistant stout
Surely all the rout
That heres hym shall doubt
He wyll be in and out
Prowlynge rounde about
275 To get forth the snout
If prayer maye do good
All the whole broode
Skuruy, skabed, and skalde
Shauen, shorne, and balde
280 Pore priestes of Baule

---

We praye for hym all
Unto the God of breade
For yf he be deade
We maye go to bed
285 Blyndefylde and be led
Without rag or shred
But I am sore adred
I se hym loke so red
Yet I durste ley my heade
290 As doctor fryer sayde
He hath some what in store
Well you shall knowe more
Herken well therfore    [Sig Avii]
Some shall paye the skore
295 He hath ben a pardoner
And also a garddener
He hath ben a vytailer
A lordly hospytelar
A noble teacher
300 And also³ a preacher
Thoughe Germyn his man
Were hanged what than?
Saye worsse and you can
Best let hym alone
305 For Peter Iames and Iohn
And Apostles euery one
I gyue you playne warnynge
Had neuer suche learnynge
As hath this famous clarke
310 He is learned beyond the marke⁴
And also maister huggarde
Doth shewe hym selfe no sluggarde
Nor yet no dronken druggarde

---

³ also] so so 1548.
⁴ beyond] be beyond 1548.

But sharpeth vp his wyt
315 And frameth it so fyt
These yonkers for to hyt
And wyll not them permyt
In errour styll to syt
As it maye well apeare
320 By his clarkely answere     [Sig Avii<sup>v</sup>]
The whiche intitled is
Agaynst what meaneth this
A man of olde sorte
And wryteth not in sporte
325 But answereth earnestly
Concludynge heresy
And yet as I trowe
Some bluster and blowe
And crake (as they crowe)
330 But nettes wyll we laye
To cache them yf we maye
For yf I begynne
I wyll brynge them in
And feche in my cosens
335 By the whole dosens
And call them coram nobis
And teache them dominus vobis
With his et cum spiritu tuo
That holy be both duo
340 When they be sayde and songe
In holy latyn tongue
And solemne belles be ronge
But these babes be to yonge
Perkynge vpon theyr patins
345 And fayne wolde haue the mattens
And eueninge⁵ songe also     [Sig Aviii]
In Englishe to be do

---

⁵ eueninge] eueinge 1548.

With mariage and baptysinge
Buryalles and other thynge
350 In vulgare tongue to saye and synge
And so they do it newly
In dyuerse places truly
Sayinge they do but duely
Mayntainynge it in any wyse
355 So shulde they do theyr seruyce
Alas who wolde not mone
Or rather grunt or gro[n]e
To se suche seruyce gone
Whiche saued many one
360 From deadly synne and shame
And many a spote of blame
From purgatorye payne
And many showre of rayne
Well yet I saye agayne
365 Some honest men remayne
And kepe theyr customes styll
And euer more wyll
Wherfore in dede my read is
To take you to your beades
370 All men and women I saye
That vseth so to praye.
That suche good priestes maye                [Sig Aviii<sup>v</sup>]
Contynue so alwaye
Or els none other lyke
375 But al lyeth in the dyke
And loke ye do not faynt
But praye to some good saynt
That he maye make restraint
Of all these straunge facions
380 And great abomynacions,
Because I maye not tary
I praye to swete syr Harry
A man that wyl not vary
And one that is no sculker

13

385 But kan. knyghte of the Sepulchre
That he maye stande fast
And be not ouer cast
Or els to be the last
Of all them that do yelde
390 In cyte towne or fielde
For yf he stike therin
No doubt he shall not blyn
Tyll he come to eternytie
With all his whole fraternyte
395 Amen therfore saye ye
That his partakers be
Ye get no more of me.
Finis.

*The vpcheringe of the messe:*

[Imprinted at London by Iohn Daye and Willyam Seres.]

Who hath not knowen or herd     [Sig Ai<sup>v</sup>]
How we were made afeard
That magre of our beard
Our messe shulde cleane awaye
5    That we did dayly saye
And vtterly decaye
For euer and for aye
So were we brought in doubte
That all that are deuout
10   Were like to go withoute
The messe that hath no peere
Which longe hath taried here
Yea many an hundreth yere
And to be destitute
15   Of that whiche constitute
Was of the highe depute
Of Christe and his apostles
Althoughe none of the Gospels
No mencion maketh or tells
20   We must beleue what ells?
Of things done by councells.
Wherin the high professours
Apostlique successours
Take holde to be possessours
25   And some wer made confessours
Some of them were no startars
But were made holi marters     Aii
Yet plowmen smythes & cartars
With such as be their hartars
30   Will enterprise to taxe
Thes auncyent mens actes
And holy fathers factes
Thoughe messe were made bi men
As popes nyne or ten
35   Or many more what then?

15

Or not of scripture grounded
Is yt therfore confounded
To be a supersticion?
Nay nay they mysse the quission
40 Make better Inquysicion
Ye haue an euyll condicion
To make suche exposicion
Ye thinke nothing but scripture
Is only clene and pure
45 Yes yes I you ensure
The messe shalbe hir better
As light as ye do set hir
　The scripture hath nothing
Wher by profyte to bryng
50 But a lytyll preaching
With tattling and teaching
And nothing can ye espie
Nor se with outwarde eye　　　　　　　　　　[Sig Aiiᵛ]
But must your ears applie
55 To learnyng inwardlye
And who so it will folowe
In goods though he may walow
If scripture once him swalowe
She wyll vndo him holowe
60 Wherefore no good mes singers
Will come wᵗ in hir fyngers
But are hir vnder styngers
For she wolde fayne vndo
All such as lyueth so
65 To the messe she is an enymye[6]
And wolde distroye hir vtterlye
Wer not for sum that frendfully
In time of nede will stand hir by
Yet is the messe and she as lyke

---

[6] Not indented in NLW copy.

16

70 As a christian to an heretike
The messe hath holy vestures
And many gay gestures
And decked with clothe of golde
And vessells many folde
75 Right galaunt to beholde
More then may well be tolde
With basen ewer and towell
And many a prety Iwelle
With goodly candellstyckes         Aiii
80 And many proper tryckys
With cruetts gilt, and chalys
Whereat some men haue malice
With sensers and with pax
And many other knackys
85 With patent and with corporas
The fynest thing that euer was
Alasse is it not pitie
That men be no more wittye
But on the messe to Iest
90 Of all suche thinges the best
For if she were supprest
A pyn for all the rest.
   But harke to me a while
And marke ye well my style
95 Al ye that speake so vyle
And woulde the messe exile
Tidynges I can you tell
She is like here to dwel
In dispite of the Gospel
100 For al his lokes so snel
And also I wyl proue
It wil the Gospel behoue
To sue to haue her loue
For within fewe yeres
105 He durst not for his eares         [Sig Aiiiᵛ]
Be sene in all this land

17

Nor harde nor had in hand
But she had by hym stande
He was hir seruaunt than
110     Let him say what he can
With him durst no man
Meddle more or lesse
But whan he harde messe
This must he nedes confesse
115     Or eles in exposicions
Or doctors dispuicions
Such were the constitutions
And also institutions
Suche were their prohibicions
120     And also inhibicions
He durste not crie creake
Till he coulde englishe speake
But lyke an huddy peake
Kepe warme hys braynes weake
125     And nowe he is full cranke
And conneth hir no thanke
But compteth hir as ranke
As any on the bancke
But maister Euangelium
130     The tyme agayne may come
But wel ther mum
Ha, Ha, Hum.
    Wel yet ther be some
That are not all dum
135     That long hath hold theyr peace
And were content to cease
Leste malice should encrese
To frie them in their grese
And nowe they be turned lose
140     They passe not of a gose
To saye the worst they can
By messe the pore woman

Aiiii

18

What did I call hir pore?
Naye some wyl cal hir whore
145  And stireth a great vprore
Some cal hir popes daughter
Some sayes she made manslaughter
Some turne hir to a laughter
Some wold they had not sought hir
150  Som cursseth hym yᵗ brought hir
And him that first taught hir
Some say she is a leache
To make whole scabes & bleache
Some saye she is good for byles
155  And good for humbled heles
And good for kowe or Oxe
That chafid be wyth yockes  [Sig Aiiii$^v$]
And good for hens and cockes
To kepe them from the fox
160  They saye she is good for the pox
And such as haue sore dockes
And as for gaulde horse backes
That chafed be with packes
With panyers and wyth sackes
165  No helpe they say she lackes
And good for meselde hogges
And also maungye dogges
But for a Winchester goslynge
They saye she passeth al thinge
170  She bringeth wether clere
And ceasonable yere
And if it neade agayne
They saye she bringeth raine
She seaceth thonder lowde
175  And scatereth euerie cloude
They say the plage and pestilence
The feuer and the epilence
The popish messe expelleth hence

19

And grasse she maketh growe
180 And fayre wynde to blowe
And rule it highe and lowe
Her power is greate I trowe
And some saye wedes & thornes [Sig Av]
She kepeth from the cornes
185 And yet some mockes & scornes
And say hir pristes make hornes
On eueninges and in mornes
Thus do they hir defame
And slaunder hir good name
190 Wherin they be to blame
For I can good witnes fet
That she neuer holpe one yet
   Thus thei speake and spare not
And what thei prate thei care not
195 For lowdly do they sounde
That missa is not founde
Within the byble boke
Who so theron shall loke
And yet they be a croke
200 Amisse the marcke they toke
Ther shal ye find misach
A wel, howe lyke ye thys knacke?
   Wherfore loke about
And serche in and out
205 For she is no lowt
I put you out of doubt
She is not cleane forsaken
But very wel taken
Yea yea be lakin [Sig Av<sup>v</sup>]
210 She is worth a flicke of bacon
And if it be well sought
She wil not so be bought
Yet may ye se hir for nought
In many holy places

20

215     Within a fewe paces
An holy holy thinge
Especially when they synge
With mery piping
And besy chauntyng
220     We maye be veri glad
That yet the messe is had
For al it is so bad
The people be as mad
As euer they may be
225     The messe to here and se
Auengaunce on it for me
For I am al moste werye
I haue taken suche payne
To bringe hir home agayne
230     Wherfore nowe totus mundus
That round is and rotundus
Be mery and Iocundus
And sing the letabundus
With al the whole chorus
235     That here hath ben before vs         [Sig Avi]
And al the sely soules
That hereth messe in poules
And in al places beside
In london that is wyde
240     Where messe is song or sayd
And be nothinge affraed
That she shal go awaye
But tary whyle she maye
For she must long continue
245     She hath suche greate retynue
Stronge men of bone and sinue
Ye can no better wyshe
They wyl sticke to their stockfish
And stande lyke lusty bloudes
250     Aduenturinge lyfe and goodes

And all to put in peril
For mastres missas quarel
And nothynge wil they shrincke
No more then for to drincke
255 To spake such as they thincke
No no they wyll not wincke
At matters to be sene
Nor let for king or quene
Ye gesse nere whom I meane
260 Yet is it sayed I wene
He caried not al cleane    [Sig Aviᵛ]
Yet hath he bolder ben
Then other fiften
 Wherefore he maye be praysed
265 That such a noyse is raysed
And thorowe Englande voysed
That he woulde be so hardy
Thoughe he were taken tardy
He thought or he went thens
270 To declare his consciens
A man of muche sapience
And ful of goodly sentence
Wel lyke to wyn the audience
By his copious Eloquence
275 If wel he might enchieued
For many men beleued
That he coulde haue remeued
And wonne by his entent
Al that there were presente
280 Alacke they were not bent
To graunt or to consent
To suche thinges as he ment
 He talked that religions
With al their prety pigions
285 For good entent were wroughte
God wotteth what he thought

22

He spake it not for noughte
Though scripture he ne brought
But if he would haue sought
290 He coulde haue proued it there
Or a horse coulde lyke his eare
That taking awaye the il
They might haue stand stil
And in lyke case by Images
295 And all maner of ceremonies
   But tushe let go thes bables
And al these fible fables
The messe he did auaunce
And highly hir enhaunce
300 To be of such perfection
As neadeth no correction
Nor yet to haue infection
For al hir late detection
Nor worthie of suspection
305 So cleare is hir confection
And purenes of complection
By catholyke election
She semes to take erection
Aboue the resurrection
310 For neuer was his lot
In hir to spie a spot
But cleane from blurre and blot
He loueth hir wel, god wot [Sig Avii<sup>v</sup>]
There can no droncken sot
315 Loue more the good ale pot
I dare saye at this howre
Thoughe he be in the towre
Yet doeth he styl honoure
The messe that swete a flowre
320 Wherfore ye priestes al
That styl continue shal
With messinge in the temple

23

Forget not thys exemple
Of thys your father
325 That ye maye the rather
Obtayne the grace
To come to the place
Wher he doeth abyde
And loke ye do not slyde
330 But sticke to hir harde
Or elles all is marde
And whan ye may not chuse
Then must ye hir refuse
Ther wilbe heauy newes
335 As euer came to the stewes
The contrye is not fayre
And she liketh not the ayre
Wherfore if she appayre
Nedes home she muste repayre                [Sig Aviii]
340 There is no such remedie
As is hir natiue contrie
And if she chaunce to dye
I can not helpe it I
But synge placebo
345 Tut let hir gooe
I wene we get no mo
   A good mestres missa
Shal ye go from vs thissa
Wel yet I muste ye kyssa
350 Alacke for payne I pyssa
To se the mone here Issa
Because ye muste departe
It greueth many an herte
That ye should from them start
355 But what then tushe a farte
Sins other shifte is none
But she must neades be gone
Nowe let vs synge eche one

24

Boeth Iak and gyll and Ione
360     Requiem eternam
Lest penam sempiternam
For vitam supernam
And vmbram infernam
For veram lucernam
365     She chaunce to enherite             [Sig Aviii$^v$]
According to hir merite
    Pro cuius memoria[7]
Ye maye wel be soria
Full smale maye be your gloria
370     When ye shal heare thys storia
Then wil ye crie and roria
We shal se hir no moria
Et dicam vobis quare
She may no longer stare
375     Nor here with you regnare
But trudge ad vltra mare
And after habitare
In regno plutonico
Et Eue acronyco
380     Cum cetu babilonico
Et cantu diabolico
With pollers and pillers
And al hir well willers
And ther to dwel euer
385     And thus wil I leaue hir.
               FINI[S]

---

[7] Bodleian copy (Tanner 47 [1]) is torn here.

## III  *Pathose, or an inward passion of the pope for the losse of hys daughter the Masse.*

WHat hatefull hap
What carefull clap
What rattellyng rap
Is light in my lap
5    Whiche weareth the cap
Of myghti mayntenaunce
And greatest gouernaunce
Whose only ordinaunce
And prudent puysance
10   Brought to obeysaunce
All princely power
Me to adoure
With high honoure
And towne and towre
15   To lowt and lowre
At my comaundement
Yelding to myne intent
And were beniuolent
To such as I haue sent
20   To passe in perliament
Or councells generall
Or matters speciall
I was the capitall
And ruled ouer all
25   But yet nowe heare ye shal
Of maruailles late befall
And of the greate displeasure          <Sig Aii>[8]
And myscheffe out of measure
Betid my greatist treasure
30   In whome I had moste pleasure
As ye may here at leasure
    My daughter and myne heire

---

[8] <Sig Aii>] Aiii 1548. Incorrect signature. (See note following *Pathose* l. 21.)

Most beautifull and fayre
That sat most cheiffe in chaire
35 And on the supreme stayre
Alasse doth sore appayre
My glory and my goste
My braggyng and my boste
Whome I haue loued moste
40 And ruled all the roste
In country and in cooste
And now, alasse, is tost
From pillar vnto post
I feare me she be lost
45   Ah that my daughter messe
Shuld be in suche a sickenes
And brought in such weakenes
That by all maner of lykenes
She loseth life and quiknes
50 And therfore wo is me
This doleful day to se
That my darling shulde be
In this infirmytye          [Sig Aiiᵛ]
And great calamytye
55 For poysoned is she
  Alasse sum Edomite
Some Iewe or Iacobite
Some turke or thraconite
Hath gyuen hir aconite
60 In steade of arthanite
Wherfore I must of right
With all my mayne and might
A messenger forth dight
That is both quike and light
65 To labor day and night
And seke that cursed wight
That did me this dispyte
  And well he muste hym quite
Till he cum in the sight

70      Of mighty mahomyte
        And tell hym that his nese
        The messe that prope piece
        In deadly danger is
        And that he may not mysse
75      But send some arabies
        That worthie be and wise
        In phisike and in phisnomyes
            But O most Ientill Iupiter
        That named art Diespiter                    Aiii
80      Be thou oure holy helper
        And send vs soone a messenger
        That is a perfyt passenger.
        I call to the O Iuno
        And also to Neptuno
85      To Phebe and to Phebus
        That nowe ye wolde not leue vs.
            O most fayre⁹ venus
        On whom we chiefly leane vs
        We serue the night and day
90      Let vs not nowe decaye
        And helpe vs nowe Mercurius
        Against this feuer furious
        Thi godly disposition
        Is all in expedition
95          O excellent king Aeolus
        Be not thou maleuolous
        Nor cast vs not behinde
        But temper well the wynde
        And cause it to be kynde
100     The soner shall we fynde
        The meanes to haue our mynde
        Concernyng the redresse
        Of this oure great distresse

---

⁹ fayre] faye 1548. Meter demands "fayre."

And woofull heauynesse
105 So shall my daughter messe                    [Sig Aiii<sup>v</sup>]
The goodly yong goddesse
Recouer her sickenes
To you I call and crye
That are the goddes on hie
110 That ye will all applie
To send some remedye
For sure I am that you
Will sone enclyne and bowe
To them that maketh vowe
115 As I doo to you nowe
To offer sacrifice
For that in any wyse
Ye neuer wolde dispise
It hath not ben your guise
120 I offer here therfore
Of oxen thre scoore
Of Ramys as many more
And gots no small store
With pige and sowe and bore
125 Of euery birde a brode
And washe them in their bloude
To mytygate your moode
And that ye shulde be good
And helpe vs in oure nede
130 For sore I am in dreede
Excepte you help in dede
We shal but euel spede                    [Sig Aiiii]
    O ceres goddes of grayne
Which doth the worlde sustayne
135 Let vs not cal in vayne
But rid vs from this payn
We knowe it for certayne
That of thi great humylity
Thou geuyst vs fertility
140 Of corne for our vtility

29

And we for our hability
Haue daily offered
A sacrifice of breade
To the for quicke and deade
145 Did we not worship the
That all the worlde might se
When high and lowe degre
Did bend and bowe the kne
In tyme of ministracion
150 When we did make oblacion
To the when messe my daughter
Should do as I had taught her
To offer breade of wheate
Why shouldest[10] thou vs forget
155　O Bacchus: god of[11] wyne
Who gouerneth[12] grape and vine
And sendest liquor fine
Thyn earis (to heare) inclyne
My daughters mone and myne　　　　[Sig Aiiii<sup>v</sup>]
160 Thou myghtest well behold
How willingly we woulde
The worship as we shoulde
Wyth wyne in cuppes of golde
Offering to the, thyn owne
165 Which by thi grace hath growne
And nowe compelled are we
By greate necessitye
To you our goddes to fle
To seke a remedye
170　For Christ in euery place
Away hath turned his face
And woulde nothing embrace

---

[10] shouldest] should[e]st 1548.
[11] of] o[f] 1548.
[12] gouerneth] gouernteh 1548.

Oure sacrifice with grace
I passe not of an ase
175 Though I do him forsake
Yet dare I vndertake
(At pleasure) him to make
And vse him as me listis
Betwene my holy fistis
180 I can not be debarde
To handle hym softe or harde
But if he be frowarde
He shall fynde me waywarde
I get no thing hym by
185 I Recke not of him I          [Sig Av]
For if my daughter lyue
I will dwell by his sleue
With out his loue or leaue
Yea and he shall not chose
190 But what I bynde and lose
In earth as I will proue
He muste it graunt aboue
Well wel if he me moue
I will do I wot what
195 And tell hym this and that
How barely here he sate
He scarsly had a brat
His carkas[13] for to hide
Or no good thing beside
200 Howe porely dide he ride
Vpon a pore asse
Was he a lorde, alasse
On that fation to passe[14]
Into a noble cytie?[15]

---

[13] carkas] ca[r]kas 1548.
[14] passe] p[a]sse 1548.
[15] cytie?] cyti[e?] 1548.

205 Alacke alacke for pitie.
    That I thus longe haue bene
    So lewdly ouersene
    To put so much my triste
    In this[16] beggerly Christ
210 But if I had it wist
    Some what he shulde haue myst        [Sig Av<sup>v</sup>]
    Of that that he hath had
    I was acurst or mad
    So blyndly to be lad
215 For well I do perceiue
    That he will not receiue
    Such thinges as I him send
    Wherfore I nowe intend
    No more my tyme to spende
220 Or wast to such an ende
    Well wel it shal amende
      For synce he doth neglect
    And my good will reiect
    And sacrifice despect
225 I will my ways direct
    To them that haue respect
    And will my workes affect
    For I am none abiecte
    For Bacchus and Ceres clere
230 Disdayne not to drawe nere
    And take with godly chere
    Such as I offer here
    And this I knowe certayne
    Venus will not disdayne
235 Such thinges as they retayne
    For without them twayne
    Full sone she waxeth colde        [Sig Avi]
    Leane, witherd and olde.

---

[16] this] these 1548.

Wherfore I dare be bolde
240      To say she wilbe pleased
To se my daughter eased
And euen so wil Priapus
With gentil Fauna and Fa[u]nus
     Now Dromo that arte swyft
245      Apply the and make shift
To helpe me at a lifte
And golde shalbe thi gift
The goddes appoynted the
My messenger to be
250      Be nymble and make haste
For messe begynnyth to wast
She hath cleane lost hir tast
Hir body swelleth so fast
That it is like to brast
255      Wherfore I am agast
Hir life[17] is almost past
Yet shall she not away be cast
As long as euer life wil[18] last
     A iournay moste industrious[19]
260      To Appollo y$^u$ must make for vs
And to his son Aesculapius
That Raised *from* death a*n*drogeus
As witnesseth[20] Propertius          [Sig Avi$^v$]
He dwellith at Epidaurus[21]
265      Go to Chiron Centaurus
Machon and Podalirius
That lerned medicyne precious
Of their father Aesculapius

---

[17] life] [l]ife 1548.
[18] wil] wi[l] 1548.
[19] industrious] indu[s]trious 1548.
[20] witnesseth] winesseth 1548.
[21] Epidaurus] Epidauus 1548.

33

But come not at Archagathus
270 And conninge men of Egypt
In no wise may be ouerhipt
The wise men asclepiades
Of whom chiefe was hipocrates
Must say their minde in this disease
275 Forget not Dioscorides
No nor doctor Galenus
Whom some call Pergamenus
Full well he will demeane vs
In Rome longe did he dwell
280 And their in phisicke mell
Maruaill it were to tel
How much he did excell
All that were hym before
Syx hundreth yere and more
285 I dare lay all my landes
If it lye in his handes
Upon hym will he take
Euen for the contreiths sake
My daughter hole to make                    [Sig Avii]
290 But harke gentill Dromo
Remembre that ye go
To the learned woman Areta
And to Paulus aginita
To doctores of vienna
295 And also to rauenna
And then to auicenna
To Rasis and to Mesue
The learned men of Arabie
And like wise to all other
300 That worshippeth my brother
Machomet the stronge
Declare them amonge
All the whole matter
And let them se hir water
305 And tidinges loke thou bring

How they do like the thing
And whether by their connyng
They hope of hir amending
  For vntill thou retorne
310 I shall but mone and morne
And inwardly shall burne
With the most feruent fyre
And depnes of desyre
Wherfore I the require
315 Right quickly to retyre
  Oh what inwarde passion        [Sig Avii<sup>v</sup>]
Doth torment on this fassion
Who wold not take compassion
To heare my Lamentacion
320 For who can me blame
Synce I take such shame
That bare the great name
They count but a game
My messe to defame
325 Oh so I inflame
My hart with heate
Doth bolke and beate
I swell and sweate
I can not eate
330 My sorowes greate
Do me replete[22]
My papall seate
They will defeate
And put me by
335 My papasye
If my glorye
My daughter dye
For if she faile
It will not auaile

---

[22] replete] rep[l]ete 1548.

340      To wepe or to waile  
         To rage or to Rayle  
         I shal not preuaile          [Sig Aviii]  
         In cootis of maile  
         To make battaile  
345      Or them to assayll  
         If she be once gone  
         Comfort get I none  
         But lefte post alone  
         To mourne and make mone  
350      With hert as colde as stone  
           Yet may I haue some hope  
         Though she be slyd a slope  
         Some frendes to fele and grope  
         In Affrike and Europe  
355      How they will with me cope  
         Bicause I am the pope  
         They will my part take  
         Euen for my daughters sake  
         I trowe they will awake  
360      Thes Rigors to aslake  
         And cause them all to quake  
         That did this mischefe make  
         And thos that poyson gaue hir  
           Alasse I quake and quauer  
365      And also swarue and swauer  
         I quiuer and I wauer  
         I stacker and I stauer  
         For feare I shall not haue hir      [Sig Aviii<sup>v</sup>]  
         To lyue here wyth me styll  
370      According to my will  
         Hir sicknes doth me spill  
         But hir death should me kyll  
         My sorows do me fyll  
         And will encreace vntill  
375      Some tidinges I may gete[23]

---

[23] gete] [g]ete 1548.

That Dromo fare hath fete
Alacke I feare me yet
The man hath had some let
Or with our enimyes met
380    The which hath him beset
    Beholde he cometh I trowe
Some news now shall I knowe
Which way the wynde wil blow
Me thinke he is not slowe
385    As by his pace doth showe
Dromo, welcum thou art
For synce thou did depart
Full heauy was my hert
And still in payne and smart
390    But now thou art retorned
My care shalbe adiourned
For mycle haue I mourned
And in desire bourned
But nowe I thinke it best
395    That thou go take thi rest
For I haue made beheste
No meate within my breste
Nor body to be drest
Tyl I haue sene and sought
400    The writinge that thou brought
Full longe therfore I thought
I gyue the thankes in dede
For thy greate hast and spede
Haue golde here for thy meede
405    And I wyl go to reede
These letters missiue,
No longer wil I driue
The tyme labefactiue
While messe is yet alyue
410    And lyeth in payne passiue
I truste she shal reuiue
Though some against hir striue

Bi

And woulde hir life depriue
    Halasse what find I here?
415 Nowe doth it playne apere
That sure my daughter dere
Which dwelt in churche & quere
And euery mans chapel
With candell boke and bel
420 No longer here maye dwel                    [Sig Biᵛ]
As these phisicions tel
For they gyue their iudgemente
That hir nature is spent
Hir reynes be al to Rente
425 This answere haue they sent
To me wyth one consent
Affirminge that by nature
She shoulde be grosse of stature
Wherfore she must corrupt
430 Since she was interrupt
From hir pristine volupt
And since she brake hir diete
She coulde neuer be quiete
Nor like to be none other
435 But grosse by father and mother
So shewe they plaine to vs
To be morbus hereditari[u]s
But this venenum²⁴ pestiferus
Doeth make it mortiferus
440 And thus they sey that sure
She is without recure
    O worlde vnstable
And most variable
O man miserable
445 And infortunable
Which was honorable                             Bii

---

²⁴ venenum] venum 1548.

Nowe I am not abel
Longe to perseuer
Wyth al mine endeuer
450 I am loste for euer
My daughter decayed
That was my chiefest aide
My pompe is allayed
Wheron I most stayed
455 I am afrayede
And so sore dismayde
I knowe not which way
Nowe turne me I may
Nor what I shal say
460 I may not delay
Nor tyme portraye[25]
But applie me lightly[26]
And gyue hir aquauite
Or sum thynge that is mighty
465 As vinum absinthite
Or vinum apitie
Or eles abrotonite
Uinum chamedryte
Or eles aromatite
470 To comfort with hir herte
Oh that she myght reuert
And turne agayne to sanitye          [Sig Bii$^v$]
I swere by myne humanitye
I speake it not in vanitie
475 They that hir death conspired
And hath it most[27] disired
As fast as time required
With faggottes shalbe fired

---

[25] portraye] protraye 1548.
[26] lightly] lygtly 1548.
[27] most] must 1548.

O wher is my Gardnerus
480 That his good hert doth beare vs,
And more did and fisherus?
I feare he do not wel
Because we heare not tel
How he hath done his parte
485 I know I haue his herte
And also of many more
There is no smal store
That yet wyll sing and rore
Dayely my messe before
490 Though she be sicke and sore
But sore I am adred
Sum hath not wel sped
Or sume of them be dead
Or eles to prison led
495 For were they in prosperitie
I knowe it for a veritie
Sum what they woulde haue prouid
These thinges to haue remoued          [Sig Biii]
The whiche they neuer loued
500 That wrought were by lutherus
With helping of Bucerus
Zuingle and Bullingerus
Melancthon and Althamerus
Uitus, Theodor and musculus
505 And subtile Spaugelbergius
And by Urbanus regius
Alesius and Brentius
And by Otho Brumfelsius
By fagius and Pistorius
510 Petrus martir and sarcerius
And by Oecolampadius
And also Carolstadius
By cursed Uadianus
And also Pomeranus

40

515 And perilous Pellicanus
Lykewyse by Iohn cauinus
And spitfull Spalatinus
Coruinus and Epinus
And barkinge Bernardinus
520 Also by Osiander
Crucinger and Megander
And bablinge Bibliander
By Ionas and Capito
And by that heritike Hedio          [Sig Biiiᵛ]
525 And then by Latymers
By bilnie and Turners
By bayle and by Tailers
And other of their faction
Beyond dinumeracion
530 That sprange in euery nacion
To put mo to thys passion
  But where is my cochleus
Iohn Faber and Emserus
My champion Hofmisterus
535 Wher is my seruant Ecchius
And welbeloued Bilikius?
Where is my maluelda
With my most trusty Nausea
My Catharinus fyne
540 And Alfonsus my diuine
Al you wyth Sadoletus
Beholde how they entrate vs
Ech of you is a lim
To helpe vs interim
545 Ech of you is by right
My champion and my knight
For me and myn to fyght
As fast as ye may wright
For my knightes of England
550 As I may vnderstand          [Sig Biiii]

41

Ar far behinde the hande
And like to byde in bande
Ye knowe that for certaine
My daughter messe in peyne
555 And weaknes doeth remayne
Alasse she is but slayne
No medicine can I get
That wil amend hir yet
Wherfore ye may not let
560 Some comforting to fet
In England them amonge
That hath me serued long
Phisicians that ther be
I haue a skore and thre
565 That still doth worship me
And also my daughter
For stil haue they soughter
And glad when they coughter
As for communion
570 They set not an onion
But holde theyr opinion
My messe to be better
Eche one is hir detter
Agayne vp to setter
575 I neade not them name
For men can wel ame                    [Sig Biiii<sup>v</sup>]
That thei be the same
The which I do meane
Though I make no deane
580 For they wil not leane
But al one my syde
And so to abide
What so euer betide
Wythin the worlde wide
585 Ye thes be they that are
For messe so full of care
That nothynge wyll they spare

42

To make their purses bare
So they myght her repare
590    Wherefore it is lyke
That they wil not stike
To minister phisicke.
As muche as may be founde
Or sought aboue the grounde
595    To make hir hole and sounde
Nowe hie ye fast thyther
That you and they together
May bring some thinge hither
Hir life for to length
600    And q[u]iken hir strength[28]
Yet am I in feare
Nothinge to be there                    [Sig Bv]
That hir stomach wil beare
I thinke that she wil weare
605    Awaye for al this geare
Beholde she doeth teare
And rende her golden heare
    Oh so my herte doeth pricke
To se my childe[29] so sycke
610    For she is frenticke
Distraught and lunaticke
Wo worth that heretyke
That firste beganne
To shewe any man
615    Hir nature to scan
For before than
No creature knewe
But that she was true
For whan she was newe
620    I did her endue

---

[28] strength] strenght 1548.
[29] childe] chide 1548.

Wyth clothynge of Gospel
And of the Epistel
And nowe they be gon
She semeth as one
625   That is but skin and bon
As leane as a rake
As flat as a cake
As stife as a stake     [Sig Bvᵛ]
Hir lippes be pale
630   Hir eyes were smale
Hir checkes thyne
With a yealowe skine
And nought wythin
Hir nose is sharpe
635   And a wrye doeth warpe
As heauy as leade
She is neare deade
Or eles in swonne
I am but vndone
640     Thou son and thou mone
And the plannetes seuen
That ruleth in heauen
And also beneth
My daughter I bequeth
645   In to your holy handes
To louse hir from these bandes
And from the cruel death
That sone wyll stoppe hir breth
And shortly deuoure
650   Thys beautiful flowre
Except by your powre
Ye send hir succoure
And that spedily
Or eles she must dye     [Sig Bvi]
655     Iupiter ceraunus
Send doune vulcanus

And fire doune cast
Al suche to deuast
As causeth this carke
660 By theyr woful warcke
O Mars Mauors
With strength and force
Reuenge wyth war
Both nere and far
665 Thys tresspasse cruell
Done to my Iuell
For well I espye
They set not a flye
By my greate cursse
670 They be not the wors
For mine interdiction
It is none affection
My strength[30] doth decrease
My doctrine doth cease
675 My daughter doth perishe
Nothinge wyll cherishe
Yet hath she good keping
Boeth waking and slepinge
But I wyth much wepinge
680 Wyth crouchinge and creping       [Sig Bviᵛ]
Wyth bassing and kissing
Wil gyue hir my blessing
O pulchra proles
Miranda moles
685 Infandum doles
Hactenus que soles
Quidquid ad nutum
Habere tutum
Corpus imbutum
690 Mollibus indutum

---

[30] strength] strenght 1548.

45

Heu stat exutum
Descistunt[31] gentes
Tot[32] deridentes
Meque abnuentes
695 Minime credentes
Te fore veracem
Asserunt mendacem
Garrulam loquacem
Esse et Rapacem
700 Te dicunt vagam
Ueneficam sagam
Heu michi quid agam
Nunc peribis filia
Olim dans vtilia
705 Supra mille millia
En sequar et ego         [Sig Bvii]
Quique reges rego
Uiuere sed nego
Tu quum defungeris
710 Sacro que vngeris
Oleo papali
Hoc genus sed mali
Ingruit infestans
Nostraque detestans
715 Ecce scripture
Predicantur pure
Quo perit (audito)
Lex mea quam cito,
  O darlynge dere
720 I leaue the heare
With heauy chere
Holde here take this
A careful kysse

---

[31] Descistunt [sic].
[32] Tot] To 1548.

I wil the blisse
725     That thou maist the rather
Cum to thy grandfather
Pluto the king
Of whose ofspring
You cum by dissent
730     Wyth you shalbe sent
A godly conuent
To wayte on ye than          [Sig Bvii<sup>v</sup>]
Lyke a noble woman
Lent and gange dayes
735     Shal shewe ye the wayes
Wyth the dayes embringe
To kepe ye remembringe
Of your Iournay
For going astraye
740     And pilgrimage
In your voiage
Shalbe your page
Auricular confession
And popishe procession
745     Aboute ye shal ride
On euery syde
The colettes by kynde
Before and behinde
Your fote men shalbe
750     Ful comly to se
The cannone playne
Your chamberlay[n]e
Shalbe at your hande
When ye do commaund
755     The post communion
Shalbe your minion          [Sig Bviii]
To shewe you sporte
For your comforte
Thus shall ye not trauile

760 Lyke beggar nor Iauel
But passe like a quene
Right comly besene
To Stix and Acheron
Ye shall cume anone
765 And when they be past
Ye shal cum at the last
To the porter[33] Cerbrus
Whiche though he be barbarus
Ye shal hym intreate
770 Quickly in to get
Then shall ye se the Emperoure
Sitting stout and stoure
Hym shall ye honoure
Then open your coffer
775 And vnto him offer
Holy breade and water
And then strewe and scatter
About hys vgly fete
Some of your palmes swete
780 Then shal ye lowly     [Sig Bviiiᵛ]
Offer ashes holy
Beades and sacring belles
And al other Iuelles
Then shal he take you
785 And his heire make you
Nowe wyl I forsake you
And gyue you my blessing
I wyl not be missing
But wyth expedience
790 Shewe myne obedience
To the prince infernal
In derknes eternal
Who gaue to me my name

---

[33] porter] potter 1548.

And did to you the same
795 For both did come him fro
An to hym must they go
And there wyth fendes[34]
To make ther endes
As felowes and frendes
800 Thus Pope and messe
I must confesse
To be no lesse
Then deuelishnes

Imprinted at London by Iohn Daye and Wylliam Seres.

---

[34] fendes] fende 1548.

*Iohn Bon and Mast person*

Alasse poore fooles, so sore ye be lade
No maruel it is, thoughe your shoulders ake
For ye beare a great God, which ye yourselfes made
Make of it what ye wyl, it is a wafar cake
And betwen two Irons printed it is and bake
And loke where Idolatrye is, Christe wyl not be there
Wherfore ley downe your burden, an Idole ye do beare
                    Alasse poore
                    Fooles.

**The parson**
WHat Iohn Bon good morowe to the
**Iohn Bon**
Nowe good morowe mast parson so mut I thee
**Parson**
What meanest yᵘ Iohn to be at worke so sone
**Iohn**
The zoner I begyne the zoner shall I haue done
5    For I tende to warke no longer then none
**Parson**
Mary Iohn for that gods blessinge on thy herte
For surely some therbe wyl go to ploughe an carte
And set not by thys holy, corpus christi euen
**Iohn**
They aer the more to blame I swere by saynt Steuen
10    But tell me mast parson one thinge and you can
What saynt is copsi cursty a man or a woman?
**Parson**
Why Iohn knoweste not that? I tel the it was a man,
It is Christe his owne selfe and to morowe is hys daye
We beare hym in prosession and thereby knowe it ye maye
**Iohn**
15    I knowe mast parson? and na by my faye
But methinke it is a mad thinge that ye saye
That it shoulde be a man howe can it come to passe
Because ye maye hym beare with in so smal a glasse

**Parson**

Why neybor Iohn and art thou nowe there?

20 Nowe I maye perceyue ye loue thys newe geare

**Iohn**

Gods forbod master, I should be of that facion

I question wy your mashippe in waye of cumlication

A playne man ye may se wil speake as cometh to mind

Ye muste holde vs ascused for plowe men be but blynd

25 I am an elde felowe of fifty wynter and more     [Sig Aii]

And yet in all my lyfe I knewe not this before

**Parson**

No dyd, why sayest thou so, vpon thy selfe thou lyest

Thou haste euer knowen the sacramente to be the body of Christ

**Iohn**

Ye syr ye say true, all that I know in dede

30 And yet as I remember it is not in my crede

But as for cropsy cursty to be a man or no

I knewe not tyll thys day by the waye my soule shal to

**Parson**

Why folishe felowe, I tel the it is so

For it was so determined by the churche longe ago

35 It is both the sacramente and very Christ him selfe

**Iohn**

No spleaser mast parson then make ye Christe an elfe

And the maddest made man that euerbody sawe

**Parson**

What? peace mad man thou speakeste lyke a dawe

It is not possible hys manhode for to se

**Iohn**

40 Why sir ye tell me it is euen verye he

And if it be not his manhode, his godhed it must be

**Parson**

I tell the none of both, what meaneste thou, art y$^u$ mad?

**Iohn**

No nother mad nor druncke, but to learne I am glade

But to displease your mashippe I woulde be very loth

45 Ye graunt me here playnly that it is none of boeth
Then is it but a cake, but I pray ye be not wroth.

**Parson**

Wroth quod ha, by the masse yᵘ makest me swere an othe
I hade leuer wyth a docter of diuinitie to reason
Then wyth a stubble cur that eateth beanes and peason

**Iohn**                                                    [Sig Aiiᵛ]

50 I crie ye mercye mast person pacience for a season
In all thys cumlicacion is nother felony nor treason

**Parson**

No by the masse but herest thou, it is playne heresye

**Iohn**

I am glade it chaunced so, theyr was no witnes by
And if ther had I cared not, for ye spake as yl as I
55 I speake but as I harde you saye I wot not what ye thought
Ye sayd it was not God nor man & made it worsse then nought

**Parson**

I ment not so, thou tokeste me wronge

**Iohn**

A sir ye singe another songe
I dare not reason wyth you longe
60 I se well nowe ye haue a knacke
To saye a thynge and then go backe

**Parson**

No Iohn I was but a littyll ouersene
But thou mentest not good fayeth I wene
In all thys talke that was vs betwene

**Iohn**

65 I? no trowe it shannot so beene
That Iohn Bon shall an heretike be calde
Then myght he saye him so fowle befalde.

**Parson.**

But nowe if thou wylt marke me well
From begynninge to endynge I wyl the tell
70 Of the godly seruice that shalbe to morowe
That or I haue done no doubte thou wylt sorowe

To here that suche thynges shoulde be fordone
And yet in many places they haue begun
To take a waye the olde and set vp newe
75   Beleue me Iohn thys tale is true                    [Sig Aiii]

**Iohn**
Go to mast parson saye on and well to thryue
Ye be the Iolest gemman that euer sawe in my lyue

**Parson**
We shal firste haue matins, is it not a godly hereynge?

**Iohn**
Fie? Yes, me thinke tis a shamefull gay chearynge
80   For often times on my prayers, when I take no greate kepe
Ye sing so arantly well, ye make me fal a slepe

**Parson**
Then haue we prosession and Christe aboute we beare

**Iohn**
That is apoysone holy thinge for God him selfe is ther

**Parson**
Than comme we in and redy vs dresse
85   Full solempnely to goo to Messe

**Iohn**
Is not here a mischeuous thynge?
The Messe is vengaunce holye for all ther sayeinge

**Parson**
Then saye we Confiteor and misereatur³⁵

**Iohn**
Ieze Lorde tis abbominable matter

**Parson**
90   And then we stande vp to the auter

**Iohn**
Thys geere is as good as oure ladies sawter

**Parson**
And so gose fourth wyth the other dele

---

³⁵ misereatur] miseriatur 1548.

53

Tyll we haue rede the Pistell and Gospell
**Iohn**
That is good mast person I knowe ryght well
**Parson**                                    [Sig Aiii^v]
95   Is that good? why what sayste thou to the other
**Iohn**
Mary horrible good I saye none other

**Parson**
So is all the messe I dare auow this
As good in euery poynte as Pistell or Gospel is
**Iohn**
The fowle euyll it is, whoe woulde thynke so muche
100   In fayeth I euer thought that it had bene no suche
**Parson**
Then haue we the canon that is holyest
**Iohn**
A spightfull gay thynge of all that euer I wyst
**Parson**[36]
Then haue we the memento euen before the sacringe
**Iohn**
Ye are morenly well learned I se by your recknynge
105   That ye wyll not forget suche an eluyshe thynge
**Parson**
And after that we consecrate very God and man
And turne the breade to fleshe wyth fyue wordes we ca*n*
**Iohn**
The deuell ye do I trowe. Ther is pestilence busines
Ye are much bou*n*de to god, for suche a spittell holines
110   A galows gay gifte wyth fyue wordes alone
To make boeth God and man and yet we se[37] none
Ye talke so vnreasonably well, it maketh my herte yerne
As elde a felow as yche am I se well I maye learne

---

[36] Parson] Person 1548.
[37] we se] wese 1548.

**Parson**

Yea Iohn and then wyth wordes holy and good

115  Euen by and by we tourne the wyne to bloude

**Iohn**

Lo wyll ye se lo? who woulde haue thought it

That ye could so sone, from wine to bloud ha brought it [Sig Aiiii]

And yet except your mouth, be better tasted than myne

I can not fele it other but that it shoulde be wyne

120  And yet I wote nere a cause ther maye be whye

Perchaunce ye ha dronke bloude ofter then euer dyd I

**Parson**

Truely Iohn it is bloud though it be wine in taste

As soone as the worde is spoke the wyne is gone & past

**Iohn**

A sessions on it for me my wyttes are me benumme

125  For I can not study where the wyne shoulde become

**Parson**

Study quod ha, beware and let suche matter go

To meddle muche wyth thys may brynge ye sone to wo

**Iohn**

Yea but mast parson thynk ye it were ryght

That if I desired you to make my blake oxe whight

130  And you saye it is done, and styl is blacke in syght

Ye myght me deme a foole for to beleue so lyght

**Parson**

I maruell muche ye wyll reason so farre

I feare if ye vse it, it wyll ye mar

**Iohn**

No no sir I truste of that I wylbe ware

135  I praye you wyth your matter agayne fourth to fare

**Parson**

And then we go forth and Christes body receyue

Euyn the very same that mary dyd conceyue

**Iohn**

The deuill it is, ye haue a greate grace

To eate God and man in so short a space

**Parson**

140 And so we make an ende as it lieth in an order,
But now the blessed messe[38] is hated in euery border    [Sig Aiiii$^v$]
And railed on & reuiled, w$^t$ wordes most blasphemous
But I trust it wylbe better w$^t$ the help of Catechismus
For thoughe it came forth but euen that other day
145 Yet hath it tourned many to ther olde waye
And where they hated messe and had it in disdayne
There haue they messe and matins in latyne tonge againe
Ye euen in London selfe (Iohn) I tel the troeth
They be ful glade & mery to here of thys God knoweth

**Iohn**

150 By my trueth mast parson I lyke full wel your talke
But masse me no more messinges. The right way wil I walke
For thoughe I haue no learning yet I know chese from chalke
And yche can perceiue your iuggling as crafty as ye walke
But leue your deuilish masse & y$^e$ communion to you take
155 And then will Christ be w$^t$ you euen for his promisse sake

**Parson**

Why art thou suche a one and kept it so closse
Wel al is not golde that hath a fayre glosse
But farewel Iohn Bon god bringe the in better mind

**Iohn**

I thanke you sir for that you seme verie kynde
160 But praye not so for me for I am well Inoughe
Whistill boy, driue furth God spede vs and the plough
Ha browne done, forth that horson crabbe
Ree comomyne, garlde, wyth haight blake hab[39]
Haue agayne bald before, hayght ree who,
165 Cherly boy cum of that whomwarde we maye goo
FINIS.

---

[38] messe] me[ss]e 1548.
[39] blake hab] blake ha 1548.

# IOHN BON AND MAST PERSON

Imprinted at London by Iohn Daye, and Willyam
Seres, dwellinge in Sepulchres Parishe at the signe
of the resurrection a littel aboue Holbourne conduite.

Cum gratia & priuilegio ad imprimendum solum.

# V    *Antipus,*

**To heare of such thinges ye be not wont**
**Nam horum contraria verissima sunt**

AS verily as Adam created firste his God
So verily he tasted not, the fruite that was forbod

As verily as Abell, dyd kyll hys brother Kayn
So verily the shyppe made Noye this is playne

5    As verily as Isaac, hys father dyd begette
So verily the Sodomytes remayn vnburned yet

As verily as the Isralites, the Egiptians dyd oppresse
So verily dyd Moyses gyue God the lawe dowbtles

As verily as Sampson was, slayne of the lion rampynge
10    So verily dyd Goliad distroye Dauid the Kynge

As verily as in Babilon the meates were eate of Bell
So verily the dragon of brasse deuoured Daniell

As verily as Christe dyd crucifye the Iewes
So verily the Aposteles the gospell dyd refuse

15    As verily as Simon Magus the Apostels dyd confute
So verily the Apostels dyd princes persecute

As verily as the deuyll hath perfecte loue and hope
So verily goddes worde doth constitute the pope

As verily as Isesicles wythin be hote and holowe
20    So verily proude prelates oure master Christe do folowe

As verily as bread doeth make and bake the baker
So verily these thefes the prestes can make their maker.

If Leighton wyll neades his maker make
That these are true he can not forsake
25    A Papiste he is and the popes owne knight
That preacheth falshed in stead of ryght
He knowith not howe to pay hys dettes
But wyth catchinge his creditors in the Popes netts
A thefe, a robber, by preachinge sedition
30    Is better regarded than the kings commission.
                    Amonge Papistes.

*The comparison betwene the Antipus and the Antigraphe or answere therunto, with. An apologie or defence of the same Antipus. And reprehence of the Antigraphe.*

## Antipus, [Sig Aii]

**To heare of suche thynges ye be not wont**
**Nam horum contraria verissima sunt**

AS verily as Adam created firste his God,
So verily he tasted not, the fruite that was forbod
　As verily as Abell, dyd kil his brother Kayn
So verily the shippe made Noe, this is playne
5　As verily as Isaac, his father did begette
So verily the Sodomites remayne vnburned yet
As verily as the Isralites, the Egiptians dyd oppresse
So verily did Moyses gyue God the law doubtles
As verily as Sampson was, slayne, of the lion rampinge
10　So verily dyd Goliath distroye Dauid the Kynge
As verily as in Babilon the meates were eate of Bell
So verily the dragone of brasse deuoured Daniell
As verily as Christe dyd crucifye the Iewes
So verily the Apostles the Gospel dyd refuse
15　As verily as Simon Magus the Apostles dyd confute
So verily the Apostles dyd princes persecute
As verily as the deuel hath perfecte loue and hope
So verily goddes worde doeth constitute the pope
As verily as Isicles within be hote and holowe
20　So verily proude prelates our maister Christe do folowe
As verily as breade doeth make and bake the baker
So verily these thefes the priestes can make their maker

　If Leighton wyll neades his maker make
That these are true he can not forsake
25　A Papiste he is and the popes owne knyght [Sig Aiiᵛ]
That preacheth falshed in stead of ryght

60

He knoweth not howe to paye his dettes
But wyth catchinge his creditors in the Popes nettes
A thefe, a robber, by preachinge sedicion
30  Is better regarded then the kinges commission

Amonge Papistes.

## Antigraphium

**Heare of suche true thinges,**
**As ye haue ben wont**
**Nam ea audite verissima sunt**

AS verely as Adam was create by God
So verely he tasted the fruite was forbode
As verely as Abel was killed of Cayn
35  So verely made Noy the ship, this is plaine
As verely as Isaac was of his father gotte
So verely was the Sodomites consumed by fire hot
As verely as the Egiptians God did opresse
So verely gaue God Moyses the lawe doubteles.
40  As verely as Sampson killed the lion rampinge,
So verely was Golias killed of dauid the Kinge
As verely as in Babilon the meates were not eaten of Bell
So verely the dragon of brasse deuowred not Daniel
As verely as Christe was crucified of the Iewes
45  So verely y$^e$ Apostles taught vs gods word & true newes
As verely as the deuel hath not perfecte loue and hope
So verely consente not I to the falsenes of the pope
As verely as the Isickelles with in be not hot and hollow
So verely meke prelattes oure master Christe do folowe  [Sig Aiii]
50  As verely as breade is made of the baker
So verely by gods worde we consecrate our maker
As verely as gods worde did tourne Moyses rod
So verely gods word consecrates the body of God
As verely saynt Paulle with me doth well accorde
55  Who makes no difference is giltie of y$^e$ body of our Lord.
    Leiton can neuer of his owne pore his maker make

But only gods word no christian can this forsake
No papiste he is nor yet the popes knight
That preacheth the trueth and abhorteth the vnright
60 He willeth to paye his creditors his dettes
Desiringe God to kepe him frome the popes nettes
No thefe nor robber but voide of sedicion
A man well regardynge oure soueraignes commission

### The writer.

And you that call you Gospellers that in Ire do swell
65 You are as fare frome the Gospell as heauen is from hell
Amende your liues and folowe charitie
Leaue your presumptuouse and folishe vanitye
The misteries of God ye knowe thys is playne
Ye cannot conceyue in your fantasticall brayne
70 Commite your selfes to God, and the Kynge
And folowe holy churche to your endynge
For vnto these three I wyll sticke
And neuer regarde no false[40] hereticke
But praye vnto God that I maye se hym burne
75 If he from heresy wyll not tourne

### Of the Sacrament.

The breade which I wyl gyue, so cleane so pure
Christe sayeth is very fleshe stedfaste and suer
I thinke him a beast and a moste vile noddy [Sig Aiii$^v$]
That wyl not beleue Christ that sayth it is hys body
80 I beleue it with stedfaste herte and mynde
As gods owne wordes doth me commaunde and bynde
So as I beleue he made althinges of nought
So I beleue it is the body y$^t$ on the crosse me boughte
And the verye bloude as scripture maketh mention
85 Was shed on the crosse for mankinde redemption.
FINIS.

---

[40] false] flalse 1548.

62

## Apologia Antipi,

**To speake false latine, I perceyue ye be wont
By your writinge, ea audite verissima sunt.**

RIght rougheli and rashli, and wel ouersene
With ruggid reason, vnclerkly conueied
Ye cowcher of stones, reproued I wene
The proper antipus, that truly had saide
90    Without lyne or leuel, foundacion ye laide
Wherfore it apereth, your worke muste decaye
For thinges euill grounded, will moulder awaye.

To builde your baggage, on an other mans grounde
As it hath ben the costome, so wil ye stil vse
95    But the trade of your trechery, shall sone be confounde
Wher with ye were wont, the trueth to abuse
Your doctryne and order, are bothe but confuse
To maynteyn your errours, the scripturs ye frame
So that ye muste be ouerthrowe with the same.
100    To comende your diligence more then your wyt          [Sig Aiiii]
It is my parte, I can it not denaye
Your learning and connyng, I will not omyt
For thoughe it be not muche, it is not very gaye
Paraduenture ye will thinke, this is but homly play
105    So hastily your wit and learnyng to reproue
But ther be suche occasions, as me therto moue
How chaunced you to stomake at Antipus the littel
Sythen he taxed none, but such as papistes were
But it most nedes be so, a fooles brayne is shittil
110    And alwaies dothe showe, which way the hert doth bere
And euyn so did you nowe, without wisdom or feare
That ye haue ben and be? Right earnestly expresse
A papist most pestilent, no man will Iudge lesse.

And in your antigraphe, you shew your selfe full wise
115    Which ye wrote to antipus, whose contraries be iust

63

And yet, I thinke ye toke some other dawes deuise
As of some smoky Smyth, and other that ye truste
To the which antigraphe, an answere make I muste
Wherin I trust the lorde, wilbe my helpe and ayde
120     To proue you an heritique, I am nothing afrayde

In all your hole Antigraphe, ye vary nothing fro
The antipus: but the contrayes do declare
A boy of twelue yere olde, as well coulde haue done so
Wherfore ye showe your wyt, to be but weake and bare
125     To inter in correction, of thinges that perfect are
But in the latter lines, great grieffe, ye seme to take
Because he sayd such theues, could not their maker make

Ye bryng a pece of scripture, your heresy to maintaine
That as gods worde in Egipt, made a serpent of the Rod
130     So goddes worde maketh God, ye haue a peuish brayne    [Sig Aiiii$^{v}$]
Knowe ye not ye Romayne, that the very word is god?
Then howe can he make him selfe, thou heretical clodde?[41]
Art thou not ashamed, suche poison to spewe yet?
Christe is not made, nor create, but onely was beget.

135     I knowe full well thy shifte,[42] & what thou wylt obiect
I knowe well thou wilt saye, it is by concecration
For that is al the holde, of thy most cursed sect
And by that worde consecrate, came all the abhominacion
For as ye haue abused it ye made it execration
140     A worde I saye it is inuented but by man
Serch all the euangely and find it if ye can

As verily saint Paule with your sayinges doth accorde
As light doth with darcknes whiche easely maye be spied
For where he speaketh of difference of the body of the Lorde

---

[41] clodde?] c[l]odd[e]? 1548.
[42] thy] they 1548.

145      He meaneth not as you flesh flies do, and that shalbe tried
       The christians the bodye, so Christ the heade, he applied
       Prouinge the pore his members[43] as well as the riche to be
       The whiche when ye regarde not no difference make ye

         As when the congregation to the lordes supper shal come
150      To eate the breade worthely the Lordes death to betoken
       They must accept al lyke and not some more then some
       For all they be partakers of Christes body broken
       This is the very meaning of that saint Paul hath spoken
       Because this bread doth signifie yᵉ lords dath in our presence
155      Betwen yᵉ bread & other heades[44] must we make a difference

         To eate christes fleshe & eke to drynke hys bloud
       As so to dwel in Christ as he maye dwell in vs
       Lo here ye maye se playne it is a spirituall foode
       Beleue and thou hast eaten saynte A[u]gustine sayde thus          Bi

160      Christe when he gaue the breade, wyth handes so glorious
       Sayde when ye shall, do this do it remembringe me
       He sayde not when ye do it, my body shal it be

         Thys is my body sayde he, which for you shalbe geuen
       What thinke ye, dyd he meane a body made of bread?
165      No, but it that was present and was betrayed that euen,
       He sayde for them and many, sone after shoulde be dead
       He created not an other, no such thinges shal ye reade
       The death of that one body, for all men is sufficient
       So wyth his holy memory, let al men be contente

170      He toke the cup and sayde, this is the testament newe
       In my bloud, How thinke ye, made he his bloud of wine?
       He gaue it for a witnesse, of his bloude shedynge true
       Why should you any other wise, his holy wordes define

---

[43] members] menbers 1548.
[44] heades] [h]eades 1548.

Or as men nothinge spirituall to fleshelynes incline
175 And take his wordes grosly after their Iwishe wayes
As saint Iohn the euangeliste in the sixt Chapter sayes
But O thou grosse pharisey, for go thy fleshely mynde
Let scripture the Illuminate, thy Iudgment is but crasse
A man God made the, reasonable by nature in thy kynde
180 And y^e by thyn vnthankefulnes wilt make thy self an asse
Treadinge within the trade, of the moste wicked Masse
Wherin thou kepest compasse, as a blind horse in the myl
God graunte the to se better, when it shalbe his wyll
FINIS.

NOwe where as ye stande in Leytons defence,
185 Papisticall actes, ye seme to commence
For standing by him stowtly as a champion cheife
It is foly to axe you, and your felowe be a thefe
Ye haue vndertake he shall his dettes paye
But that shalbe the morowe after domes daye
190 Ye saye the kinges commission, full well he doeth regarde [Sig Bi^v]
Regarde ye it better boeth, or ye shall haue rewarde
With papistes.
Your other wordes also intituled the writer
A man maye sone perceyue sprange from some shepebiter
Ye cal men Gospellers, and saye they swel in Ire
195 But you be full of charitie, ye wishe them in the fire
Ye wyl teache men their duitie to God and to the Kynge
Which knowe their duitie, better then you in that thyng
Ye wil folowe holy church, ye saye to your endynge
The holy church of Rome, no dought is your meaninge
200 Ye saye in your Antigraphe that you forsake the Pope
But no thanke to you, gramercy gentyll Rope.

In your writing of y^e sacrament, ye playe sir hoddy doddy,
In vnderstanding the scriptures as crafty as a calfe
He that beleueth not as you, ye call him a vile noddy
205 But you proue more a dawe, then I wold take ye by halfe,

I leaue ye as ye be, and make no more a do.
Nothinge haue you written, but ye be answered there to.
FINIS.

A Mason, a Smyth, and a Paynter fyne
Wyth a Mugge, and a Gray, and a Perkens grosse
210   Be fooes to Antipus, at whom thei repine,
And hym with great anger, thei turne and thei tosse.
As cruel as Iewes, that dyd Christ on the crosse,
To put hym to rebuke, thei do what they may,
But they mysse of their purpose, and go the wrong way.

215   The Mason first at Babilon began,
Byldyng of the towre that men cal Babel,
Though he be a Babilonite, Nemprothes owne man.
That nowe raineth in Rome, it is no great maruaile
Thubalkaim the first smyth, and grauer of metell,
220   For antiquitie and frendshyp, must nedes stande hym by   [Sig Bii]
To forge him his toles, to buylde Idolatrie.

An other ther is, that hyght master Mugge
An ayder and adbettour, with all his hole power
As nymble in cariyng, as is my spaniell rugge,
225   He wyll catch a lye by the ende, & wythin halfe an hower
Bear it a myle of, for feare it shoulde be sower,
The Paynter shal go wyth hym, to painte y$^e$ matter faire
Whoso lacketh papistes, here he may haue a paire.

Then is there one Perkens, with a belly somwhat large
230   Of kin to Perken Warbeck, as by his name appereth
Which for his good conditions, maye rowe in the barge,
At good he stoppeth hys eares, but euyl he sone heareth,
And al such as are papistes, full earnestly he chereth,
And Gray that badgerd, maye not be lefte behynde
235   Nor their sword bearer of s. Mildredes who knoweth all their mind

67

In knauery.
In heresy
In baudry.
In popery.
Etcetera.

240

Gyue place ye Poetes fine
Bow doune now & encline
For nowe yᵉ Muses nyne
So Sacred and Diuine
5   In Parnase holy Hyll
Haue wrought theyr worthy wyll
And by theyr goodly skyll
Uppon that myghty Mountayne
In Hellycons Fountayne
10  (That alwayes doth remayne
Synce Pegase made it flowe
As by your bokes we knowe)
Haue washed the lyppes of one
That slepte not longe agone
15  That forked Hyll vpon
Who after that anon
As he had sene the Muses
Newe Poetry he vses
And yours he cleane refuses.
20  For wakyng sodenly                    [Sig Aiiᵛ]
He wrote ryght wortheily
Suche kynde of Poetrye
As neuer one of you
Had hearde or sene tyl nowe
25  He wrote I tel you playne
An Antygraphe full mayne
None suche on thys syde Spayne
Antipus to suppresse
And clerly to compesse
30  Wherein he fayneth no lesse
But that yf God were dead
He myght be raysed in Bread
Wherfore ye Poetes al
And clarkes bothe greate and smal
35  Submyt your selues ye shal
And downe before hym fall

And neuer not to ryse
For you cowlde not deuyse
So greate an interpryse
40    As thys new poet dyd
Whose connyng is yet hyd
And many other workes
That secretly yet lurckes        Sig Aiii
None suche amonge the Turkes
45    Nor Saracens can be founde
The Gospellers to confounde.
Hys workes are so well bownd
And buylded on suche grounde
As cannot wel decay
50    Tyl the sande be washed away.
He is skylled so wonderously
In the scyence of Masonrye.
Wherfore I wyl not spare
Hys learnyng to declare
55    Although wyth myckle care
Because I want the wayes
Thys Poete for to prayse
And fame vpon hym rayse
That floweth in these dayes,
60    Wythe suche exceadynge Eloquence
And Superfluous Sapyence
Imbute wyth[45] Insuffycyence
Of learnyng and Intellygence
Whose wrytynges are laudable
65    So new founde and notable
I tell you wythout fable        [Sig Aiiiᵛ]
That no man vnder skye
Can prayse them worthely
They shewe them selues so fayer
70    That none can them appayer

---

[45] wyth] wtyh 1548.

And therfore now beholde
And see how well he coulde
Describe them that are bolde
To marry beyng sworne
75 To kepe them chast beforne
Makyng theyr vow a scorne
And takyng to them wyues,
Wyth them to leade theyr lyues
But wyth these blooddes he stryues
80 And out of towne them dryues
Wyth eloquent taxacions
And vyolent vexacyons
And earneste exprobracyons
Wythe instant insultacions
85 And straunge denomynacyons
That none among all nacyons
Can shew suche learned fasshyons
As can thys noble scholer                    Sig Aiiii
He may well weare a coller
90 Of .H. for hys humanitee
And for hys greate Urbanytye
He may weare vppon hys Bonnet
A double .P. well set
And wyth a traye aboue
95 In tokenynge of the loue
That towarde hym he beareth
Whyche men to Chastenes sweareth.
Wherfore loke vp and see
Yf ye beleue not me
100 Your owne Iudges to be
For easely may ye spye
Yf ye looke earnestly
And well hys latten trye
That oute of Barbarye
105 Hys learninge he hath fett
And all hys knowledge gett.

71

For thys I dare well Sweare
Here can no suche fyne gear      [Sig Aiiii<sup>v</sup>]
Be had but onely theare,
110      Aduise it well and reade
For here it doth succede.
O Insensati
All marryed preistes that be Nupti
Barbis disguisati
115      Carnales hedos Uocati
Quorum deus venter
To y<sup>e</sup> belly they be bound by Indenture
Uentri semper obedire
Uulueque seruire
120      Quorum Sathan est Pater
Et Lecheria Mater
Thys Genera Uiperarum
Runnes per Orbem Terrarum
O God omnipotent
125      Qui regnas et viuis
Sende shame and punishement
To all Prestes and theyr wyues
And let them goo voyde of all grace
Et infernorum supplicia
130      Wyth Lucyfer to haue a Place
In sempiterna supplicia.

### The Prayse of the Meter.

O meter passing measure
Prouokinge sporte and pleasure      [Sig Av]
O treatise of hygh treasure
135      So Typycal in fygure
None suche from lyn to lygure
Lapte vp in suche fyne latyn
As passeth both sylk[46] and satyn

---

[46] sylk] syl[k] 1548.

O Homer so Heroicall
140 And Percius Satyricall
Where are your workes Poetycale
O Horace where art thou
Uyrgyll and Ouide now
And all the rest of you
145 Let se who dare auow
One suche a worke to shew
No no, ful wel I know
Take al you on a rowe
Ye cannot do it I trow
150 Not one of you that wrote
Suche Satyres wel I wot
Yf he your bokes had sene
He wolde haue shamed them clene
You had no Peers you wene
155 Because wyth lawrel grene
Crowned you were by ryght
But oure newe Poete myght                    [Sig Av<sup>v</sup>]
Be crowned wyth the Uyne,
And Garland Canaby[n]e
160 For engyne and for wytt
The muses dyd admytt
Not onely hym to yt
But gaue hym so muche grace
That yf he vewe the face
165 Of one In any place
He maye make hym wyth spede
A Poete to procede.
The profe therof indede
Ful playnly dyd appere
170 Wythin thys halfe yere
For one that was a Smythe[47]

---

[47] Smythe] Smytthe 1548.

73

A forger at the stythe[48]
A myghtye man of pytthe
And stronge of lym and lytthe
175   When he had bene hym wythe
And talked but a whyle
He wrote so hygh a style
As none wythin a myle
Coulde fashyon wyth a fyle
180   Wyth al hys wyt and wyle,                     [Sig Avi]
Wel wel for all ye smyle
Certes I tel you treuth
A lack yt is greate ruth
That men wyl not beleue
185   The gyftes that Muses geue
Besyde all thys hys Smythery
Uulcanus taught hym certanly
Wherw$^t$ he wroughte[49] right curyously
As ye may se yt euydently
190   Conteyned in the testymony
And latter wylle of Heresy.
For there He sheweth Poetry
Hyghly professyng Romery
Lo, now I say therfore
195   Your bokes we nede no more
They maye be rent and tore
What though ye crye and rore
We nede not now your lore
For yf thys arte were drownd
200   Agayne it may be found
Euen by the very sound
Of these new Poetes Tooles
They be no smalle fooles,                          [Sig Avi$^v$]
If they be red In scholes

---

[48] stythe] stytthe 1548.
[49] wroughte] wroughe 1548.

205 You may syt downe on stooles
And so to take your rest
As I suppose it best.
But well ye thyncke I Geyst
By cocke for all your lokes
210 You maye claspe vp your bookes
And then go kepe the roockes
Or els wyth hangle hookes
Go fyshe and take some flookes
For cleane your cleargy crookes
215 And goeth nomore on ryght
Synce these beganne to wryght
Ye haue no more no might
To florysh in theyr syght
But thys I wyll you tell
220 The Mason doth excell
Wherfore he may full well
Aboue all beare the Bell
Wherfore wyth all my power
I wyll eche daye and hower
225 Aduaunce hys hyghe honour
Praiyng these Muses Sacre       [Sig Avii]
Wyth Hellicons Lauacre
To washe me by theyr ayde
To do as I haue saide.

### The prayse of the Poete.

230 O Poete so impudent
Whyche neuer yet was studente
To thee, the Goddes prudente
Minerua is illudente
Thou wrytest thynges dyffuse
235 Incongrue, and confuse
Obfuscate and obtuse
No man the lyke doth vse
Among the Turckes or Iewes

Alwayes inuentyng newes
240  That are incomparable
They be so fyrme and stable
Lyke as a Shyppe is able
Wythout Ancre and Cable
Roother Maste or Sayle
245  Pully Rope or Nayle
In Wynde Weather or Hayle
To guyde both top and tayle          [Sig Aviiᵛ]
And not the course to fayle
So thys our Poet maye
250  Wythout a stopp or staye
In cunnynge wend the way
As wel by darke as day
And neuer go astray
Yf yt be as they say.
255  O Poet rare and Recent
Dedecorate / and endecent
Insolent and insensate
Contendyng and condensate
Obtused and obturate
260  Obumbylate, obdurate
Sparyng no Prest or Curate
Cyuylyan or Rurate
That be alredy marryed
And from theyr vow bene varyed
265  Wherto the scrypture them caried
They myght as wel haue taryed
I sweare by the north doore Rood
That stowte was whyle he stood
That they had bene as good
270  To haue solde theyr best blew hood          [Sig Aviii]
For I am in suche a moode
That for my power and parte
Wyth al my wyt and arte
Wyth whole intent and harte

275 I wyl so at them Darte
That some of them shal farte
Before they feele it smarte.
Coulde not these bloods be pleased
Wyth mens wyues to be eased
280 And in their daughtars seased
As wel as the other greased
Though thus they had not preased?
In fayth they shalbe feased
For I set to my hand
285 In fyght wyth them to stand
By water and by lande
By grauell and by Sande
And by the salte sea strond
Beholde here is a wand
290 To beate them back and bone
I trow a thyng alone
To make these gallantes grone
And withe our poetes ayde                    [Sig Aviiiᵛ]
They shalbe so dismayde
295 So fearfull and afrayde
That downe they shalbe layde,
As thycke as hoppes and hayle.
Nowe wyll I them assayle
And threashe them withe my Flayle
300 To marre these married Preistes
I fyghte wyth bothe my Fystes
Looke on the fraye who Lystes.

**A Latten Clubbe, or Hurle Batte.**

O UOS Insensati
Ex Sathana Nati
305 Satyrique Uocati
Barbis Detonsati
Loti Leuigati
Corollis designati

|     |                              |     |
|-----|------------------------------|-----|
|     | Quo sic effeminati           |     |
| 310 | Molles et Parati             |     |
|     | Sitis, Stupro dati           |     |
|     | Petulantes Hoedi             |     |
|     | Turpes et Cinoedi            |     |
|     | Per quos Pios ledi           |     |
| 315 | Ac Insontes Cedi             |     |
|     | Certo possit⁵⁰ Credi         |     |
|     | Procreantes Hibride          |     |
|     | Sed Amicti Nebride           |     |
|     | Quod non estis Nupte         | Bi  |
| 320 | Eo plus Corrupti             |     |
|     | Castum profitentes           |     |
|     | Non custodientes             |     |
|     | Uerum odientes               |     |
|     | Falsamque Docentes           |     |
| 325 | Uxores non habentes          |     |
|     | Alias Conquerentes           |     |
|     | Nubere abnuentes             |     |
|     | Incestui cedentes            |     |
|     | Lupi Existentes              |     |
| 330 | Lupam subsequentes           |     |
|     | Priapo seruientes            |     |
|     | In Deum statuentes           |     |
|     | Ipsum que Colentes⁵¹         |     |
|     | Uuluas Indagantes            |     |
| 335 | Illecebras Amantes           |     |
|     | Uelut Scortatores            |     |
|     | Aliorum Uxores               |     |
|     | Filias et Sorores            |     |
|     | Seruas et Ancillas           |     |
| 340 | Seducentes Illas             |     |
|     | Rapitis Ubique               |     |

---

⁵⁰ possit] [p]ossit 1548.
⁵¹ Colentes] Colentess 1548.

Uiuentes quam obliq*ue*
Nigri Necromantici
Hydri Hydromantici
345      Putridi Piromantici
Incantantes Idolatres
Publici Pseudolatres
Iuvum[52] Sathanam habetis
Patrem Papamq*ue* Tenetis
350      Matris Gremioq*ue* sedetis
Gomor eam Nominetis
Cum his Penasq*ue* Luetis
Lupinis Uestibus
Caudis et Testibus              [Sig Bi<sup>v</sup>]
355      Dediti Incestibus
Uiperarum Genus
Quorum dea Uenus
Infernorum Tenus
Ducet Imperpetuum
360      Ad Ditis Supplicium
Id quod Uetet Ille
Qui Seruat Millia Mille.

## ECQUID UOS BEO?

Lo now how like you thys?
I trowe I dyd you Blisse
365      And them, as woorthy is
To dyng tyll they shall Pisse
Me thynke I doo not misse
Though my Crowne be not scraped
Nor I in Order mysshaped
370      Nor for suche woorshyppe gaped
Nor anoyted Preyste wyth Oyle

---

[52] Iuvum] Iuum 1548.

79

Nor Creame or other Soyle
Nor tooke suche fylthy Foyle
Yet wyll I tugge and Toyle
375 Tosse turne and Turmoyle
Cumbre Clowte and Coyle
Dismembre and Dispoyle     Bii
All them that I maye catche
That dayly wayte and watche
380 Feacte wenches to vpsnatche
And marrye to their Matche
But I wyll them dispatche
And byggely on them beate
For all their wyues so feacte
385 That are so Nyce and Neate
Whiche sittyng on their Seate
Of Scriptures wyll Intreate
And fayne woulde vs defeate⁵³
Wyth woordes grymme and greate
390 From Beades of woodde and Geate
And from our myghtie Meate
That is, our God of wheate
Puffe, so I Swelle and Sweate
I fridge: I frothe and freate
395 Of thys Uncowthe: to thynke
But suerly shall they Drynke
Tyll aboue the grounde they stynke
Wyth a Lyryeum Twynke
For I can neuer Swynke
400 As longe as our Uulcanus     [Sig Biiʸ]
And lusty Longimanus
Wyll sticke whyle he is Sanus
For though he be Prophanus
He is not nothyng Uanus
405 Nor learned lyke Alanus

---

⁵³ defeate] defeacte 1548.

80

I tell you he is no Nanus[54]
But one of stature stoute
No Lubber nor no Loute
He wyll reache rounde aboute
410  And ventyng wyth hys snoute
Wyll touche them toppe and towte
And all theyr rufflyng rowte
Wyth Clarckly clubbes to cloute
For fyersly hath he fought
415  Endeuouryng to dryue oute
The reader in our queare
That draweth to hym here
Men commyng farre and neare
There dyd oure Smythe appeare
420  With countenaunce so cleare
Full chaungeable in cheare
And dapper as a deare
Chefely he dyd hym charge     [Sig Biii]
How he had caught at large
425  More then he coulde dyscharge
Or fynde in text or Marge
Concernyng Consecratyon
And Transubstanciation
Or all oure Transmutacion
430  And Substaunce Alteracion
Deniyng Ueneracion
And also Adoration
In tyme of Ministration
And that Non dentibus
435  Panem Prementibus
Nullis Euentibus
Christum Gustari
Nec Mancipari
Posse vel decipi

---

[54] Nanus] Na[n]us 1548.

81

| | |
|---|---|
| 440 | Sensus, cum Recipi |
| | Dabitur Panis |
| | Sed Smyth Immanis |
| | Abiit Inanis |
| | But or he wente awaye |
| 445 | He trymmed hym I saye |
| | Wyth goodly tantes and gaye |
| | And wyth a tryggum tray |
| | Lyke a fyne Philologus |
| | Or rather a Pantolobus |
| 450 | He called hym Spermologus |
| | And wold haue a Dialogus |
| | But were there a Catalogus |
| | Of hym and al hys sect |
| | He myght be chef elect |
| 455 | These reders to correct |
| | For wel can he obiect |
| | And Subtelly suspect |
| | In thynges that be dyrect |
| | But sure yf he be chect |
| 460 | Your corrage is deiect |
| | And al your hope in vayne |
| | Yet styl wyl I remayne |
| | To take for you greate payne |
| | Yf ye wyl me retayne |
| 465 | And put myselfe in parrel |
| | To fyght thus in your quarrell |
| | Yf thou O Poet once |
| | That well canst cowche thy stones |
| | Or faber wyth hys wall |
| 470 | To me for helpe wyll call |
| | Either wyth boke or word |
| | Soone wyl I be the thyrd |
| | So if I fynde you kynde |
| | Certes you shal me bynde |

[Sig Biii<sup>v</sup>]

[Sig Biiii]

475        To shew that is behynd
Wel wel ye know my mynde.

      LO thus Philogamus
After thys sorte
Helpeth Misogamus
480        Hym to comforte
Agaynst Monogamus
That dothe reporte
That youre Apogamus
Is but aborte.

      FINIS.

QUOD PHYLOGAMUS.
Alias. I. What call Ye Hym.

## VIII

*Doctour doubble ale.*

Although I lacke intelligence
And can not skyll of eloquence
Yet wyll I do my diligence
To say sumthing or I go hence
5    Wherin I may demonstrate
The figure gesture and estate
Of one that is a curate
That harde is and endurate
And ernest in the cause
10    Of piuish popish lawes
That are not worth two strawes
Except it be with dawes
That knoweth not good from euels
Nor Gods worde from the Deuels
15    Nor wyll in no wise heare
The worde of god so cleare
But popishnes vpreare
And make the pope Gods peare
And so them selues they lade
20    Wyth bables that he made
And styll wyll holde his trade
No man can them perswade
And yet I dare say
Ther is no day
25    But that they may
Heare sincerily
And right truly
Gods worde to be taught
If they wolde haue sought
30    But they set at nought
Christes true doctrine
And them selues decline[55]
To mens ordinaunce
Which they enhaunce

Aii

---

[55] decline] de[c]line 1548.

35 And take in estimation
Aboue Christes passion
And so this folish nacion
Esteme their owne facion[56]
And all dum ceremonies
40 Before the sanctimonies
Of Christes holy writ
And thinke their owne wit[57]
To be far aboue it
That the scripture to them teachis
45 Or honest men preachis
They folowe perlowes lechis
And doctours dulpatis
That falsely to them pratis
And bring them to the gates
50 Of hell and vtter derkenes
And all by stubborne starkenes
Putting their full trust
In thinges that rot and rust
And papisticall prouisions
55 Which are the deuels dirisions
Now let vs go about
To tell the tale out
Of this good felow stout
That for no man wyll dout
60 But kepe his olde condicions
For all the newe comyssyons     [Sig Aii<sup>v</sup>]
And vse his supersticions
And also mens tradicyons
And syng for dead folkes soules
65 And reade hys beade rolles
And all such thinges wyll vse
As honest men refuse

---

[56] facion] [f]acion 1548.
[57] wit] wi 1548.

But take hym for a cruse
And ye wyll tell me newes
70 For if he ons begyn
He leaueth nought therin
He careth not a pyn
How much ther be wythin
So he the pot may wyn
75 He wyll it make full thyn
And wher the drinke doth please
Ther wyll he take his ease
And drinke ther of his fyll
Tyll ruddy be his byll
80 And fyll both cup and can
Who is so glad a man
As is our curate than
I wolde ye knewe it a curate
Not far without newgate
85 Of a parysh large
The man hath mikle charge
And none within this border
That kepeth such order
Nor one a this syde Nauerne
90 Louyth better the ale tauerne
　　But if the drinke be small　　　　　　　[Sig Aiii]
He may not well withall
Tush cast it on the wall
It fretteth out his gall
95 Then seke an other house
This is not worth a louse
As dronken as a mouse
Mon syre gybet a vous
And ther wyll byb and bouse
100 Tyll heuy be his brouse
Good ale he doth so haunt
And drynke a due taunt
That alewiues make ther vaunt

Of many a peny rounde
105 That sum of them hath founde
And sometyme mikle strife is
Amonge the alewyfes
And sure I blame them not
For wrong it is God wot
110 When this good dronken sot
Helpeth not to empty the pot
For sumtime he wyl go
To one and to no mo
    Then wyll the hole rout
115 Upon that one cry out
And say she doth them wronge
To kepe him all day longe
From commyng them amonge
Wherfore I geue councell
120 To them that good drinke sell
To take in of the best                    [Sig Aiii<sup>v</sup>]
Or els they lese their gest
For he is redy and prest
Where good ale is to rest
125 And drinke tyll he be drest
When he his boke shulde study
He sitteth there full ruddy
Tyll halfe the day be gone
Crying fyll the pot Ione
130 And wyll not be alone
But call sum other one
At wyndowe or at fenestre
That is an idell ministre
As he him selfe is
135 Ye know full well this
The kinde of carion crowes
Ye may be sure growes
The more for carion stinking
And so do these in drinking

140 This man to sum mens thinking
Doth stay hym muche vpon the kyng
As in the due demaunding
Of that he calleth an head peny
And of the paskall halpeny.
145 For the cloth of corpus Christy
Four pens he claymith swiftely
For which the sexton and he truly
Did tog by the eares earnestly
Saying he can not the king well paye
150 If all such driblars be take away
Is not this a gentill tale      [Sig Aiiii]
Of our doctour doubble ale
Whose countenaunce is neuer pale
So wel good drinke he can vphale
155     A man of learning great
For if his brayne he wolde beat
He coulde within dayes fourtene
Make such a sermon as neuer was sene
I wot not whether he spake in drinke
160 Or drinke in him how do ye thinke?
I neuer herde him preach God wot
But it were in the good ale pot
Also he sayth that fayne he wolde
Come before the councell if he coulde
165 For to declare his learning
And other thinges concerning
Goodly councels that he coulde geue
Beyond all measure ye may me beleue
His learning is exceding
170 Ye may know by his reading
Yet could a cobblers boy him tell
That he red a wrong gospell,
Wherfore in dede he serued him well
He turned himselfe as round as a bell
175 And with loud voyce began to call

Is chere no constable among you all,
To take this knaue y<sup>t</sup> doth me troble?
With that all was on a hubble shubble
There was drawing and dragging
180      There was lugging and lagging
And snitching and snatching        [Sig Aiiii<sup>v</sup>]
And ketching and catching
And so the pore ladde
To the Counter they had
185      Some wolde he shuld be hanged
Or els he shulde be wranged
Some sayd it were a good turne
Such an heretyke to burne
Some sayde this and some sayd that
190      And som dyd prate they wist not what
Some did curse and some did ban
For chafing of oure curate than
He was worthy no lesse
For vexing with his pertnesse
195      A gemman going to Messe,
Did it become a cobblers boy
To shew a gemman such a toy?
  But if it were wel wayde
Ye shuld fynde I am afrayde
200      That the boy were worthy
For his reading and sobrietie
And iudgement in the veritie
Among honest folke to be
A curate rather then he.
205      For this is knowen for certentie
The boy doth loue no papistry
And our Curate is called no doubte
A papist london thoroughout.
And truth is it they do not lye,
210      It may be sene wyth halfe an eye.       [Sig Av]
For if there come a preacher,
Or any godly teacher

To speake agaynst his trumpery
To the alehouse goth he by & by
215 And there he wyl so much drinke
Tyll of ale he doth so stinke,
That whether he go before or behynde
Ye shall him smell without the winde
For when he goeth to it he is no hafter[58]
220 He drinketh dronke for two dayes after
With fyll the cuppe Ione,
For all this is gone
Here is ale alone
I say for my drinking
225 Tush, let the pot be clinking
And let vs mery make,
No thought wyll I take
For though these fellowes crake
I trust to se them slake
230 And some of them to bake
In smithfelde at a stake
And in my Parysh be some
That if the tyme come
I feare not wyll remember
235 (Be it august or september
October or Nouember
Or moneth of December)
To fynde both wood and timber
To burne them euery member
240 And goth to borde and bed
At the signe of the kinges head.          [Sig Av^v]
    And let these heretikes preach
And teach what they can teach
My parish I know well
245 Agaynst them wyll rebell
If I but once them tell

---

[58] hafter] haf[t]er 1548.

Or geue them any warning
That they were of the new learning.
For with a worde or twayne
250      I can them call agayne
And yet by the Messe
Forgetfull I was
Or els in a slumber
There is a shrewde nomber
255      That curstly do comber
And my pacience proue
And dayly me moue
   For some of them styll
Continew wyll
260      In this new way
Whatsoeuer I saye
   It is not long ago
Syns it chaunsed so
That a buriall here was
265      Without dirige or Masse
But at the buriall
Chey song a christmas carall
By the Masse they wyll mar all
If they continew shall
270      Some sayd it was a godly hearing
And of their hartes a gay chering[59]
Some of them fell on weping           [Sig Avi]
In my church I make no leasing
They harde neuer the lyke thing
275      Do ye thinke that I wyll consent
To these heretikes intent
To haue any sacrament
Ministred in English?
By them I set not a rysh

---

[59] a gay chering] The bottom of the page is cut away here 1548. See also note l. 271.

280 So long as my name is hary George
I wyll not do it spight of theyr gorge.
Oh Dankester Dancastre
None betwene this and Lancaster.
Knoweth so much my minde.
285 As thou my speciall frynde
It wolde do the much good
To wash thy handes in the bloude
Of them that hate the messe
Thou couetest no lesse
290 So much they vs oppresse
Pore priestes doubtlesse
And yet what than
There is not a man
That soner can,
295 Perswade his parishons
From such condicions
Then I perse I
For by and by
I can chem conuert
300 To take my parte
Except a fewe
That hacke and hew            [Sig Aviᵛ]
And agaynst me shew
What they may do
305 To put me to
Some hynderaunce
And yet may chaunce
The bisshops visitour,
Wyll shewe me fauour
310 And therfore I
Care not a fly,
For ofte haue they
Sought by some way
To bring me to blame
315 And open shame

But I wyll beare them out
In spight of their snout
And wyll not ceasse
To drinke a pot the lesse
320 Of ale that is bygge
Nor passe not a fygge
For all their malice
Away the mare q*uod* walis
I set not a whitinge
325 By all their writing,
For yet I deny nat
The Masses priuat
Nor yet forsake
That I of a cake
330 My maker may make
   But harke a lytle harke
And a few wordes marke                    [Sig Avii]
Howe this caluish clarke
For his purpose coulde warke
335 There is an honest man:
That kepte an olde woman
Of almes in hyr bed
Liyng dayly beddered
Which man coulde not I say
340 Wyth popishnes a way
But fayne this woman olde
Wolde haue Messe if she coulde
The which this priest was tolde
He hearing this anone
345 As the goodman was gone
Abrode aboute his busines
Before the woman he sayd Messe
And shewed his prety popishnes
Agaynst the goodmans wyll
350 Wherfore it is my skyll
That he shulde him endight

For doing such dispight
As by his popish wyle
His house wyth Masse defyle
355     Thus may ye beholde
This man is very bolde
And in his learning olde
Intendeth for to syt
I blame him not a whyt
360 For it wolde vexe his wyt
And cleane agaynst his earning
To folow such learning                    [Sig Avii<sup>v</sup>]
As now a dayes is taught
It wolde some bring to naught
365 His olde popish brayne
For then he must agayne
Apply him to the schole
And come away a fole:
For nothing shulde he get
370 His brayne hath bene to het
And with good ale so wet
Wherfore he may now iet
In feldes and in medes
And pray vpon his beades
375 For yet he hath a payre
Of beades that be right fayre
Of corall gete, or ambre
At home within his chambre
For in matins or Masse,
380 Primar and portas
And pottes and beades
His lyfe he leades
    But this I wota
That if ye nota
385 How this idiota
Doth folow the pota
I holde you a grota

Ye wyll rede by rota
That he may were a cota
390   In cocke losels bota
    Thus the durty doctour
The popes owne proctour         [Sig Aviii]
Wyll bragge and boost
Wyth ale and a toost
395   And lyke a rutter
Hys latin wyll vtter
And turne and tosse him
Wyth tu non possum
Loquere latinum
400   This alum finum
Is bonus then vinum
Ego volo quare
Cum tu drinkare
Pro tuum caput
405   Quia apud
Te propiciacio
Tu non potes facio
Tot quam ego
Quam librum tu lego,
410   Caue de me
Apponere te
Iuro per deum
Hoc est lifum meum
Quia drinkum stalum
415   Non facere malum
Thus our dominus dodkin
Wyth ita vera bodkin
Doth leade his lyfe
Which to the ale wife
420   Is very profitable
It is pytie he is not able
To mayntayne a table         [Sig Aviii<sup>v</sup>]
For beggers and tinkers

And all lusty drinkers
425 Or captayne or beddle
Wyth dronkardes to meddle
Ye cannot I am sure
For keping of a cure
Fynde such a one well
430 If ye shulde rake hell
 And therfore nowe
No more to you
Sed perlegas ista,
Si velis Papista,
435 Farewell and adewe
With a whirlary whewe
And a tirlary typpe
Beware of the whyppe.
 Finis.
440 Take this tyll more come.

## IX

*Cauteles preseruatory concerning the preseruation of the Gods which are kept in the pixe* [Sig Ai]

Aii

For as muche as I se that most me*n* in theyr sience be diligent and circum-
specte as craftes men in their occupacions dooe exquisitly laboure and searche
out the knowledge not onely of workemanshippe and connynge: but as well
of the order and preseruinge of the stuffe and mater whereof they shall frame
and fassion theyr worke, ye and when it is wrought and finished, to the
perfection of theyr forecaste or imagination: they do not lyghtly and negli-
gently regard the same worke, But lyke as they dyd before studye to bring to
passe and to performe their workemanshippe and take paynes in practisynge
thereof: Euen so wil they studie and loke for the preseruacion of the same that
the thynge where wyth they haue so muche laboured & broken theyr witte
should not by slouth and rechelesse lokeing to, be suffered to decaye in a
shorte [**Sig Aii**ᵛ] space: I maruaile therfore that you who are of yᵉ most high
science or artifice yᵗ as ye say your selues are not workers⁶⁰ only of worldli
thi*n*ges. But also the workers of the great workeman & makers of the greate
maker whom ye can make & fassio*n* at your owne wyl and pleasures:* wil not
regarde the workes yᵗ ye make* which⁶¹ oughte moste worthily to be pre-
serued from anye dispayre or corruption (if it be as you saye) but let your
gods whom ye haue made corrupt, molde, stinke, rotte, muste, cleaue to-
gether bred wormes* wᵗ diuerse other mishappes, as some time to be eaten of
a mouse, ratte or munkay* & to be borne away of robin redbrest or philip
Sparowe* the whiche woulde greue any manes or womans hert (whoe beleu-
ethe in the same great God of youre makeinge) and causeth many to forsake
yᵗ fayth which they had in him and all thys is by youre owne foly and slender
ouer <Aiii> sight. Wherefore ye are much worthy disprayse amonge al other
craftes men. Men se dayly how the appothecaries and grossers in theyr
occuptynges haue waies and meanes to co*n*serue and preserue diuerse thynges
as fruites rotes & herbes.

Thei preserue Damasene prunes, cheres, Quinces, peachis, peares, Oliues,
Cappars, Orenges walnuttes, melons, Citrones & manye other thynges
wherin they be worthie to be co*mm*endid & ye co*n*trariwise are worthy to be

---

⁶⁰ workers] workres 1548.
⁶¹ make which] make (which; no close paranthesis 1548.

discommendid, yea rather to be greately punished because, ye be no more studious in yᵉ preseruing of yo[u]re. God from filthe and putrifaction. The which god you say is not only yᵉ creator of herbes fruites rotes & al other like but as wel of yᵉ appoticaries & grossers them selues & all other, yea & yᵉ creator & maker of you also. Though you make him whi do ye not therfore find some wais how to kepe him swet, but let him pe [**Sig Aiiiᵛ**] rishe so vilely howe wyll you haue men to beleue in hym as in a God when ye youre selues set so lyght by him that ye⁶² wyll not take the paine to kepe hym swete and cleane from filthines.

And thoughe ye can make newe when the olde be rotten and burned or buried,* yet I woulde not haue you so rechels and slouenly aboute them as ye be al the sorte of you, but to be as net fyne and Ielous ouer them as ye maye be, leste the people (seinge youre slouenly and sowterly faction aboute them) regard nother youre goddes nor you that are the makers of them.

And because ye shall the easlier and soner attayne the knowledge of the preseruacion of them: I intend⁶³ in thys lytell worke to prescribe to you the order therof wherby ye may also auoide and put by the hanous infamy obloquie & slaunder whych both your godes & you the makers [**Sig Aiiii**] of them do daiely sustayne and beare, I feare⁶⁴ me to youre vtter exinanicion, and derogation of all youre greate power of God makinge and to thentent that ye maye the rather find the waies to preuente the same I haue composed thys lytell boke for you to beare in youre handes* or in your bosomes as a necessary vtensile concerninge youre craft and occupacion, wherein be conteyned these rules folowinge.

Firste it is requisite that ye shoulde knowe whether the wafer maker be an honest man, & of good conscience, and connyng in the feate,* or no, for by his vnconninge or couetousnes he maye be a great cause of the decaye of them. As if he make them of musty wheate, or make hys batter to thynne for couetuousnes. Or if by rechelesnes take not head whether hys Irons be hote inoughe or to coulde, for so by slackenes of bakynge maye they be the soner mu [**Sig Aiiiiᵛ**] stye and hore mouldyd.

---

⁶² ye] he 1548.
⁶³ intend] inted 1548.
⁶⁴ beare, I feare] beare, (I feare; no close paranthesis 1548.

Item ye shal haue a close boxe to put them in and that shal ye sette in youre chimneis ende to kepe them drye til ye shall consecrate them. And this is to be done in yᵉ winter quarter, or rainy and foggy whether.

Item ye must chose of the fairest roundest and whighteste,* or elles if neade be ye maye clip them rounde with a payer of sheres, or pare them with a sharpe knife. The clippinge or paringes whereof, maye paruenture be a refreshing to youre clarke or to the boye that healpeth you to saye Masse.*

Item it shalbe neadefull for you when ye be in consecratyng, to blow or breath as nicely and featly as ye may deuise, leste by youre much brethinge and anhelation ye myght irrorate*⁶⁵ & enmyst* them so much, yᵗ they shall neuer be swete or good after.

Item it behoueth not hym that hath a stinkinge breath or pthisic* [Sig Av] or aposteme* in hys longes or stomake, or hath the pokkes to blowe or breath so much on them as he that hath not, for by such stinkinge exhalacions and out breathinges youre goddes are so corrupte and infecte, that they be corrupted and infectuous both to body and soule of them that eate them as their God.

Item ye ought (as neare as ye may) to consecreate on a fayre cleare & sunny day for if the aire be moist darke or misty they will become the soner fautie.* And what by corrupte breathynge and whether together, they may be so muche danke and soddy, that they wyll neuer be broughte to good, and so your laboure conning stuffe and all is but loste.

Item it will become you to loke to them often, leaste they ron to far into putrificacion. Prouided alway that ye do it in cleare whether.

Item remember yᵗ ye torne them & remoue them, for cleauyng together [Sig Avᵛ]

Item if it be so yᵗ they be molde or any thing clammy (as ofte times they be) ye shal carie them into the churche yard or into some garden or vpon the leades of the church, and laye them abrode one by one vpon a fayre cloth to take the sun and then bestowe them vp agayne.

Item ye must prouide a net of silke or fine threde to leye on them in the time of driynge and also to wache warely for feare that birdes should take any of them awaie.

---

⁶⁵ irrorate] irroate 1548.

Item ye must consider the wind whither it be great or in what quarter it bloweth. For some wyndes be infectuous more then some, as the southe, south weste, or southest & to take heade y$^t$ none of them be blowe*n* awaie with the wind, for they be but light and of smale substaunce.

Item ye must marke wel y$^e$ nu*m*bre of the*m*, y$^t$ ye may put into the pixt as many as ye take out, and so shall ye be sure that ye haue lost none of the*m*.[66] **[Sig Avi]**

Item you shal remember y$^t$ ye must all wayes haue an od God, for they maye not be euen in numbre.*

Item if they be mold or musty or grene or euil coloured ye shal wype the*m* w$^t$ a fine cloth vpo*n* a fram* made of four stickes & ley the*m* on it one by one eche one by him selfe & hold the same frame ouer a chafinge dishe of coles into y$^t$ which coles ye shal cast the pouder of brimstone* which wyll make the*m* white againe but ye must remember to torne them oft.

Item it shalbe co*n*uenient for you to know how to preserue them fro*m* mites or wormes which thing ye may wel do if it be possible on this wise. Ye shal anoint or rub the inner side of y$^e$ pixt or cup wherein, ye kepe the*m* w$^t$ a lytel wormwode, tansey or rue,* in time of yere whe*n* ye may haue the herbes. And when ye can not cume by the herbes conueniently, the*n* shal ye take a litel of the pouder of mintes and strewe amonge them, or the **[Sig Avi$^v$]** pouder of coloquintida* whyche is white & wil agre wel w$^t$ the colour of the*m* & wyl not suffer anye wormes to breade where it is, by the meanes of the bitternes thereof.

Item ye shal take good hede and reme*m*ber vnto whom and what persons these that be so trimmed ought to be ministred for if ye shall minister them to healthey and well tasting persons it wil be easily espied, and may perad-uentre cause the*m* to spit them out agayne* whereof may arise diuerse in conueniences wherfore ye shall all waye kepe them for sicke folke and suche as can not sauoure thinges wel in ther mouthes (for they wyl impute it to their euyl tast) ye & it may so proue that they maye the soner recouer theyr health for by y$^e$ bitternes & proprietie* therof they beynge prouoked to laxe or vomite may eiecte and cast out such humors as be the cause of their sicknes

---

[66] the*m*.] the*m* 1548.

& so become hole* whiche[67] thinge [**Sig Avii**] the comon people wyll repute as a greate miracle and giue much glory to your goddes therefore.

Item to auoyde the mishappes that might betide them by vermyne as mouse, rat, wesel, munkay or spaniel ye must be circumspecte and take hede on euery hand especially when ye take them out or put them in the boxe and loke that ye leaue none abrode, for ofte tymes it hath be sene that they haue benne* deuoured by suche meane and wyth suche kynde of vermine.

Item ye oughte to caste an eye toward your God when ye be in your bisy memento* & after the leuation,* for whilse ye wincke* and hold your handes before youre nose and eies, it may chaunce some robin redbrest (whiche amonge all other birdes is most hardy, sauce, pert and homely) to season vpon it & flie away cleane therewith whiche done ye knowe in what perilous and daungerous case [**Sig Avii**ᵛ] ye stande in. Wherefore it standeth in youre hande to be well ware and wise therof.

Item if ye haue any tame sparowe or other thinge which is familier with you, take good hede to them or eles leaue them at home for the time, for straunge things hath happened by suche, to the disworshippe of youre goddes.

Item haue in minde that whyle he lieth on the altare, ye set the fote of the chalice vpon the edg of your God, lest the wind by whipynge sodenly get vnder him & blowe him away or about the chauncel* to youre shame & dishonour of your goddes which he defend that dwelleth in the pixt aboue, dayly sensing in & out bi a stryng betwene the altare and the roffe,* to whom be honoure worship and prayse worthye Amen.*

If any or al of these wil not healpe: then ye must vse your olde order of burning, or buriyng of them, wher [**Sig Aviii**] in I know wel ye be expert inough and so well practised yᵗ I nede not to instruct you therin, or shewe you any thyng therto belonginge.

These haue I wrytten to you vndesired to thend that ye shoulde auoyde sla[u]nder and infamy. More shal ye haue shortly God willinge, the whiche I thinke wilbe very necessary for you. And be you assured that as long as I am able to wryte say or do: ye shal not fayle of healp or ayde after the blout sorte as ye se I haue shewed in this litel treatise, the which I doubt not ye wil acept

---

[67] whiche] whcihe 1548.

noneother wise the*n* I iudge in you to do, for sure I am that ye forget me not in your prayers and beneditions, wherein ye be more besy and deuout then I woulde ye should be for my parte. Neuerthelesse I trust I spede not the worsse for them but the better, by defe*n*ce and goodnes of the Lord Iesus Christe, who sitteth on the right hand of God the father* [**Sig Aviii**ᵛ] with the holy gost and from thence shall come a very man vnite wythe his godhead, to iudge all the world in whose sight al vile false and stinkyng godes and Idoles with their worshippers and makers* shalbe co*n*founded, And vnto him with the father and the holy spirite be honoure and praise for euer and euer and to all that beleue only in hym* eternal ioye thorowe the same Lorde Iesus Christe. Amen.

# TEXTUAL NOTES

## Printing History and Collation

All of Luke Shepherd's verse satires were published anonymously and printed individually in London, except for *Apologia Antipi* which was printed only in the compilation, *The comparison betwene the Antipus and the Antigraphe or answere thereunto, with An apologie or defence of the same Antipus And reprehence of the Antigraphe.* In his catalogue of English authors, John Bale lists all of Shepherd's satires, except *Pathose, or an inward passion of the pope for the losse of hys daughter the Masse.*[1] *Iohn Bon and Mast person, Pathose, or an inward passion of the pope for the losse of hys daughter the Masse,* and *The vpcheringe of the messe* bear the printers' names, those of John Day and William Seres, either at the beginning or the end of the text; the rest are printed anonymously. *A pore helpe* carries the same title page border as these texts, but not the printers' names. *The comparison betwene the Antipus and the Antigraphe or answere thereunto, with An apologie or defence of the same Antipus And reprehence of the Antigraphe* bears a different title page border with John Day's name on it.[2] The *STC* gives 1548 as a probable printing date for all of Shepherd's works,[3] although internal evidence suggests that 1547 is a possible date for some of them.

---

[1] Bale, *Index*, 283.

[2] See title page border: Anthony Cope, *A godly meditacion vpon .XX. select and chosen Psalmes of the Prophet Dauid, as wel necessary to al them that are desirous to haue y darke wordes of the Prophet declared and made playn: as also fruitfull to suche as delyte in the contemplation of the spiritual meanyng of them* (London, 1547, *STC* 5717), in R. B. McKerrow and F. S. Ferguson, *Title-page Borders Used in England & Scotland 1485–1640* (London: Oxford University Press for The Bibliographical Society, 1932), 65.

[3] A. W. Pollard and G. R. Redgrave, *A Short-Title Catalogue of Books Printed in England, Scotland, & Ireland and of English Books Printed Abroad 1475–1640*, 2nd ed., revised by W. A. Jackson, F. S. Ferguson, and Katherine F. Pantzer, 3 vols. (London: The Bibliographical Society, 1976–91), 2: 329.

*A pore helpe* 8° (*STC* 13051.7). Robert Wyer probably printed this satire, two identical copies of which exist at the Bodleian Library, Oxford.[4] John Day and William Seres printed another edition (*STC* 13052), copies of which exist, in different states, at the University Library, Cambridge, and at the National Library of Wales.[5] Bale assigns *A pore helpe* to Shepherd under the title *Adiutorium exile* and accurately Latinizes as its opening the words: "Nolit quisquam in tota hac terra."

I have followed the *STC* with regard to the chronological order of these two editions, but collation does not provide clear evidence of sequence. What follows is a discussion of two hypotheses regarding the chronology of the extant copies of *A pore helpe*. I have arranged them in order of preference.

If we hypothesize that Oxford is the first edition, then collation suggests that Cambridge has been hastily and badly set from it, as the latter lacks two lines in Aii and four lines in Av. All of these lines are printed in the National Library of Wales copy which was set from Cambridge, with reference to Oxford, and which has manipulated lines in Aii, Aiv^v, Av, and Av^v in order to avoid resetting the whole poem. Both the Wales copy and the Cambridge copy are different states of the same edition.

Stemma for *A pore helpe* (hypothesis 1):

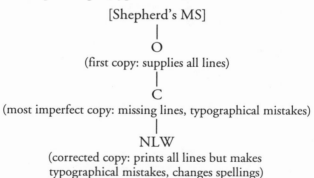

We can also hypothesize that Cambridge is the first edition of this work, set from the author's manuscript but accidentally omitting six lines. In this

⁴ *STC* 3: 192.

⁵ *STC* 3: 52. The *STC* erroneously lists the NLW text as the same edition as *STC* 13051.7; the NLW text lacks the first leaf.

case the Oxford copy could not have been set from Cambridge because Oxford prints the lines which Cambridge lacks. Oxford could have been printed from the Wales copy (which inserts the missing lines from Shepherd's manuscript), its printer correcting mistakes which Wales makes, for example, lines 30, 31, 80, 357, 366, and 380 (see List of Variants), but failing to correct "which" (instead of "with") in line 30 and "our" (instead of "your") in line 80. Oxford also prints the wrong catchword ("And" instead of "By") on Avii.

Stemma for *A pore helpe* (hypothesis 2):

[Shepherd's MS]

|

C

(first copy, but lacks 6 lines)

|

NLW

(inserts missing lines, corrects some errors, makes
typographical mistakes, changes spellings)

|

O

(corrected copy: prints missing lines,
corrects some mistakes, changes spellings)

The only theories which seem certain with regard to *A pore helpe* are the close relationship (different states of the same edition) between the Cambridge copy and the Wales copy, that Wales follows Cambridge, and that Oxford cannot have come from Cambridge without some corrected text to supply the missing lines. While both the hypotheses I have proposed are possible, I suggest that Oxford is probably the first edition. The Oxford copy is the most complete of all the copies and is the copy text for this edition.

W. K. Jordan proposes a likely printing date for *A pore helpe* of 1547, based on internal evidence[6] and, although he is not specific about the details, he presumably refers to the lines in the poem that suggest the imprisonment of Bishop Gardiner in the Fleet from 25 September 1547 to 8 January 1548.[7]

---

[6] W. K. Jordan, *Edward VI: The Young King* (London: George Allen & Unwin, 1968), 137 n. 4.

[7] Philip Hughes, *The Reformation in England*, 3 vols. (London: Hollis and Carter, 1953–54), 2: 93, 102.

Shortly after his release from prison, Gardiner was placed under house arrest until 20 February 1548[8] and Shepherd may have written this poem early in that year, rather than in 1547. M. Channing Lenthicum dates the tract as probably late 1548, basing her argument on an allusion in *A pore helpe* to Gardiner's incarceration, and on a reference in the poem to one of Miles Hogarde's works.[9] She further argues that the physical condition of the compartment of the title page in the Day and Seres copy of the text "indicates a date 1548–9" for this work.[10] However, internal evidence indicates that the Mass was not yet officially celebrated in English at this time, which suggests a composition date before May 1548 when the English service was established in most London churches.[11]

John Strype edited *A pore helpe* in 1721,[12] and William Carew Hazlitt edited it in 1866.[13] Samuel Egerton Brydges printed thirty-one lines of it in *Censura Literaria* in 1815.[14] None of these editions is entirely reliable. Alexander Dyce accurately printed ninety-nine lines of this work in 1844.[15]

---

[8] Glyn Redworth, *In Defence of the Church Catholic: The Life of Stephen Gardiner* (Oxford: Basil Blackwell, 1990), 268.

[9] M. Channing Lenthicum, "*A Pore Helpe* and Its Printers," *The Library*, 4th ser. 9 (1929): 169–183, passim. Lenthicum suggests that lines 124–143 of *A pore helpe* refer to the years 1548–53, during which Gardiner was imprisoned in the Tower (Lenthicum, "*A Pore Helpe*," 179, 181). She does not consider lines 182–183, which, I suggest, refer to Gardiner's earlier imprisonment in the Fleet (25 September 1547–8 January 1548), or to his placement under house arrest (19 January–20 February 1548). Shepherd refers openly to Gardiner's incarceration in the Tower in *The vpcheringe of the messe* (317).

[10] Lenthicum, "*A Pore Helpe*," 183.

[11] *A pore helpe* (345–350); C. W. Dugmore, *The Mass and the English Reformers* (London: Macmillan, 1958), 126.

[12] Strype, *Memorials*, 2: pt. 2, 333–337.

[13] William Carew Hazlitt, ed., *Remains of the Early Popular Poetry of England*, 4 vols. (London: John Russell Smith, 1864–66), 3: 249–266.

[14] Samuel Egerton Brydges, *Censura Literaria. Containing Titles, Abstracts, and Opinions of Old English Books, with Original Disquisitions, Articles of Biography, and Other Literary Antiquities*, 2nd ed., 10 vols. (London: printed for Longman, Hurst, Rees, Orme, and Brown, 1815), 1: 66–68.

[15] John Skelton, *The Poetical Works of John Skelton*, ed. Alexander Dyce, 2 vols. (London: Thomas Rodd, 1843, with addenda 1844; New York: AMS Press, 1965), 1: app. 3, cix–cxii.

*The vpcheringe of the messe* 8° (*STC* 17630). John Day and William Seres printed this satire.[16] Of five extant copies, two copies exist at the Bodleian Library, Oxford. These two copies (Tanner 47 (1) and Douce MM 296) are almost identical. In the Tanner copy a letter in one word on Ai^v is omitted, the catchword on Avi has an uninked letter, and Aviii–Aviii^v are mutilated. In the Douce copy an end-letter in one word on Aviii^v is omitted and an extra space is included.[17] A copy of *The vpcheringe of the messe* exists at the Huntington Library, San Marino, California, and another copy is in the University Library, Cambridge. Finally, an imperfect copy, lacking the first leaf, is preserved at the National Library of Wales. These five copies represent five different states of the same edition. All copies have the catchword "Whe" on the penultimate page which is a mistake for "She." Collation suggests that Oxford is the first copy because subsequent copies emend typographical faults. (I am unable to determine which of the two Oxford copies precedes the other.) The Huntington copy has fewer corrections than the Oxford copy, and the Cambridge copy has even fewer. The Wales copy is the most perfect, despite the missing pages. Therefore, the copy text for this edition is the Wales copy, except for the leaf Ai which it lacks. The copy text for pages Ai–Ai^v is the Cambridge copy.[18]

Stemma for *The vpcheringe of the messe*:

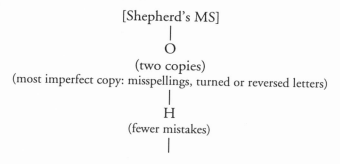

[Shepherd's MS]

|

O

(two copies)

(most imperfect copy: misspellings, turned or reversed letters)

|

H

(fewer mistakes)

|

---

[16] *STC* 3: 52.

[17] Prior to my collation, these two copies were thought to be identical, apart from the mutilation. I am grateful to Clive Hurst, Head of Rare Books and Printed Ephemera at the Bodleian Library, for his help regarding this text.

[18] Ai–Ai^v are identical in the Cambridge, Huntington, and Oxford (Douce) copies.

C
(fewer mistakes)

|

NLW
(most perfect copy)

*The vpcheringe of the messe* must be the work that Bale refers to as *Stomachum misse* because his opening lines correspond with those of Shepherd's satire: "Quis non nouerit vel non audiuerit."

Jordan suggests a probable printing date of 1547, but offers no evidence.[19] However, internal evidence indicates that Gardiner was in the Tower by the time this satire was written:

> I dare saye at this howre
> Thoughe he be in the towre
> Yet doeth he styl honoure
> The messe that swete a flowre
> (316–319)

*The vpcheringe of the messe* must, therefore, have been composed after 30 June 1548, when Gardiner was incarcerated.[20] Friedrich Germann edited *The vpcheringe of the messe* in 1911.[21] This edition is not completely reliable. Dyce accurately printed one hundred and thirty-one lines of it in 1844.[22] Hazlitt accurately reprinted the complete text in 1875.[23] David Norbrook and H. R. Woudhuysen printed an extract from it in 1992.[24]

---

[19] Jordan, *Edward VI*, 138 n. 1.

[20] Hughes, *Reformation*, 2: 105; MacCulloch, *Cranmer*, 404.

[21] Friedrich Germann, *Luke Shepherd, ein Satirendichter der englischen Reformationszeit* (Augsburg: Theodor Lampart, 1911), 97–101.

[22] Dyce, *Skelton*, 1: app. 3, cxii–cxv.

[23] William Carew Hazlitt, ed., *Fugitive Tracts Written in Verse Which Illustrate the Condition of Religious and Political Feeling in England and the State of Society There during Two Centuries*, 2 vols. (London: Chiswick Press, Printed for Private Circulation, 1875), n.p.

[24] H. R. Woudhuysen, ed., *The Penguin Book of Renaissance Verse, 1509–1659*, intro. David Norbrook (Harmondsworth: Penguin Books, 1992), 529–530.

*Pathose, or an inward passion of the pope for the losse of hys daughter the Masse* 8° (*STC* 19463). John Day and William Seres printed this satire.[25] An imperfect copy exists at the University Library, Cambridge, and a second imperfect copy of the same edition exists at the National Library of Wales. The latter is not listed in the *STC*. In both copies Aiii is incorrectly signed and should be Aii. The Wales copy corrects various spelling mistakes in the Cambridge text, rectifies the omission of single words in two different lines, and also prints lines 543 and 544 in their correct order. The copy text for this edition is the Wales copy since it contains the leaves Aiii–Avi^v that are missing from the Cambridge copy. Of these pages only Aiii is signed. As pages Ai–Ai^v are missing from the Wales copy, the copy text for Ai–Ai^v is the Cambridge copy. Bale does not list this satire in his catalogue. *Pathose, or an inward passion of the pope for the losse of hys daughter the Masse* appears to act as a sequel to *The vpcheringe of the messe* which, therefore, suggests a probable printing date of later than the end of June 1548. Germann edited most of this satire in 1911.[26]

*Iohn Bon and Mast person* 4° (*STC* 3258.5). John Day and William Seres printed this satire, copies of which exist at the British Library, London, and at the Newberry Library, Chicago.[27] The two copies are different states of the same edition whose differences are caused through instances of bad inking and extra spaces. Although the two copies are almost identical, the British Library copy is in a cleaner state and is the copy text for this edition. *Iohn Bon and Mast person* incorporates an illustration in its text.[28] The picture is situated above the prefatory verse (Ai) and depicts the carrying of the pyx containing the consecrated host in a Corpus Christi procession. Richard Pynson used the same woodcut in 1517 in a work entitled *Here begynneth the Rule of seynt Benet*. The design of Pynson's woodcut was based very closely on a woodcut William Caxton originally used in 1490 in the work *Saint*

---

[25] *STC* 3: 52.

[26] Germann, *Luke Shepherd*, 104–111; Germann assigns this text to Shepherd on the basis of style (72–73).

[27] *STC* 3: 52.

[28] Non-ironic use of woodcuts depicting religious scenes of this kind was banned from 1535. Ironic use of woodcuts was permissible, but in actuality it was extremely uncommon.

*Bonadventura Speculum vite Christi* which Wynkyn de Worde reprinted in 1494. Bale lists Shepherd's work under the title *Ioannem Bonne* and gives its opening lines: "Precor tibi auroram felicem Ioan."

Edward Underhill, a contemporary, states that Shepherd wrote it "in the tyme off kynge Edwarde,"[29] and relates that the report of the tract so angered Sir John Gresham, Mayor of London (October 1547–October 1548), that he sent for John Day, intending to punish the printer and find out the name of the author.[30] Strype claims that *Iohn Bon and Mast person* was written in "the first year of King Edward" (i.e., 28 January 1547–27 January 1548), but gives no exact date.[31] Susan Brigden states that the poem was printed in 1547,[32] but provides no proof. Some internal evidence suggests a reference to Hugh Latimer's *Sermon on the Ploughers* which he delivered on 18 January 1548.[33] Hazlitt simply gives the date of the satire as 1548 without elaborating.[34] Dickie Allen Spurgeon places the work sometime between July and October 1548. He bases his dating on the publication of Thomas Cranmer's *Cate-chism* (i.e., *Cathechismvs: That is to say a shorte Instruction into Christian Religion for the synguler commoditie and profyte of children and yong people*) which he assigns to July 1548, and on Gresham's term of office as Mayor of London which ended in October 1548.[35] John King suggests that Day and Seres may have printed this tract to coincide with Cranmer's disestablishment of Corpus Christi in 1548.[36] If Shepherd wrote *Iohn Bon and Mast person* as propaganda before the feast of Corpus Christi was disestablished, then it must have been composed earlier than 31 May (1548) when the feast day occurred that year. However, some internal evidence in the poem indicates that it was composed soon after the printing of Cranmer's *Catechism*, which Gardiner

---

[29] Underhill, "Anecdotes," 172.

[30] Underhill, "Anecdotes," 172.

[31] Strype, *Memorials*, 2: pt. 1, 182.

[32] Brigden, *London and the Reformation*, 438.

[33] See Commentary on *Iohn Bon and Mast person* (145–147).

[34] William Carew Hazlitt, ed., *Faiths and Folklore: A Dictionary of National Beliefs and Popular Customs, Past and Current, with Their Classical and Foreign Analogues, Described and Illustrated*, 2 vols. (London: Reeves and Turner, 1905), 1: 150–151.

[35] Dickie Allen Spurgeon, "An Edition Of Three Tudor Dialogues," Ph.D. diss., University of Illinois, 1967, 11.

[36] King, *English Reformation Literature*, 258.

dated "about the time" of his St Peter's day sermon of 29 June 1548[37] and to which John Ab Ulmis refers as having been "lately published" in a letter written to Henry Bullinger on 18 August 1548.[38] Margaret Aston, J. I. Packer and G. E. Duffield, and Cranmer's most recent biographer, Diarmaid MacCulloch, give June (no date) 1548 as the publishing date of Cranmer's *Catechism*.[39] The most recent editor of Cranmer's works, D. G. Selwyn, corroborates Gardiner's dating of the *Catechism*.[40] While Shepherd's ironic lines[41] are possibly an allusion to something other than Cranmer's work, for instance, Justus Jonas's *Catechismus pro pueris et juventute*, I believe that they do refer to Cranmer's *Catechism* and that Shepherd wrote *Iohn Bon and Mast person* soon after the *Catechism* was published in June 1548, either in support of the abrogation of Corpus Christi, or because even though the feast itself had already been disestablished, he believed that there was an ongoing need for Protestant propaganda against images and idolatry.

Brydges printed the first thirty lines of *Iohn Bon and Mast person* (with Joseph Haslewood's comments) in *Censura Literaria* (1805–09), and reprinted it in the second edition in 1815.[42] In 1807 J. Smeeton reprinted the whole work in facsimile from the only then known copy which had formerly belonged to Richard Forster.[43] William Henry Black edited it for the Percy

---

[37] Foxe, *Acts*, 6: 126.

[38] Hastings Robinson, ed., *Original Letters Relative to the English Reformation, Written during the Reigns of King Henry VIII., King Edward VI., and Queen Mary: Chiefly from the Archives of Zurich*, 2 pts (Cambridge: The University Press, 1846–47), 2: 379–381.

[39] Margaret Aston, *England's Iconoclasts: Laws against Images* (Oxford: Clarendon Press, 1988), 430; J. I. Packer and G. E. Duffield, eds., *The Work of Thomas Cranmer* (Appleford: Sutton Courtenay Press, 1965), xvi; MacCulloch, *Cranmer*, 387.

[40] D. G. Selwyn, ed., *A Catechism set forth by Thomas Cranmer* (Appleford: Sutton Courtenay Press, 1978), 94. This work is Cranmer's translation into English of Justus Jonas's 1539 Latin translation of Andreas Osiander's and Johannes Brenz's earlier German text.

[41] "But I trust it wylbe better w$^t$ the help of Catechismus / For thoughe it came forth but euen that other day / Yet hath it tourned many to ther olde waye," *Iohn Bon and Mast person* (143–145).

[42] Brydges, *Censura Literaria*, 1: 59–62.

[43] Leslie Stephen and Sidney Lee, eds., *The Dictionary of National Biography from the Earliest Times to 1900*, 21 vols. (London: Smith Elder, 1908–09), 18: 54–55.

Society in 1852,[44] and Hazlitt edited it in 1866.[45] Edward Arber edited it in the *English Garner* (1877–95),[46] and A. F. Pollard reprinted it in Arber's collection in 1902.[47] Spurgeon edited it with two other Tudor dialogues in 1967.[48] King edited it in 1992.[49] The editions by Black and Spurgeon are entirely reliable.[50]

*Antipus*, **a single sheet folio printed on one side only (*STC* 683).** John Day probably printed this text because he printed a later work, *The comparison betwene the Antipus and the Antigraphe or answere thereunto, with An apologie or defence of the same Antipus And reprehence of the Antigraphe*, that incorporates it and uses the same ornamental capitals.[51] Bale does not list *Antipus* separately. The unique copy of *Antipus* exists at the Bodleian Library, Oxford.

*The comparison betwene the Antipus and the Antigraphe or answere thereunto, with An apologie or defence of the same Antipus And reprehence of the Antigraphe* 4° (*STC* 5605a). John Day printed this compilation, which contains three short works arranged sequentially in the order in which the components originally appeared.[52] In it, *Antipus* has been completely reset and is, therefore, a different edition from *Antipus STC* 683. The second poem in this work is entitled the *Antigraphium* and is Sir John Mason's reply to

---

[44] William Henry Black, ed., "Iohn Bon and Mast person," *Early English Poetry, Ballads and Popular Literature of the Middle Ages. Edited from Original Manuscripts and Scarce Publications.* 30 vols. (London: T. Richards, 1840–52), 30: xi–xxviii.

[45] Hazlitt, *Remains*, 4: 1–16.

[46] Edward Arber, *English Garner*, 8 vols. (Westminster, Archibald Constable, 1877–95), 4: 101–111.

[47] A. F. Pollard, *Tudor Tracts, 1532–1588* (Westminster: Archibald Constable, 1903), 159–169.

[48] Spurgeon, *Tudor Dialogues*, 1–25.

[49] John N. King, "Luke Shepherd's *John Bon and Mast Person*," *American Notes and Queries* n.s. 5 (1992): 87–91.

[50] Mostly the errors involve misread or transposed words; both the 1807 facsimile edition and Hazlitt's edition print Caxton's, not Pynson's woodcut on the title page.

[51] *STC* 3: 52.

[52] *STC* 3: 52.

Shepherd's *Antipus* text.[53] Presumably, the *Antigraphium* was earlier printed as a single-sheet folio, but no copy of it survives outside of Shepherd's text. The third poem, *Apologia Antipi*, is Shepherd's reply. The unique copy of *The comparison betwene the Antipus and the Antigraphe* exists at the Huntington Library, San Marino, California. While Bale does not list this work under its actual title, he refers to *Antipi amicum* and suggests that it begins with the words: "Est Lathomus quidam, floridus." Although *The comparison betwene the Antipus and the Antigraphe* does not open with these lines, the work is concerned with rebutting a conservative writer named Mason ("Lathomus" translates as "stone cutter"), and Bale frequently Latinizes writers' names in this way. Presumably, Bale did not have this satire in front of him when he described it, or he had only heard about the work and had not read it, or else he described a now lost installment of this flyting. Internal evidence suggests a probable printing date for *The comparison betwene the Antipus and the Antigraphe* some time after the printing of the *Order of Communion* (8 March 1548), as some of its lines echo words contained in the new rite of communion.[54]

*Phylogamus* 8° (*STC* 19882). William Hill probably printed this satire.[55] A copy without title page exists at All Souls College, Oxford, and an imperfect copy, lacking leaves Ai, Aiiii, and Av, exists at the British Library, London. The Oxford copy and the British Library copy are different states of the same edition. In both copies Aii has the same decoration of a cut tree trunk beside the title.[56] Differences in the two copies are the presence of a final "e" in two words, two turned letters, and one extra space (probably the result of a furniture shift). Bale lists the work as *Phylogamum* and accurately renders its opening lines into Latin: "Date locum emuncti poete lepidi." The copy text for this edition is the Oxford copy as this text is more complete than the British Library copy. *Phylogamus* was written after *The comparison betwene the Antipus and the Antigraphe* because it contains a reference to Mason's

---

[53] *Phylogamus* (25–26); *STC* 1: 251.

[54] See Commentary on *The comparison betwene the Antipus and the Antigraphe* (156–157).

[55] *STC* 3: 83.

[56] This decoration, inverted and reversed, appears beside the title of a similar Protestant work also printed by Hill; see Punt, *Endightment*.

authorship of the *Antigraphium*.[57] Dyce accurately printed fifty-five lines of it in 1844,[58] and Germann printed a fragment of it in his doctoral dissertation in 1911.[59]

*Doctour doubble ale* 8° (*STC* 7071). Anthony Scoloker probably printed this satire, the sole copy of which exists at the Bodleian Library, Oxford.[60] Bale ascribes *Doctour doubble ale* to Shepherd under the title *Doctorem double ale* and accurately renders its opening words as: "Quamuis intelligentia caream."

Patricia M. Took states that *Doctour doubble ale* "almost certainly dates from 1547" and describes the poem as "a fine example of the type of lampoon" that the Injunctions of that same year complained about.[61] However, internal evidence indicates that the poem was printed sometime after the printing of the Privy Council's Proclamation forbidding private Masses (February 1548) and *The Order of Communion* (8 March 1548).[62] Additional evidence also supports this later dating. According to Gordon Duff, Scoloker printed only seven works at Ipswich before he moved to London, where he was established by June 1548.[63] As Duff does not list Shepherd's poem as one of the works printed at Ipswich, *Doctour doubble ale* seems to have been printed in London sometime in 1548. Charles Henry Hartshorne edited *Doctour doubble ale* in 1829,[64] and Hazlitt edited it in 1866.[65] Both are unreliable editions. Dyce accurately printed one hundred and forty-seven lines of it in 1844.[66]

---

[57] *Phylogamus* (25–26).

[58] Dyce, *Skelton*, 1: app. 3, cxv–cxvii.

[59] Germann, *Luke Shepherd*, 101–104.

[60] *STC* 3: 151.

[61] Patricia M. Took, "Government and the Printing Trade, 1540–1560," diss., University of London, 1978, 142.

[62] See *Doctour doubble ale* (61, 326–330).

[63] Gordon E. Duff, *The English Provincial Printers, Stationers, and Bookbinders to 1557* (Cambridge: Cambridge University Press, 1912), 106–107.

[64] Charles Henry Hartshorne, ed., *Ancient Metrical Tales: Printed Chiefly from Original Sources* (London: William Pickering, 1829), 227–245.

[65] Hazlitt, *Remains*, 3: 297–321.

[66] Dyce, *Skelton*, 1: app. 3, cxix–cxxiii.

Shepherd's prose work has caused difficulty for scholars in the past. Bale identifies the work in his catalogue under the title *Cautelas preseruatorias*, and bibliographers originally thought that *A godlye and holesome preseruatyue against desperation at all times necessarye for the soule: but then chiefly to be vsed and ministred when the deuill doth assault vs moost fiersely, and deth approcheth niest* (*STC* 20203.5) was Shepherd's prose work.[67] No evidence exists to corroborate the previous assertion of Shepherd's authorship of *A godlye and holesome preseruatyue*, as neither the title, nor the beginning lines of this work, correlate in any way with those that Bale quotes. *Cautelas preseruatorias* may be translated as "a (pre)cautionary preservative," but the words: "Quia video maiorem hominum nu"[68] do not correspond convincingly to anything in Shepherd's Preface or in the opening of the work, although it could possibly be argued that they are a paraphrase of the first lines of a paragraph on Avi: "Seinge therefore the multitude of people is great, and the ministers of the gospel very few." However, Bale is unlikely to record a line six pages into the body of a text as that work's opening, unless the work lacked its initial pages. In that case, we could reasonably expect Bale to describe the text as incomplete. Furthermore, Shepherd's putative authorship of *A godlye and holesome preseruatyue* is suspect in that this work differs from the rest of his writing in its subject matter and purpose. All of his other texts adopt a controversial Protestant point of view, ridiculing the Mass and sacramentals. Unlike them, *A godlye and holesome preseruatyue* is not satire. Offering a remedy against despair and comfort for those about to die, this religious work lacks a radically Protestant stance. Moreover, while authorship of *A godlye and holesome preseruatyue* does not preclude authorship of another prose composition, I believe it does preclude authorship of the work now ascribed to Shepherd, as he is unlikely to have written two prose works with titles so similar they could be mistaken for each other. In addition, if Shepherd published two prose works in 1548, Bale would almost certainly be aware of both texts. Bale identifies Shepherd's prose work under the title *Cautelas preseruatorias*, and the Latin incipit that he quotes corresponds exactly with the first words of the

---

[67] *STC* 2: 247. John Herford probably printed this work for James Burrell in 1548; William Copland printed another edition (*STC* 20204) for Richard Keele in 1551 (this edition includes four extra pages of prayers at the end); see *STC* 3: 32, 45, 96.

[68] Bale, *Index*, 283.

work entitled *Cautels* which the *STC*'s Addenda and Corrigenda attributes to Shepherd.[69]

*Cauteles preseruatory concerning the preseruation of the Gods which are kept in the pixe.* 8° (*STC* 4877.2) was printed anonymously in London in 1548.[70] John Day probably printed this work since the ornamental initial capital "F" which begins the text of *Cauteles preseruatory* is one Day uses in his 1551 Bible (known as the Becke Bible). I have been unable to trace any other printer's contemporary usage of this ornament.[71] Moreover, certain other ornaments that Day uses in his Bible also appear in some of Shepherd's works. For example, the ornamental initial capital "A" that Day uses in *Antipus* and at the beginning of the *Antigraphium* in *The comparison betwene the Antipus and the Antigraphe* appears fourteen times in Day's Bible, and the ornamental initial capital "W" that begins Shepherd's *Iohn Bon and Mast person* appears five times in the same Bible.[72] Both the initial capital "A" and "F" feature an elfish figure inside the alphabetical letter and appear to be from the same series. If this is the case, then Day almost certainly printed *Cauteles preseruatory*.

Since the extant text of Shepherd's prose work lacks a title page, I have taken its title from the entry in Andrew Maunsell's 1595 English bibliography.[73] *Cauteles preseruatory* begins: "For as muche as I se that most me[n] in theyr sience be diligent and circumspecte as craftesmen in their occupacions dooe exquisitly laboure and searche out the knowledge not onely of workemanshippe and connynge: but as well of the order and preseruinge of the stuffe and mater whereof they shall frame and fassion theyr worke." The rest of this satire is concerned with irreverent instructions to Catholic clergy

---

[69] *STC* 3: 271.

[70] *STC* 1: 617; 3: 271.

[71] The ornamental initial capital "F" occurs three times in the Becke Bible: Judges: ix, Ciii<sup>v</sup>, Matthew xx, Cccci<sup>v</sup>, and a prologue to the Epistle of St Paul to the Romans, Mmmmi. For illustration of this ornamental initial capital, see C. L. Oastler, *John Day, the Elizabethan Printer* (Oxford: Oxford Bibliographical Society, 1975), 50.

[72] The ornamental initial capital "A" occurs in Books 1–4 on Liii<sup>v</sup>, Nv<sup>v</sup>, Aii, Bv<sup>v</sup>, Fvi, Miiii, Oii<sup>v</sup>, QQiii<sup>v</sup>, BBgi<sup>v</sup>, JJivi, KKkiii, KKkv<sup>v</sup>, DDoiii, and DDov; the ornamental initial capital "W" occurs on Hiiii, CCi, BBiii, DDdv, and DDoii<sup>v</sup>.

[73] Maunsell, *Catalogue*, pt. 1, Civ<sup>v</sup>.

on how to preserve communion hosts. Everything about the expression and tone of the tract points to Shepherd's authorship. In its subject and style the tract complements Shepherd's other satires, and its impious voice recalls that of *A pore helpe*, especially in its catalogue of the misfortunes that can befall unconsumed communion hosts.

The unique copy of *Cauteles preseruatory* exists, at present disbound, at the National Library of Wales. The work lacks its title page, but is otherwise complete. It came to the National Library of Wales as part of the collection of the Welsh bibliographer John Humphrey Davies (1871–1926).[74] Previously, it was bound with ten other rare tracts (including *Pathose, or an inward passion of the pope for the losse of hys daughter the Masse, A pore helpe*, and *The vpcheringe of the messe*) whose subject matter is the Mass. Since its presentation to the National Library, this volume of Mass tracts has been broken up and the other works individually bound.

### Collation Formula
[N.B.: * denotes copy text]

*STC* 13051.7 *A pore helpe,*
*Bodleian (Douce H 100; Tanner 47 (3)) 8º: A8 [signed Aiii, Aiiii, Av]

*STC* 13052 *A pore helpe,* [another edition]
Cambridge (Syn. 8. 54. 94) 8º: A8 [signed Aii, Aiii, Aiiii]
National Library of Wales [erroneously described as 13051.7 in the revised *STC*] (13051.7) 8º: A8 (—A1) [signed Aiii, Aiiii]

*STC* 17630 *The vpcheringe of the messe:*
Bodleian (Douce MM 296; Tanner 47 (1)) 8º: A8 [signed Aii, Aiii, Aiiii]
Cambridge (Syn. 8. 54.114) 8º: A8 [signed Aii, Aiii, Aiiii]
Huntington (RB 50444) 8º: A8 [signed Aiii, Aiiii]; Aii trimmed, signature and catchword absent
*National Library of Wales (17630) 8º: A8 (—A1) [signed Aii, Aiii, Aiiii]

---

[74] I am grateful to Charles Parry, Department of Printed Books, National Library of Wales, for kindly providing this information and for his help regarding Shepherd's texts.

*STC* 19463  *Pathose, or an inward passion of the pope for the losse of hys daughter the Masse.*
Cambridge (Syn. 8. 54. 113) 8o: A–B8 (—A3–A6) [signed Aii, Bi, Bii; A2 signed "Aiii"]
*National Library of Wales [not listed in the revised *STC*] (19463) 8o: A–B8 (—A1) [signed Aii, Aiii, Bi, Bii; A2 signed "Aiii"]

*STC* 3258.5  *Iohn Bon and Mast person*
British Library (C. 95. a. 9.) 4o: *A*4
*Newberry (Case 3A 528) 4o: A4

*STC* 683  *Antipus,*
*Bodleian (Arch. A d. 6 (2)) [reprinted in 5605a] s.sh.fol.

*STC* 5605a  *The comparison betwene the Antipus and the Antigraphe or answere thereunto, with. An apologie or defence of the same Antipus. And reprehence of the Antigraphe.*
*Huntington (RB 31220) 4o: A4 B2 [signed Bi]

*STC* 19882  *Phylogamus*
*All Souls (Codrington Library no longer allows its call-numbers to be published) 8o: A8 (—A1) B4 [signed Aii, Aiii, Aiiii, Bi, Bii]
British Library (C. 40. m. 9. (26.)) 8o: A8 (—A4, A5) [signed Aii, Aiii]; lacks B

*STC* 7071  *Doctour doubble ale.*
*Bodleian (Arch. A f. 83 (9)) 8o: a8 [signed aii]

*STC* 4877.2  *Cauteles preseruatory concerning the preseruation of the Gods which are kept in the pixe.*
*National Library of Wales (4877.2) 8o: A8 (—A1) [signed Aii, Aiii]

## Editorial Method

All significant editorial interventions, including obvious mistakes which are emended in the text, are footnoted. (These footnotes indicate only editorial variations from the copy texts.) The original spelling and punctuation are retained in all the texts, but the letter "s" replaces the long "ſ" used throughout the black letter texts and the letter "z" replaces the yogh symbol in *Iohn Bon and Mast person*. Turned letters in all of Shepherd's works are corrected within square brackets and all contractions except for wᵗ, yᵉ, yᵗ and yᵘ are expanded in italics. Elisions are left unmarked, and word divisions are unaltered in all of the texts. Line breaks in the poems are preserved, but the initial letters are capitalized. Paragraph indentations are regularized in the prose work, but preserved in the verse texts. Signature numbers are inserted on the page to which they refer. Signature numbers without brackets indicate signed pages, and signature numbers within square brackets indicate unsigned pages. Signature numbers for signed pages are enclosed within angle brackets where they occur in the middle of words in the prose text. Sigla references specify only verso. When a reference is to the recto side of a leaf, the signature number alone is given and recto can be inferred. Some titles of works quoted or referred to in this edition are shortened for convenience, and some original capitalization is changed. The titles of all works are cited in the original spelling and punctuation of their title pages, with the exception of final periods or commas, which are omitted for the sake of clarity. The publishing dates and volume numbers of works quoted are cited in Arabic numerals. Final punctuation marks in the titles of Shepherd's works are included in the texts, but excluded generally elsewhere in this edition. In the absence of a title page, the title *Cauteles preseruatory* is adopted from the spelling given by Andrew Maunsell in his 1595 bibliography.

# COMMENTARY

The Commentary is primarily intended to elucidate difficult lines, to explain historical allusions, to expand religious references, and, where possible, to translate the Latin and pseudo-Latin lines. The titles of Shepherd's works are quoted in the original spelling and capitalization, but are abbreviated for convenience. Extraneous, final punctuation marks are excluded in all instances apart from headings. Unless otherwise stated, all biblical quotations or references are from *The Bible*, New Revised Standard Version with the Apocrypha (Oxford: Oxford University Press, 1989).

Since the doctrine of transubstantiation is the most crucial theological point of contention between Protestants and Catholics, and because satirizing transubstantiation is such an intrinsic part of Shepherd's work, it may be useful to include a concise summary of the doctrine at this point: "In the moment of transubstantiation, according to Roman doctrine, the sacrificial body of Christ materializes as substance under the accidental appearance of the bread. The bread as material signifier becomes transparent to or dissolves into the signified reality of Christ's body. The distance between the sign and the reality to which it refers collapses, as Christ fully inhabits the blessed and broken host" (Shullenberger, "Poetics of the Eucharist," 28).

## I *A pore helpe,*

heading *bukler*] "His faithfulness is a shield and buckler" (Psalm 91:4; Ephesians 6:16–17; Thessalonians 5:8–9).

7 *tratlynge tales telles*] Idle talk.

53–54 *Ryght holy thynges to make / Yea God within a cake*] Refers to the sacramental element of bread and to the doctrine of transubstantiation. See also *Pathose* (177); *Antipus* (22); *The comparison betwene the Antipus and the Antigraphe* (51; 127); *Doctour doubble ale* (329–330), and *Cauteles preseruatory* (Aii^v).

64 *boke, bell and candell*] Refers to the ritual of excommunication (Myrc, *Instructions*, 21–24). See also *Pathose* (419).

79 *christined belles*] Protestants regarded "christening" church bells as blasphemous (Foxe, *Acts*, 1: 82; 6: 383).

80–82 *longe gownes*] Ecclesiastical garb.

*shauen crownes*] Clerical tonsures. See also lines 279–280.

*typettes*] Tippets. A band of silk or fur worn round the neck, with the two ends hanging from the shoulders in front.

81f. *your . . . ye . . . you*] Error for "our," "we," and "us." The narrator pretends a Catholic viewpoint, but mistakenly reverts to a Protestant voice in this and other lines. See also lines 82, 86–87, 94, 98, and 102.

86 *wyll none of your owne*] Clerical marriage was not legalized in England until February 1549 (Haigh, *Reformation Revised*, 100).

96 *brabble on the Byble*] To debate scriptural interpretation.

101 *Paraphrasies*] The *Paraphrases* of Erasmus. The Injunctions of 31 July 1547 required each parish church to provide a copy of this work for the instruction of the laity.

139 *or faggottes bere*] Bearing faggots in public signified recantation of heresy. See also *Pathose* (478).

141 *our learnynges olde*] Catholic teachings; as opposed to the "new learning" i.e., Protestantism or evangelicalism.

144 *laye mannes boke*] Images and pictures. Originating this trope, Gregory the Great argues: "a picture is introduced into a church so that those who are ignorant of letters may at least read by looking at the walls what they cannot read in books" (quoted in Watt, *Cheap Print And Popular Piety*, 160 n. 111).

148 *I wysse*] Assuredly (variant of "iwis"). See also line 219.

153–57 *Christes body aboue . . . Fleshe bloude and bone present*] Protestants argued the impossibility of Christ's simultaneous corporeal presence in heaven and on all the altars where Mass was celebrated (e.g., Martin Bucer, see MacCulloch, *Cranmer*, 382).

160–63 *The wordes of consecracion . . . be not in the crede*] Shepherd points out the absence of reference to transubstantiation in any creed. See also *Iohn Bon and Mast person* (30).

164 *these felowes newe*] Protestants.

180 *a box*] A pyx; a box or vessel in which the consecrated host is reserved or carried about in during processions. See also "boxe" *Cauteles preseruatory* (Aiv^v, Avii); "glasse" *Iohn Bon and Mast person* (18); "pixe" *Cauteles preseruatory* (title), and "pixt" *Cauteles preseruatory* (Av^v, Avi, Avii^v). A contemporary reference refers to the Eucharist as "Jacke of the boxe" (*Grey Friars*, 55).

182 *a fox*] Stephen Gardiner (1483–1555), Bishop of Winchester (see Appendix). William Turner seems to have coined the term "the fox" for Gardiner; he identifies Gardiner as the pope's son in *The Rescvynge Of The Romishe Fox Othervvyse called the examination of the hunter deuised by steuen gardiner* (Ai^v). John Bale also uses the image "Fox of wynchester" for Gardiner in *A breue Cronycle of the Bysshope of Romes blessynge, and of his Prelates beneficiall and charitable rewardes, from the tyme of Kynge Heralde vnto this daye* (Avi).

183 *presoner vnder lockes*] Refers to Gardiner's imprisonment, either in the Fleet (25 September 1547 to 8 January 1548), or under house arrest (19 January to 20 February

1548). Shepherd refers to Gardiner's later imprisonment in the Tower in *The vpcheringe of the messe* (317).

187 *Nor eatyn of a mouse / Nor rotten is*] A reference to the traditional theological question as to what happens when the host is profaned by being eaten by an animal or when it goes moldy. The reformers denied that the host contained Christ's physical substance. See similar expression in *Cauteles preseruatory* (Aiiᵛ).

195 *offered vp agayne*] The prime point of contention in reformist opposition to the propitiatory notion of the Mass. See also note on *The vpcheringe of the messe* (147) and note on *Pathose* (144).

200–01 *in playes / In tauerns and hye wayes*] The narrator ridicules Protestant plays by consigning them to taverns and the streets.

205–06 *synge pype mery annot / And play of wyll not cannot*] See similar phrase in Bale's *Three Laws*, line 396 (*Complete Plays*, ed. Happé, 78; 162 n. 396). A reference to Matthew 11:17; Luke 7:32.

211 *them*] The Gospellers.

213–17 These lines appear to refer to Gardiner's now lost verses against the Protestants (Took, "Government and the Printing Trade," 140–141). See also lines 231–234. Gardiner's only extant poem is *Theyr dedes in effecte, my lyfe wolde haue.*

214 *theyr bonettes vale*] Doff their hats.

218 *what a man*] Gardiner.

237 *take my marke amys*] Proverbial (Tilley, *Proverbs*, M 669).

239 *his*] Hiss.

241 *twelue men*] A jury. No record exists of this court case. See also line 335.

243 *the bar*] King's Bench court, Westminster.

248 *coram nobis*] In the sovereign's presence. Refers to the court of the King's Bench. See also line 336.

249 *vobis*] You. See also line 337.

251 *pulled the henne*] Deceived.

253 *porage*] Variant of "porridge."

256–57 *to wagge / Upon a wodden nagge*] To be hanged.

264 *my Lorde*] Gardiner.

270 *popistant*] Nonce-word for a papist.

*stout*] Resolute. A reference to Gardiner's intractable support of the Catholic Church. Turner describes Gardiner as "steuen my son both fierce and stout" in *The Rescuynge Of The Romishe Fox Othervvyse called the examination of the hunter deuised by steuen gardiner* (Aiᵛ).

275 *get forth the snout*] John Ponet, who replaced Gardiner as Bishop of Winchester, described him as having "a nose hooked like a buzzard, wide nostrils like a horse, ever snuffing into the wind" (quoted in Dixon, *History of the Church of England*, 2:419 n.*).

280 *priestes of Baule*] Catholic priests, likened to the priests of Baal (the Canaanite pagan god) in 1 Kings 18.

289  *I durste ley my heade*] I dared wager.

290  *doctor fryer*] Doctor John Fryer (1499–1563), physician. Imprisoned in the Fleet (1528) on suspicion of heresy and in the Tower (1561) for his Catholic sympathies (Emden, *Register*, 220–221).

291  *in store*] In abundance.

294  *paye the skore*] Avenge.

296–97  *garddener*] Gardiner.

*vytailer*] As Purveyor General, Gardiner was responsible for victualling the troops during the Scottish and French wars. See also *The vpcheringe of the messe* (248).

301  *Germyn his man*] Germain, Gardiner's nephew and secretary, was hanged at Tyburn on 7 March 1544 for denying the Royal Supremacy.

311  *maister huggarde*] Miles Hogarde (Myles Huggarde). Generally considered to be the first artisan to write for the Catholic cause, Hogarde published at least seven tracts in verse and one in prose (in two very different editions) between 1548 and 1557; as well, two of his poems survive in manuscript. From at least 1540, Protestants attacked Hogarde for his lack of academic learning; Robert Wisdom names him as one of his persecutors in that same year (Martin, *Religious Radicals*, 84 n. 4). See also Commentary on *A pore helpe* (311) and on *The comparison betwene the Antipus and the Antigraphe* (209).

322  *Agaynst what meaneth this*] A contemporary anonymous ballad, *What meaneth this guyse*, which is answered by Hogarde and contained, along with Hogarde's work, in Robert Crowley's *The Confutation of the mishapen Aunswer to the misnamed, wicked Ballade, called the Abuse of y̑ blessed sacrament of the aultare*.

337–38  *dominus vobis[cum]* ... *et cum spiritu tuo*] The antiphon and response recited throughout the Mass. Shepherd may be using these words ironically as John Skelton does in *Ware the Hauke*, line 286 and in *Collyn Clout*, lines 230–281, when he implies that "Dominus vobiscum" is as much Latin as ignorant priests actually know (*Poems*, ed. Scattergood, 69, 252; 404 nn. 286–295, 468 n. 230).

342  *solemne belles be ronge*] Sanctus bell, also rung at consecration: abolished in the vernacular communion service.

344  *patins*] Clogs or overshoes, with a pun on "patin" (paten), the plate on which the Eucharist is placed during the Mass.

345–52  Matins and evensong now celebrated in English; also refers to vernacular marriage and baptism services, and the litany (Brigden, *London and the Reformation*, 402; MacCulloch, *Cranmer*, 160; 301; 328). See similar reference in *Pathose* (569).

363  *And many showre of rayne*] Benefits obtained through the Mass. See similar expressions in Jerome Barlowe and William Roye's *Rede me and be nott wrothe* (Bii^v) and William Punt's *A new Dialoge Called The Endightment agaynste mother Messe* (Aiiii^v–Av). See also *The vpcheringe of the messe* (170–184).

382–85  *syr Harry* ... *of the Sepulchre*] Harry (Henry) George, conservative curate of the church of St Sepulchre. Originally a member of the community of Black canons of the Order of St Austin at St Bartholomew's Hospital, Duck Lane, West Smithfield (Dugdale, *Monasticon*, 6: pt. 1, 297), Henry George is listed in the Court of Augmentations as receiving a pension after the dissolution of that monastery (*Letters and*

*Papers*, 21: 775, f.16). St Sepulchre's was situated between St Paul's and Smithfield and, like St Faith's parish under Paul's or Ludgate in St Martin's parish, it was well-known in London as a church where the Mass was still said in Latin.[1] Shepherd identifies Harry George as the curate in *Doctour doubble ale* (280).

*kan.*] Possibly a mistake for "a" — the compositor mistakenly anticipating the initial letter of the next word.

397 *Ye get no more of me*] Compare identical expression in *The Image of Ypocresye* (2574).

## II *The vpcheringe of the messe:*

title *vpcheringe*] Encouragement.

3 *magre of our beard*] In defiance of our purpose.

15–19 The narrator insists the Mass be accepted as doctrine as a matter of faith.[2] See also lines 36 and 196–197.

21 *councells*] The early Church councils.

25 *confessours*] Those who avow their religion under persecution, but who do not suffer death as martyrs.

26 *no startars*] Those who remain conservatives (i.e., do not start away from the Roman faith).

29 *hartars*] Abettors.

39 *mysse the quission*] Miss the cushion, i.e., make a mistake. Proverbial (Whiting, *Proverbs*, C 641).

48–55 Scriptural understanding and preaching are the basis for Protestant religion.

59 *vndo*] Destroy, with a pun on "expound."

60 *mes singers*] Priests.

62 *styngers*] Stingers, i.e., those with sharp tongues.

71–86 An ironic attack on the outward show of the Mass.

74 *many folde*] Manifold.

77 *basen ewer and towell*] The basin, ewer, and towel used for the Lavabo, the ritual cleansing of hands during the Mass.

81 *cruetts*] Liturgical vessels for wine, water, or oil.

*chalys*] Chalice.

83 *sensers*] Censers.

*pax*] A carved tablet that the celebrant and the congregation at Mass kissed. The pax

---

[1] Punt suggests that those who sought such a service would find the Mass "In one of those plasys wytheoute fayle," Punt, *Endightment*, Avi.

[2] The Council of Trent (1545–47) reaffirmed the medieval doctrine of transubstantiation maintained by St. Thomas Aquinas and defined the Mass as Christ's sacrifice and the Church's sacrifice, a mystery which can only be accepted by faith.

was frequently used "as substitute for reception of communion" (Rubin, *Corpus Christi*, 74).

85 *patent*] Obsolete form of "paten."

*corporas*] Corporal cloth. A square linen cloth used for covering the elements of the Eucharist.

92 *A pyn for all the rest*] Proverbial (Whiting, *Proverbs*, P 210). See also *Doctour doubble ale* (72).

97 *Tidynges*] Often a synonym for the Gospel. Used ironically here.

99 *In dispite of*] In spite of.

100 *snel*] Keen-witted.

105 *durst not for his eares*] Refers to ear-boring, or the loss of ears or ear-lobes, as a penalty, especially for vagrancy (Exodus 21:6).

113–14 Puns on hearing Mass and auricular confession.

116 *dispuicions*] Arguments, debates (probably a misspelling of "disputisoun").

121 *crie creake*] Confess oneself in error. Proverbial (Tilley, *Proverbs*, C 810).

121–22 The sacraments are now administered in English rather than Latin. Shepherd argues that until people had access to the Gospel in English, they did not know first-hand which religious practices were based on Scripture and which were merely traditional. Once they could read the Gospel they could interpret God's laws for themselves.

123 *an huddy peake*] A fool (variant of "hoddypeak"). See also "hoddy doddy" in *The comparison betwene the Antipus and the Antigraphe* (202).

125 *full cranke*] In high spirits.

126–28 *And conneth hir no thanke / But compteth hir as ranke / As any on the bancke*] The narrator complains that the Gospel does not acknowledge his gratitude to the Mass, but treats her like a common prostitute. "The bancke" refers to the south bank of the Thames (an area famous for its brothels and inns), which was part of the Southwark estate of the Bishop of Winchester. See also note to line 168.

131 *mum*] Proverbial (Whiting, *Proverbs*, M 803).

138 *To frie them in their grese*] Leave vindictively alone. Proverbial (Tilley, *Proverbs*, G 433). Here it also refers to the burning of heretics.

140 *passe not of a gose*] Care not at all.

144–46 *some wyl cal hir whore . . . Some cal hir popes daughter*] Contemporary Protestant image of the Roman Church as the whore of Babylon (Revelation 17–18).

147 *she made manslaughter*] Shepherd links the Mass with Cain (Genesis 4:8–10). Catholic doctrine describes the Mass as a sacrifice as well as a sacrament, whereas the Protestants rejected the notion that Christ's one true sacrifice on the Cross could be repeated (Ketley, *Two Liturgies*, 534–535).

152–57 Popular contemporary Catholic claim that the Mass is a cure for all ills. See also lines 170–184.

155 *humbled heles*] Chapped or chilblained heels (variant of "hummelled").

168 *a Winchester goslynge*] A prostitute and the vulgar name for venereal disease (the expression is usually "Winchester goose"). Also a reference to Gardiner who, as

Bishop of Winchester, had the licensing of the brothels in Southwark.

170–84 Benefits obtained through the Mass. See also note on *A pore helpe* (363).

186 *make hornes*] Commit adultery (horns of cuckoldry).

196 *missa*] A disparaging term for the Mass[3] used by the Protestants who pointed out that the word "missa" is not found in any biblical text. See also lines 252 and 347. "Mistress Missa" derives from the words "Ite, missa est," which are said by the priest in the Blessing at the end of the Mass. For discussion, see Foxe, *Acts*, 6: 356–357; 377.

200 *Amisse*] And miss.

201 *misach*] Probably the Old Testament figure, Mishach (Daniel 3:8–30).

209 *be lakin*] An oath — "by Our Lady" (corruption of "ladykin").

210 *flicke of bacon*] A flitch (side) of bacon. Chaucer's Wife of Bath mentions the practice at Dunmow, near Chelmsford, in Essex, of a flitch of bacon being offered to any couple who lived together for a year and a day without regretting their association or quarreling. See *The Wife of Bath's Tale*, lines 217–218.

230–33 An example of Latin and pseudo-Latin words. See also lines 347–351.
   *totus mundus*] All the world.
   *rotundus*] Round.
   *Iocundus*] Happy, jesting, joking.
   *the letabundus*] "Laetabundus exultet fidelis chorus"; "Full of joy, let the faithful chorus rejoice." The opening line of a medieval Christmas sequence. See Skelton's *Collyn Clout*, lines 247–248 (*Poems*, ed. Scattergood, 253; 468 nn. 246–249).

237 *poules*] St Paul's Cathedral.

246 *men of bone*] (a pun) Edmund Bonner (1500–69), Bishop of London (see Appendix).

248 *stockfish*] Stockfish, i.e., smoked cod traditionally eaten on the fast days of Lent. Gardiner's nickname originated when he was appointed to victual the navy and made Wednesday a fish day; the day became known as the Bishop's fasting day (Foxe, *Acts*, 6: 32). Gardiner jests about his nickname in a letter to Protector Somerset on 21 May 1547 (Foxe, *Acts*, 6: 34).

258 *king or quene*] M. Channing Lenthicum suggests a contemporary allusion, but does not identify specific persons (Lenthicum, "*A Pore Helpe*," 171 n. 1).

261 *He*] Gardiner.

263 *other fiften*] The Regency Council provided for in Henry VIII's will and from which Gardiner was excluded.

272–74 Refers to Gardiner's eloquent sermons.

---

[3] John Foxe recounts John Mailer saying "that the mass was called beyond the sea, 'miss,' for that all is amiss in it" (Foxe, *Acts*, 5: 447).

275 *enchieued*] Raised up (old French "cheve").

291 *Or a horse coulde lyke his eare*] i.e., Never. Proverbial (Tilley, *Proverbs*, H 630).

294–95 *Images . . . ceremonies*] (A unique example of near rhyme rather than exact end rhyme in Shepherd's texts.) The Injunctions (31 July 1547) insisted that images be removed from churches and forbade the lighting of candles before the paintings of saints or the use of beads for praying.

305 *cleare*] Pure.

*confection*] The performance of the sacrifice of the Mass.

317 *he be in the towre*] Gardiner was imprisoned in the Tower on 30 June 1548, the day after his famous sermon at Paul's Cross, in which he publicly refused to accept the authority of the Privy Council over religious matters. He was released on Mary I's accession in 1553.

335 *stewes*] Brothels.

344 *synge placebo*] The first antiphon of Vespers for the Dead in the Latin rite begins "Placebo Domino in regione vivorum"; "I will walk before the Lord in the land of the living" (Psalm 114:9, *Vulgate*).

347–51 Another example of mock-Latin endings:

*mestres missa*] Mistress Missa.

*thissa*] Thus.

*kyssa*] Kiss.

*pyssa*] Piss.

*Issa*] Truly (from "iwis").

359 *Iak and gyll*] Jack and Jill. A catch phrase for "everyone." Also proverbial (Whiting, *Proverbs*, J 2).

*Ione*] Joan. Common name for an alewife. See also *Doctour doubble ale* (129).

360–61 *Requiem eternam / Lest penam sempiternam*] Eternal rest; lest everlasting pain. An ironic inversion of the opening prayer that is repeated throughout the Mass for the Dead: "Requiem aeternam dona eis, Domine: et lux perpetua luceat eis"; "Eternal rest grant unto them, O Lord, and let perpetual light shine upon them" (2 Esdras 2:35–36; 4 Esdras 2:35–36 in the *Vulgate*). Compare with *Phylogamus*: "In sempiterna supplicia"; "In everlasting pain/torture" (131). For a similar use of parody, see *Pathose* (142–153; 709–711).

362–64 *For vitam supernam*] For heavenly life.

*And vmbram infernam*] And infernal shade.

*For veram lucernam*] For the true light.

367–81 *Pro cuius memoria*] For whose memory.

*soria*] Sorry.

*gloria*] The chant of joy and also a prayer from the Ordinary of the Mass. The combination of "smale" and "gloria" in this line creates a pun since the Gloria is not recited in the Mass for the Dead.

*storia*] Story.

*roria*] Roar.

127

*moria*] More.

*Et dicam vobis quare*] And therefore I tell you.

*stare*] Be pre-eminent.

*regnare*] Rule.

*ad vltra mare*] Beyond the sea.

*habitare*] Live.

*In regno plutonico*] In Pluto's domain. See also *Pathose* (727).

*Et Eue acronyco*] And timeless Eve. Refers to Eve and her connection with Satan. Shepherd consigns the Mass to dwell with Pluto and Eve (Eva) in hell, making a pun on "vae" (Latin for "woe") and mocking the Catholic veneration of Mary by "ave" ("Ave Maria") as the reverse of "Eva."

*Cum cetu babilonico*] With [all] the Babylonian gang. The realm where the Mass is now going to dwell is the home of papists. Also refers to the Babylonian captivity of the "true" Church, i.e., Protestant image of the Roman Church as Antichrist. "Cetu" can also mean "whale" and the line may refer to the great fish which swallowed the prophet Jonah, who prefigures Christ. There may also be a reference to the annihilation of the Leviathan by God (Psalm 74:14) and a foreshadowing of the eventual destruction of the Catholic Church.

*Et cantu diabolico*] And a diabolical song.

382 *pollers and pillers*] Extortionists, plunderers.

---

## III  *Pathose, or an inward passion of the pope for the losse of hys daughter the Masse.*

5–6 *the cap / Of myghti mayntenaunce*] The crimson velvet cap of maintenance, a papal honor and mark of fealty bestowed on Henry VII in 1488 and 1505 (King, *Iconography*, 21) and on Henry VIII in 1514 (Legg, "Gift," 193–195). As well as the cap and sword, Henry VIII had previously received the pope's golden rose. On her accession, Mary I also received the pope's golden rose; her consort, Philip of Spain, was given the cap and sword (King, *Iconography*, 42; 184–185).

21 *councells generall*] e.g., Council of Trent (1545–47) which the reformers planned to counter with a council of their own (MacCulloch, *Cranmer*, 394).

*Aiii*] This is an incorrect signature. Aiii is signed twice in the Wales copy of this text. This page should be signed Aii. Leaves Aiii–Avi$^v$ are missing in the Cambridge copy. The only signature in the "A" gathering in the Cambridge copy is on this page. See Printing History and Collation.[4]

---

[4] See also Janice Devereux, "The Missing Pages of Luke Shepherd's *Pathose*: A Hypothesis," *Notes and Queries* n.s. 42 (1995): 281–283.

# COMMENTARY

29 *my greatist treasure*] The Mass. See similar phrase in Barlowe and Roye's *Rede me and be nott wrothe* (Bii).

40 *ruled all the roste*] Rule the roast (as distinct from rule the roost); have full sway of authority. Proverbial (Whiting, *Proverbs*, R 152).

43 *From pillar vnto post*] Hither and thither. Proverbial (Whiting, *Proverbs*, P 313).

56–58 *sum Edomite / Some Iewe or Iacobite / Some turke or thraconite*] Terms of abuse. Jews (Edomites), Turks, and Saracens are traditionally enemies of the Roman Church; Jacobites are heretical followers of the early sixth-century Syrian, Jacobus Baradaeus, who were held to have denied the dual nature of the Son of God. "Thraconite" is probably used here for its rhyme. See also "Turkes" and "Saracans" *Phylogamus* (44–45).

59 *aconite*] Deadly poison obtained from wolf's-bane or monk's-hood.

60 *arthanite*] Unrecorded in *OED*; possibly a variation of "athanasy" (immortality). Turner lists "Athanasia" ("tansey") in *Libellus de Re Herbaria Novvs . . . in lucem æditus* (Aiii) and Shepherd mentions "tansey" in *Cauteles preseruatory* (Avi).

62 *mayne and might*] Proverbial (Whiting, *Proverbs*, M 537).

70–71 *mahomyte*] Mohammed (c. 570–632); see also "Machomet" (301). Protestants often used Mohammed as a type for the papal Antichrist.
*nese*] Niece.

72 *prope*] Comely.

75–77 *arabies . . . In phisike and in phisnomyes*] Arabian physicians, the translators and keepers of Greek and early Latin medicine.

78 *Iupiter*] Jupiter, highest and most powerful of the Roman gods.

79 *Diespiter*] Archaic and elevated form of "Jupiter."

83 *Iuno*] Juno, Roman goddess, guardian deity of married women.

84 *Neptuno*] Neptune, Roman god of the sea and other waters.

85 *Phebe*] Phoebe, Greek goddess of the moon.
*Phebus*] Phoebus, Greek god of the sun; see also "Appollo" (260).

87 *venus*] Venus, Roman goddess of love.

91–92 *Mercurius*] Mercury, Roman god of eloquence and messenger to the gods. Also a pun, since mercury was used as a drug in the treatment of syphilis.
*this feuer furious*] Suggesting that the Mass's illness is caused by venereal disease, Shepherd links her with the whore of Babylon (the Roman Church).

95 *Aeolus*] Aeolus, Roman god of the winds.

120–29 *I offer here therfore . . . To mytygate your moode . . . helpe vs in oure nede*] An ironic reference to Jewish sacrifices in the Temple at Jerusalem.

133 *ceres*] Ceres, Roman goddess of agriculture.

142–43 *daily offered / A sacrifice of breade*] Here the Mass is offered not to God, but to the pagan goddess, Ceres. See also lines 133–153.

144 *To the for quicke and deade*] Refers to the Catholic practice of offering Masses for the dead as well as the living. The Protestant tenet of "once and for ever" atonement

rejects the idea that Christ's redemption is repeated in the Mass and can gain remission of sins for the souls in purgatory.[5]

148 *bend and bowe the kne*] Satirizes kneeling at communion and other manifestations of venerating the eucharistic elements.

150 *oblacion*] Objected to by reformers.

155–65 Shepherd emphasizes the pope's idolatrous worship of the elements of the Mass by extending the Mass-offering to the pagan god, Bacchus.[6]

170–71 *Christ in euery place / Away hath turned his face*] Romans 11:4. Also recalls Psalms 13:1; 27:9; 143:7.

174 *passe not of an ase*] Care not even a little.

176–84 A blasphemous and lewd pun.

177 *him to make*] Also refers to the doctrine of transubstantiation. See also *A pore helpe* (53–54); *Antipus* (22); *The comparison betwene the Antipus and the Antigraphe* (51; 127); *Doctour doubble ale* (329–330), and *Cauteles preseruatory* (Aii^v).

179 *Betwene my holy fistis*] Also a satire on the elevation of the host.

190–92 *bynde and lose . . . He muste it graunt aboue*] Refers ironically to Christ's words to Peter (Matthew 16:19). See also note to line 217.

200–01 *Howe porely dide he ride / Vpon a pore asse*] Alludes disparagingly to Christ's entry into Jerusalem (Matthew 21:7).

217 *Such thinges as I him send*] Refers to the power of keys, the ecclesiastical authority Christ conferred on Peter, claimed by Catholics to have been transmitted to the popes as his successors (Matthew 16:19).

224 *sacrifice despect*] The pope complains that God no longer accepts that the celebration of the Mass repeats the work of Christ's redemption.

241 *my daughter eased*] A sexual pun. Shepherd uses a similar expression in *Phylogamus* (279).

---

[5] "The offering of Christ, made once for ever, is the perfect redemption, the pacifying of God's displeasure and satisfaction for all the sins of the whole world, both original and actual: and there is none other satisfaction for sin, but that alone. Wherefore the sacrifices of masses, in the which, it was commonly said, that the priest did offer Christ for the quick and the dead, to have remission of pain or sin, were forged fables, and dangerous deceits" ( Joseph Ketley, ed., *The Two Liturgies, A.D. 1549, and A.D. 1552: with Other Documents Set Forth by Authority in the Reign of King Edward VI* (Cambridge: The University Press, 1844), 534–535. See also MacCulloch, *Cranmer*, 509.

[6] For use of Bacchus's wine-drinking as a mock sacrament, see the *Pater noster* in the late medieval satire, *Missa de Potatoribus* (*The Mass of the Drunkards*), Harley ms. 913. fol. 13^v; Thomas Wright and James Orchard Halliwell, eds., *Reliquiae Antiquae. Scraps from Ancient Manuscripts Illustrating Chiefly Early English Literature and the English Language*, 2 vols. (London: William Pickering, 1841–43), 2: 210.

# COMMENTARY

242–43 *Priapus*] Priapus, Greek and Roman phallic god. See also *Phylogamus* (331).
*Fauna*] Fauna, Roman rural goddess (Bona Dea) identified with fruitfulness.
*Fa[u]nus*] Faunus, Roman rural god linked with fertility.

244 *Dromo*] A stock comic character usually depicted as a servant and a messenger. He
appears in contemporary drama by John Rastell, Thomas Kirchmeyer, Nicholas
Grimald, and John Foxe, and also in William Turner's prose tract against images.[7]
Shepherd uses him to ridicule the pope, who needs Dromo's help to cure his diseased
daughter, so that the celebration of the Mass can continue to free souls from purga-
tory. Because Turner's Dromo is afflicted with syphilis, Shepherd may suggest the
double irony that the pope's ailing servant infected his daughter, the Mass.
*that arte swyft*] Dromo in Greek means "runner" (Terence, *Andria*, ed. Shipp, 190).
A pun on his alacrity of catching or spreading the pox.

261 *Aesculapius*] Greek god of medicine; son of Apollo.

262 *That Raised from death*] Refers both to Aesculapius raising Androgeos from the dead
and Christ raising Lazarus.
*androgeus*] Androgeos, son of Minos, king of Crete.

263 *Propertius*] Sextus Propertius (c. 50–16 BC), Roman elegiac poet, who wrote about
Androgeus (Androgeos) in *Elegies* 2. 1. 62.

264 *Epidaurus*] City in Argolis with a famous temple to Aesculapius.

265 *Chiron Centaurus*] Chiron, centaur tutor of Aesculapius, renowned for his know-
ledge of plants, medicines, and divination.

266 *Machon*] Machaon, son of Aesculapius and famous surgeon of the Greeks.
*Podalirius*] Podalirius, another son of Aesculapius and eminent physician.

269 *come not at*] Do not seek out.
*Archagathus*] Peloponnesian surgeon and the first professional medical practitioner in
Rome (219 BC), famous for the severity of his surgery. The pope is not prepared
to risk his daughter's mutilation by allowing Archagathus to treat her.

272 *asclepiades*] The Asclepiadeans, i.e., the physicians.

273 *hipocrates*] Hippocrates (c. 460?–377 or 359 BC), celebrated Greek physician of
antiquity.

---

[7] See Thomas L. Berger and William C. Bradford, eds., *An Index of Characters in English
Printed Drama to the Restoration* (Colorado: Microcard Editions Books, 1975), 146; Thomas
Kirchmeyer (Naogeorgus), *Tragoedia Nova Pammachius*, in *Thomas Naogeorg Sämtliche Werke*,
ed. Hans-Gert Roloff, 4 vols. (Berlin: Walter De Gruyter, 1975), passim; Nicholas Grimald,
*Christus Redivivus*, ed. Kurt Tetzeli von Rosador (Hildesheim: Georg Olms Verlag, 1982), 8;
John Hazel Smith, ed., *Two Latin Comedies by John Foxe the Martyrologist* (Ithaca: Cornell
University Press, 1973), passim; William Turner, *The Rescvynge of the Romishe Fox Othervvyse
called the examination of the hunter deuised by steuen gardiner* (London, 1545, *STC* 24355),
Hiii, Hiv. For discussion, see Janice Devereux, "Dromo: A Minor Dramatic Character
Adopted for Protestant Propaganda," *Notes and Queries* n.s. 44 (1997): 27–29.

# COMMENTARY

275 *Dioscorides*] Pedanius Dioscorides, first-century Greek physician.

276–77 *Galenus*] Claudius Galen (c. AD 130–201), famous Greek physician.

*Pergamenus*] (from) Pergamum (i.e., Galen's birthplace) in Mysia.

292 *Areta*] Aretas of Cyrene (c. 400 BC), Greek philosopher.

293 *Paulus aginita*] Paul of Aegineta (Aegina, near Attica), seventh-century Greek physician.

296 *auicenna*] Avicenna (Ibn Sina, 980–1037), renowned Islamic philosopher, physician, and scientist.

297 *Rasis*] Rhazes (Al-Razi, c. 841–925), Arab physician and scientist.

*Mesue*] Mesue the Elder (Ibn Masawaih, c. 776–857) and Mesue the Younger (Masawaih Al-Mardini, 925–1015), Arabic physicians.

301 *Machomet*] Mohammed.

304 *let them se hir water*] The Galenic school of medicine relied on urine tests.

310–50 *I shall but mone and morne . . . With hert as colde as stone*] Ironic parody of traditional romantic imagery, suggesting an incestuous relationship between the pope and his daughter, the Mass.

323–24 *They*] Protestants.

*count but a game / My messe to defame*] The first act of Edward VI's first parliament was the Act against Revilers of the Sacrament and for Communion in Both Kinds (1 Edward VI c. 1), which attempted to end abuse of the sacrament of the altar.

328 *I swelle and sweate*] Echoes *Phylogamus* (393).

352 *slyd a slope*] Probably proverbial, with possible reference to "slide" (lapse morally) and "aslope" (obliquely).

353 *to fele and grope*] To discover and investigate.

354 *Affrike*] Africa.

383 *Which way the wynde wil blow*] Proverbial (Tilley, *Proverbs*, W 144).

397–98 *No meate within my breste / Nor body to be drest*] The pope resolves to fast and wear penitential garb (i.e., sackcloth and ashes).

419 *candell boke and bel*] A pun. Objects used in the rite of excommunication and in the celebration of the Mass. See also *A pore helpe* (64).

424 *reynes*] Reins, i.e., kidneys.

*to Rente*] To-rent, i.e., torn asunder.

437–39 *morbus hereditari[u]s*] Hereditary sickness.

*venenum pestiferus*] Fatal poison.

*mortiferus*] Deadly.

461 *portraye*] Prolong.

463 *aquauite*] Aqua vitae, i.e., distilled alcoholic liquor.

465–69 *vinum absinthite*] Poisonous wine of absinthe (wormwood).

*vinum apitie*] [Aromatic] wine. Possibly a wine used to create an appetite.

*abrotonite*] Wine prepared from southernwood.

*Uinum chamedryte*] Aromatic, bitter wine made from germander.

*aromatite*] Aromatites vinum, aromatic wine.

479 *Gardnerus*] Stephen Gardiner.

481 *more*] Sir Thomas More (1478–1535), humanist, writer, and Lord Chancellor (see
Appendix).

*fisherus*] John Fisher (1469–1535), Bishop of Rochester (see Appendix).

488 *sing and rore*] Compare "crie and roria" in *The vpcheringe of the messe* (371).

493 *sume of them be dead*] The pope laments those English Catholic clergy executed for
refusing to acknowledge the Royal Supremacy.

500–27 The pope quotes a list of contemporary Protestant reformers:

500 *lutherus*] Martin Luther (1483–1546), reformer, writer, and translator (see Bieten-
holz, *Contemporaries of Erasmus*, 2: 360–363).

501 *Bucerus*] Martin Bucer (1491–1551), reformer and theologian (see Bietenholz,
*Contemporaries of Erasmus*, 1: 209–212).

502 *Zuingle*] Huldrych Zwingli (1484–1531), Swiss reformer (see Bietenholz, *Contem-
poraries of Erasmus*, 3: 481–486).

*Bullingerus*] Heinrich Bullinger (1504–75), reformer, humanist, and writer (see
Bayle, *Dictionary*, 2: 194–197; *New Catholic Encyclopedia*, 2: 883).

503 *Melancthon*] Philip Melanchthon (Schwartzerdt, 1497–1560), reformer, academic,
and theologian (see Bietenholz, *Contemporaries of Erasmus*, 2: 424–429).

*Althamerus*] Andreas Althamer (Brentius, or Paldo Sphyra, c. 1500–40), reformer (see
entry on Bullinger in Bayle, *Dictionary*, 2: 196).

504 *Uitus*] Possibly Theodor Vitus (Beit Dietrich, c. 1507–49), reformer (see Germann,
*Luke Shepherd*, 75).[8]

*Theodor*] Theodore Basile (pseudonym of Thomas Becon, 1512–67), English
reformer and writer (see Appendix).

*musculus*] Wolfgang Musculus (Müslin, 1497–1563), Lutheran preacher.

505 *Spaugelbergius*] Possibly Johann Spangenberg (1484–1550), theologian (see Ger-
mann, *Luke Shepherd*, 75).

506 *Urbanus regius*] Urbanus Rhegius (Urban Reiger, 1489–1541), reformer (see
Bietenholz, *Contemporaries of Erasmus*, 3: 151–153).

507 *Alesius*] Alexander Alesius (Aless, 1500–65), reformer and theologian (see *Dictionary
of National Biography*, 1: 254–259).

*Brentius*] Johannes Brenz (1494–1570), reformer and academic (see Bietenholz,
*Contemporaries of Erasmus*, 1: 193–194).

508 *Otho Brumfelsius*] Otto Brunfels (c. 1488–1534), reformer and writer (see Bieten-
holz, *Contemporaries of Erasmus*, 1: 206–207).

509 *fagius*] Paul Fagius (1504–49), reformer, academic, and theologian (see *DNB*, 6:
984).

*Pistorius*] Johannes Pistorius (d.1583), reformer (see Germann, *Luke Shepherd*, 75).

---

[8] N.B.: Germann disregards the comma between "Vitus" and "Theodor" in this line and
combines the two names to identify a single individual.

510 *Petrus martir*] Peter Martyr (Pietro Martire Vermigli, 1500–62), reformer, academic, and theologian (see *DNB*, 20: 253–256).
*sarcerius*] Erasmus Sarcerius (1501–59), theologian (see Germann, *Luke Shepherd*, 76).

511 *Oecolampadius*] Joannes Oecolampadius (Latinized Greek for Hussgen or Hausschin, 1482–1531), reformer and theologian (see Bietenholz, *Contemporaries of Erasmus*, 3: 24–27).

512 *Carolstadius*] Andreas Bodenstein von Karlstadt (c. 1480–1541), reformer, academic, and theologian (see Bietenholz, *Contemporaries of Erasmus*, 2: 253–256).

513 *Uadianus*] Vadianus ( Joachim von Watt, 1484–1551), reformer and academic (see Bietenholz, *Contemporaries of Erasmus*, 3: 364–365).

514 *Pomeranus*] Johannes Bugenhagen (1485–1558), reformer (see Bietenholz, *Contemporaries of Erasmus*, 1: 217–219).

515 *Pellicanus*] Konrad Kürschner (1478–1556), reformer and theologian (see Bietenholz, *Contemporaries of Erasmus*, 3: 65–66).

516 *Iohn cauinus*] John Calvin (1509–64), reformer, writer, and theologian (see *Chambers Biographical Dictionary*, 1: 215–216).

517 *Spalatinus*] Georgius Spalatinus (Georg Burckhardt, 1484–1545), reformer (see Bietenholz, *Contemporaries of Erasmus*, 3: 266–268).

518 *Coruinus*] Antonius Corvinus (Rabe, 1501–53), reformer (see Bietenholz, *Contemporaries of Erasmus*, 1: 347–348).
*Epinus*] Possibly Joannes Epinus ( Johannes Aepinus), theologian and writer.

519 *Bernardinus*] Bernardino Ochino (1487–1564/5), reformer (see Bietenholz, *Contemporaries of Erasmus*, 3: 22).

520 *Osiander*] Andreas Osiander (1496?–1552), reformer and theologian (see Bietenholz, *Contemporaries of Erasmus*, 3: 35–36).

521 *Cruciger*] Caspar Cruciger (1504–48), academic (see Germann, *Luke Shepherd*, 76).
*Megander*] Caspar Megander (Grossmann, c. 1495–1545), Zwinglian theologian.

522 *Bibliander*] Theodore Bibliander (Buchmann, 1504?–64), academic (see Bietenholz, *Contemporaries of Erasmus*, 1: 145–146).

523 *Ionas*] Justus Jonas ( Jodocus Koch, 1493–1555), academic, reformer, and theologian (see Bietenholz, *Contemporaries of Erasmus*, 2: 244–246).
*Capito*] Wolfgang Faber Capito (Köpfel, 1478?–1541), reformer and academic (see Bietenholz, *Contemporaries of Erasmus*, 1: 261–264).

524 *Hedio*] Caspar Hedio (Heyd, 1494–1552), reformer and academic (see Bietenholz, *Contemporaries of Erasmus*, 2: 169–170).

525 *Latymers*] Hugh Latimer (c. 1485–1555), Bishop of Worcester and Protestant martyr (see Appendix).

526 *bilnie*] Thomas Bilney (1495?–1531), Protestant martyr (see Appendix).
*Turners*] William Turner (c. 1520–68), writer and botanist (see Appendix).

527 *bayle*] John Bale (1495–1563), bibliographer, dramatist, and reformer (see Appendix).

*Tailers*] Rowland Taylor (d.1555), Protestant martyr (see Appendix).

532–41 The pope quotes a list of contemporary Catholic writers:

532 *cochleus*] Johannes Cocklaeus (Dobeneck, c. 1479–1552), writer and theologian (see Bietenholz, *Contemporaries of Erasmus*, 1: 321–322).

533 *Iohn Faber*] Johannes Fabri (Heigerlin, 1478–1541), Bishop of Vienna (see Bietenholz, *Contemporaries of Erasmus*, 2: 5–8).

*Emserus*] Hieronymus (Jerome) Emser (1479–1527), churchman, writer, and translator (see Bietenholz, *Contemporaries of Erasmus*, 1: 429–430).

534 *Hofmisterus*] Hofmeister, "the great arch-papist, and chief master-pillar of the pope's falling church," who died while journeying to the Diet of Ratisbon in July 1546 (Foxe, *Acts*, 8: 647).

535 *Ecchius*] Johann Maier von Eck (1486–1543), academic and theologian (see Bietenholz, *Contemporaries of Erasmus*, 1: 416–419).

536 *Bilikius*] Eberhard Billick (c. 1499–1557), theologian (see *New Catholic Encyclopedia*, 2: 557).

537 *maluelda*] Malvenda, "one of the Emperor's Divines" (Burnet, *Reformation*, 3: pt. 3 bk. 4 183).

538 *Nausea*] Fridericus Nausea (twisted Latin translation of Friedrich Grau or Grawe, 1480?–1552), Bishop of Vienna after Fabri's death (see Bietenholz, *Contemporaries of Erasmus*, 3: 7–8).

539 *Catharinus*] Lancellotto de Politi (Ambrosius Catherinus Politus, 1484–1553), academic, churchman, and theologian (see Bietenholz, *Contemporaries of Erasmus*, 3: 105–106).

540 *Alfonsus*] Alphonso de Castro (1495–1558), theologian (see *New Catholic Encyclopedia*, 1: 311).

541 *Sadoletus*] Jacopo Sadoleto (1477–1547), churchman and writer (see Bietenholz, *Contemporaries of Erasmus*, 3: 183–187).

543 *lim*] Limb, i.e., a member of the church (1 Corinthians 12:27).

551 *behinde the hande*] Behind-hand, tardy.

567–68 *soughter*] Sought her.

*coughter*] Caught her.

569 *As for communion*] *The Order of Communion* (8 March 1548).[9] See also *Iohn Bon and Mast person* (73–74).

570 *set not an onion*] Proverbial (Tilley, *Proverbs*, O 66).

574 *vp to setter*] To set her up.

---

[9] *The Order of the Commvnion* (printed by Richard Grafton). See Ketley, *Two Liturgies*, iii–8.

579 *make no deane*] The Act for the Submission of the Clergy (1534) destroyed the English clergy's legislative independence and deprived the pope of his power over the Church in England.

581 *al one my syde*] All on my side.

596 *ye*] Dromo.

612–13 *Wo worth*] Woe worth. A curse — "may evil befall!"
*that heretyke / That firste beganne*] Luther.

620–27 *I did her endue / Wyth clothynge of Gospel / And of the Epistel*] The liturgical readings at the Mass.
*nowe they be gon*] Now the reformers have appropriated them (i.e., the Scriptures).
*skin and bon*] Skin and bone; no longer flesh. A reference to the Mass's sickness and an ironic allusion to Christ's promise: "Those who eat my flesh . . . have eternal life" (John 6:54).
*flat as a cake*] Wafer cake, i.e., communion host.

624–37 Compare Dalilah's description of her pox-ridden body in a contemporary interlude:

> My sinews be shrunken, my flesh eaten with pox;
> My bones full of ache and great pain;
> My head is bald, that bare yellow locks;
> Crooked I creep to the earth again.
> Mine eyesight is dim, my hands tremble and shake;
> My stomach abhorreth all kind of meat
> (*Nice Wanton* 265–270).[10]

636 *heauy as leade*] Proverbial (Tilley, *Proverbs*, L 134).

640–45 *Thou son and thou mone . . . My daughter I bequeth / In to your holy handes*] Shepherd parodies a last testament that usually bequeaths the body to the earth and the soul to God. The pope wills his daughter's body and soul to Phoebus and Phoebe.

655 *Iupiter*] Here Jupiter stands for the Holy Roman Emperor, Charles V.
*ceraunus*] Thunderbolt (Greek "κεραυνός").

656 *vulcanus*] Vulcan, Roman god of fire.

661 *Mars Mauors*] Mars also called Mavors, Roman god of war.

668 *set not a flye*] Proverbial (Tilley, *Proverbs*, F 396).

669–71 *my greate cursse* ] The pope's power of excommunication.
*mine interdiction*] Pope Paul III's bull of excommunication and deposition against Henry VIII (December 1538) was not lifted until parliament petitioned for an end to the schism (November 1554). The pope's legate, Cardinal Pole, pronounced the nation's absolution on 30 November (Redworth, *Gardiner*, 326–327).

---

[10] See *Nice Wanton* (c. 1550) in Glynne Wickham, *English Moral Interludes* (London: J. M. Dent & Sons Ltd., 1976), 154.

680–81 *Wyth crouchinge and creping*] Creeping to the cross (the adoration of the rood, especially on Good Friday). Edward VI's council suppressed this devotion in 1548.[11]
*Wyth bassing and kissing*] The Injunctions of 31 July 1547 prohibited "idolatrous" images, the kissing of images, the lighting of candles in front of them, or kneeling before them. The council forbade all images on 21 February 1548 (Cardwell, *Annals*, 1: 48).[12]

683–718 The following lament is an approximation of the Latin poem in the text that begins: "O pulchra proles." The pope addresses his daughter as though she were about to leave him bereft by dying, but several of the lines contain puns through which Shepherd presents the Mass as an ailing impostor whom the people reject. I am grateful to Seymour Baker House who very generously advised on Shepherd's Latin and contributed most of this translation.[13] Specific references to these lines follow below.

> O beautiful offspring
> Wondrous might
> Unspeakable [you grieve]
> Hitherto you are accustomed
> At whatever nod [of fate]
> To have secure
> [Your] body moistened
> [And clothed] with soft [things]
> Alas [now] she stands bare
> The people leave
> Ridiculing you
> And denying me (i.e., the pope)
> Scarcely believing
> You will be [a] truthful [one]
> They declare [you to be] a liar
> [A] garrulous [one], [a] talkative [one]
> To be rapacious
> They say you are a vagrant
> A wise witch
> Alas what shall I do?

---

[11] The paragraph concerning the creeping to the cross did not appear in the printed proclamation, but was printed by Burnet from Bonner's register. See Hughes and Larkin, *Tudor Royal Proclamations*, 1: #299.

[12] N.B.: Cardwell uses old style for dates.

[13] I am also grateful to Bernadette Hall and John Hale for their help with Shepherd's Latin.

Now you shall be lost (die), daughter
Once doing useful things
More than a thousand fold
Lo I shall follow
And rule whom you rule
But I cannot live
Since you are dying
And I anoint you with ointment
Papal oil
This generation is evil
It assaults attacking
And hating us
Behold the scriptures
Are being preached pure(ly)
Whereby [listen!]
How quickly my law dies.

709–11 *Tu quum defungeris / Sacro que vngeris / Oleo papali*] Also a parody of the rite of Extreme Unction.

734 *gange dayes*] Gang or rogation days. Three days of supplication before Ascension Day, celebrated with Rogationtide (or Crosstide) processions. Banned by the 1547 Injunctions.

736 *the dayes embringe*] Ember days. Four cycles of days of fasting and abstinence: Wednesday, Friday, and Saturday after the first Sunday of Lent, Holy Cross Day, Whitsunday, and St Lucy's Day.

743 *Auricular confession*] The act of acknowledgment of sin by a person to a priest as a religious duty. Opposed by Protestants who claimed that salvation rested on faith and repentance and that confession to God only was sufficient. Most reformers also denied that priests had the power to forgive sins.

747 *colettes*] Collects or collective prayers that are part of the Divine Office; also short prayers said between the Kyrie or Gloria and the Epistle during the Mass.

751 *cannone*] The Canon, or Rule of Consecration, in the Mass that marks the transubstantiation of the bread and wine into Christ's body and blood. See also *Iohn Bon and Mast person* (101).

755 *post communion*] Prayers after the Communion in the Mass that vary according to the feast day.

763 *Stix and Acheron*] Two of the rivers of Hades.

767 *Cerbrus*] Cerberus, guardian of the entrance to the underworld.

771 *the Emperoure*] Hades, who at this point in the poem is interchangeable with the devil. Probably also refers to Charles V.

774–79 *Then open your coffer / And vnto him offer . . . Some of your palmes swete*] With a parodic allusion to Christ's triumphant entry into Jerusalem on Palm Sunday, the pope suggests that the Mass should pay homage to Pluto (god of the underworld and receiver of treasure) by offering him eucharistic bread and wine.

781–82 *ashes holy / Beades and sacring belles*] Incense, rosary beads, and bells rung at the moment of consecration in the Mass.

790–803 *Shewe myne obedience . . . Then deuelishnes*] The pope gives the Mass to Satan as a sign of subjection and obedience. Compare Thomas Becon: "the popish mass is a very shop and store-house of wickedness and of all ungraciousness, instituted of the devil" (Becon, *Works*, 3: 376).

# IV *Iohn Bon and Mast person*

title *Bon*] Good, innocent.

*Mast person*] Mass priest.

prefatory verse Entirely separate from the rest of the satire, this illustration may have been designed to be torn off and used as a wall decoration.[14] The picture and the text below it are in ironic opposition to each other. Addressing the priests depicted in a Corpus Christi procession, the verse argues that the host does not become Christ's body in the Eucharist and that worshipping a wafer of bread constitutes idolatry.

*two Irons printed it is*] The mold in which the communion wafer was shaped, baked, and imprinted with a cross or some other decoration. Under the new communion rite (1549) the host was to be "vnleauened, and rounde, as it was afore, but without all maner of printe" (Dugmore, *Mass*, 132; Ketley, *Two Liturgies*, 97).

2 *so mut I thee*] From "mote" (may) and Old English "theon" (thrive). A kind of oath — "so may I prosper."

3 *yᵘ*] Thou. See also lines 42 and 47.

4 *zoner*] Sooner.

5 *none*] Noon. The laity were expected to fast on the eve before a feast day and were often encouraged to cease labor at noon on that day (Duffy, *Stripping of the Altars*, 156).

8 *corpus christi*] The feast of Corpus Christi (established by Pope Urban IV in 1264), celebrated on the Thursday after Trinity Sunday with a procession in which the host was carried from the church for veneration by the parishioners, often taking in the parish boundaries before being returned to the church altar. For discussion, see Rubin, *Corpus Christi*, 243–271.

9 *aer*] Are.

*saynt Steuen*] Saint Stephen, first Christian martyr.

---

[14] For examples of wall decorations in a polemical context in a later period, see Tessa Watt, *Cheap Print and Popular Piety, 1550–1640* (Cambridge: Cambridge University Press, 1991), 147–149.

11 *copsi cursty*] A pun on "Corpus Christi." See also line 31. The misquotation under-
lines the incomprehensibility of Latin to most of the laity.[15]

14 *ye*] You. Until this point the priest has addressed Iohn Bon in the second person
singular "thou" as is customary for someone speaking to a social inferior. In this line
he uses second person plural "you." See also lines 20, 132, and 133.

18 *glasse*] Pyx.

22 *mashippe*] Abbreviation of "mastership." Repeated at line 44.

    *cumlication*] See also line 51. Nonce-word probably meaning "communication" or
"conversation," with a possible pun on "complication."

30 *not in my crede*] Iohn Bon ironically points out that transubstantiation is not refer-
enced in any creed; also recalls the Roman Church's requirement that the laity
memorize the Apostles' Creed.

32 *by the waye my soule shal to*] A mild oath — "by the way my soul shall [go] toward."

36 *No spleaser*] Unrecorded in *OED*. King suggests "?If it please you" (King, "*John Bon*,"
91).

37 *euerbody*] Syncopated form of "everybody."

38 *speakeste lyke a dawe*] Speak like a jackdaw, i.e., foolishly. Proverbial (Whiting,
*Proverbs*, D 29). See also *Doctour doubble ale* (12).

47 *quod ha*] (quoth he) Quotha, indeed. Generally used with contempt when repeating
another's words. See also line 126.

49 *stubble cur*] Both words refer to an awkward, clumsy individual or low-bred person;
"stubble" also means "stubborn."

51–52 *felony . . . treason . . . heresye*] Crimes for which the penalty could be death.

53 *witnes*] Witness who attests to hearing a heretical statement. The testimony of two
people, including the person to whom the accused spoke the heresy, was necessary in
order to gain a conviction.

73–74 *they haue begun / To take a waye the olde and set vp newe*] Refers to reformist
changes (e.g., removal of the rood, statues, and pictures of saints) made within days
of Edward VI's accession and to *The Order of Communion*, which allowed for the
sacrament to be administered in both kinds.

83 *apoysone*] Peisant, i.e., ponderous (King, "*John Bon*," 89).

84 *vs dresse*] Put on vestments in preparation for saying Mass.

87 *ther*] Their.

---

[15] The prayers said by the priest at the altar during the Mass were referred to as "secrets"
and most of the parishioners did not know the meaning of the Latin words (Thomas Becon,
*Works*, ed. John Ayre, 3 vols. (Cambridge: Cambridge University Press, 1843–44), 3: 266. In
addition, the prayers were usually rushed through or mumbled in a mechanical way. The
mumblings of the priest, especially at the Consecration (perceived by many as a kind of magic
act) were derided by the Protestants as "lip-labor" (Hugh Latimer, *Sermons and Remains*, ed.
George Elwes Corrie (Cambridge: Cambridge University Press, 1845), 404.

*sayeinge*] Recitation of something that has a prescribed form (e.g., prayers).
88 *Confiteor and misereatur*] Parts of the Ordinary of the Mass.
89 *Ieze*] Jesus.
91 *Thys geere*] Gear, i.e., the Mass.
   *oure ladies sawter*] Our Lady's Psalter, a set collection of 150 psalms interspersed with
      prayers recited in honor of the Blessed Virgin Mary.
93 *the Pistell and Gospell*] Epistle and Gospel, parts of the Ordinary of the Mass.
98 Refers to the Scriptures generally, rather than to specific parts of the Mass.
101 *the canon*] The Canon (Rule of Consecration), the central part of the Mass.
103 *the memento*] Prayers for the Commemoration of the Living in the Mass.
   *the sacringe*] Consecration in the Mass.
104 *morenly*] Confoundedly (variant of "murrainly").
107 *fyue wordes*] The five words of consecration spoken over the host: "Hoc est enim
   corpus meum" ("For this is my body"). Punt has "& can w$^t$ fiue woordes make both
   god and man" in *A new Dialoge Called The Endightment agaynste mother Messe* (Av).
109 *spittell*] Diseased, foul (Spurgeon 17).
110 *A galows gay gifte*] An otherwise unknown phrase that presumably means a "body."[16]
   Iohn Bon facetiously comments that the priest is able to conjure up a body, merely
   by saying the five words of consecration.
120 *nere*] Not (obsolete form of "ne were").
124 *A sessions on it*] A mild oath — "commit me to trial."
143 *Catechismus*] Archbishop Cranmer's book, *Cathechismvs: That is to say a shorte
   Instruction into Christian Religion for the synguler commoditie and profyte of children
   and yong people* (commonly known as Cranmer's *Catechism*). The work ( June 1548)
   is mostly a translation by Cranmer of the Lutheran Nuremberg catechism which in
   turn derives from Jonas's Latin version of 1539. Jonas's work was based on the 1533
   German text by Osiander and Brenz.
144–45 *For thoughe it came forth but euen that other day / Yet hath it tourned many to ther
   olde waye*] When Cranmer's *Catechism* was printed with a woodcut showing Christ
   instituting the Eucharist, some of Cranmer's contemporaries mistakenly believed the
   illustration was the same as the picture in the Latin edition of Jonas's *Catechism*
   (published in Germany in 1539) and consequently they thought Cranmer had
   changed his views on the sacrament of the Eucharist.[17] However, Cranmer held then,

---

[16] I have been unable to find another usage of this phrase.

[17] Strype reports Gardiner claimed that the illustration in Cranmer's *Catechism* showed "an altar with candles lighted, and the priest apparelled after the old sort, putting the wafer into the communicant's mouth," John Strype, *Memorials of the Most Reverend Father in God Thomas Cranmer*, ed. Philip Edward Barnes, 2 vols. (London: George Routledge, 1853), 1: 227. See also Richard Watson Dixon, *History of the Church of England from the Abolition of*

as he did at the 1555 Disputation at Oxford, that: "Christ's flesh and blood be in the sacrament truly present, but spiritually and sacramentally, not carnally and corporally. And as he is truly present, so is he truly eaten and drunken, and assisteth us" (quoted in Dugmore, *Mass*, 187). For discussion on the evolution of Cranmer's eucharistic thought, see MacCulloch, *Cranmer*, 390–392.

145–47 *ther olde waye . . . haue they messe and matins in latyne tonge againe*] Compare with the *Sermon on the Ploughers* ( January 1548), in which Hugh Latimer laments the return to conservative practices. He likens preaching to plowing, pointing out that preachers currently neglect sowing God's word, and admonishes them to "preache and teache, and let your ploughe be doyng" (Biii). Latimer then reverses the imagery to compare the devil to a diligent preacher always ready with his plow. Where this happens: "there away with bookes, and vp with candelles, awaye with Bybles and vp with beades, awaye with the lyghte of the gospel, and vp with the lyghte of candelles . . . vp with deckynge of ymages and gaye garnyshynge of stockes and stones. Vp with mannes tradicions and his lawes, downe with Gods tradycions and his most holye worde . . . let al thynges be done in Latine. there muste be nothynge but Latine . . . Goddes worde may in no wyse be translated into Englishe" (Ciiiᵛ–Ciiiiᵛ).

154 *your deuilish masse*] See similar expression in *Pathose* (800–803).

155 *euen for his promisse sake*] John 6:54.

157 *al is not golde that hath a fayre glosse*] A variant of "All is not gold that shines," proverbial (Whiting, *Proverbs*, G 282), with a pun on "gloss" in its ecclesiastical sense (*Glossa Ordinaria*).

161 *God spede vs and the plough*] Iohn Bon's rustic farewell to the parson, with a reminder of the parable of the sower (Matthew 13:18–23; Mark 4:3–20; Luke 8:5–15) and of Christ's admonition about keeping the hand to the plow (Luke 9:62). Also proverbial (Whiting, *Proverbs*, G 239).

162–64 The plowman's commands to the oxen which are likely named according to their colorings:
*Ha*] Variant of "have" and also of the interrogative "hi."
*browne done*] Grayish-brown.
*forth*] Forwards.
*Ree*] To the right. Earliest citation in *OED*.
*garlde*] Speckled, spotted.
*haight* ] To the left.
*blake*] Black.
*hab*] As "ha" above and necessary here for the rhyme.
*agayne*] In the opposite direction.

---

*the Roman Jurisdiction*, 6 vols. (London, 1878–1902; Westmead: Gregg International, 1970), 2: 513 n. * [sic].

*bald*] White mark or blaze on a beast's face or forehead.
*before*] In front.
*who*] Whoa.

## V *Antipus,*

title *Antipus*] Etymology remains unclear. Probably refers to an opposing polemical
  stance, i.e., Protestant; literally "the other foot" from the combination of "anti"
  (contrary or opposite) and Latinized Greek "pus" (foot). Shepherd may also perhaps
  pun on "antipape" (antipope) and Herod Antipas, the biblical villain, referring to the
  corruption of the Roman Church. As well, Antipus is a minor character (one of the
  Mass's servants) in Punt's contemporary work, *A new Dialoge Called The Endightment
  agaynste mother Messe.*

heading *Nam horum contraria verissima sunt*] For the contraries of those things are truest.
3 Genesis 4:8–10.
4 Genesis 6:13–17.
8 *the lawe*] Exodus 20.
10 *Goliad*] Goliath (1 Samuel 17).
11 *Bell*] Bel and the Dragon 1–27.
15 *Simon Magus*] Simon Magus, the Samarian sorcerer (Acts 8:9–19).[18]
17 *the deuyll hath perfecte loue and hope*] Ironic. A Catholic tenet holds that because the
  devil rejected God, he can never experience hope or salvation.
18 *goddes worde doth constitute the pope*] Shepherd points out the irony of the papacy
  claiming scriptural authority, while denying people access to the word of God ( John
  21:16–17; Matthew 16:18).
22 *the prestes can make their maker*] Refers to the doctrine of transubstantiation. See also
  *A pore helpe* (53–54); *Pathose* (177); *The comparison betwene the Antipus and the
  Antigraphe* (51; 127); *Doctour doubble ale* (329–330), and *Cauteles preseruatory* (Aii˅).
23 *Leighton*] William Layton, a prebendary of St Paul's (1544–51) and a strong defender
  of the Mass. The Grey Friars' chronicler commented on the controversy roused by his
  weekly orthodox sermons (*Grey Friars*, 56–57).[19]
25 *the popes owne knight*] Catholic priest, an expression often used contemptuously.
28 *the Popes netts*] Ecclesiastical practice of imprisoning those who contravened Church
  law (e.g., for refusing to pay their tithes, or as a result of an accusation of heresy).
  This imprisonment was referred to as being "wrapt in the bishop's nets" (Foxe, *Acts,*

---

[18] For a contemporary visual satire that shows the Catholic Church as a tree trunk growing
out of the reclining figures of Simon Magus and Judas and crowned by the image of the papal
ass, see Watt, *Cheap Print*, 152.

[19] See also "Leiton, Leyton" in *The comparison betwene the Antipus and the Antigraphe* (56,
184).

5: 35) and parishioners were often only released after the payment of a large fine.[20]

30 *the kings commission*] The proclamation of September 1548 that temporarily forbade unauthorized sermons in an attempt to prevent dissension (Hughes and Larkin, *Tudor Royal Proclamations*, 1: #313).

## VI  *The comparison betwene the Antipus and the Antigraphe or answere thereunto, with. An apologie or defence of the same Antipus. And reprehence of the Antigraphe.*

title  *Reprehence*] Refutation.

*Antipus* [See previous notes]

*Antigraphium* Attributed to Sir John Mason in *Phylogamus* (25–29; 51–57), *Antigraphium* is a line-by-line refutation of Shepherd's *Antipus*.

heading  *Antigraphium*] A written reply.

*Nam ea audite verissima sunt*] For hear those things that are truest.

45  *true newes*] The Gospel is usually referred to as the good news. Mason uses "true" possibly because he does not hold that the Protestant English Gospel is a faithful rendering of God's word.

51  *So verely by gods worde we consecrate our maker*] Refers to the doctrine of transubstantiation. See also *A pore helpe* (53–54); *Pathose* (177); *Antipus* (22); *The comparison betwene the Antipus and the Antigraphe* (127); *Doctour doubble ale* (329–330), and *Cauteles preseruatory* (Aiiᵛ).

52  *gods worde did tourne Moyses rod*] Misquotation of Exodus 7–11.

55  *Who makes no difference*] A Protestant, i.e., one who denies that a priest changes bread and wine into the body and blood of Christ.

*is giltie of yᵉ body of our Lord.*] The allusion is to 1 Corinthians 11:27 and to the doctrine of the *manducatio impiorum*. For discussion of this doctrine, see MacCulloch, *Cranmer*, 405–406.

64  *Gospellers*] Contemptuous title here. See also line 194.

77  *Christe sayeth is very fleshe*] John 6:55–56.

79  *Christ that sayth it is hys body*] Luke 22:19; Mark 14:22; Matthew 26:26.

*Apologia Antipi* *Apologia Antipi* is Shepherd's reply to Mason's refutation.

title  *Apologia Antipi*] The Defense of the *Antipus*.

heading  Hear those things that are truest (i.e., a repetition of the heading of the *Antigraphium* with the exception of "nam").

88  *cowcher of stones*] A pun on Sir John Mason (1503–66), statesman, member of the

---

[20] For an illustration of the Catholic Church as the controller of "nets," see R. W. Scribner, *For the Sake of Simple Folk: Popular Propaganda for the German Reformation* (Cambridge: Cambridge University Press, 1981), 111.

Edwardian Privy Council, and Chancellor of Oxford (see Appendix).

90–95 Matthew 7:24–28; Luke 6:46–49 (based on Isaiah 28:16–18). See also *Phylogamus* (47–50).

117 *some smoky Smyth*] A pun on Dr Richard Smith (1500–63), active defender of the Mass (see Appendix).

127 *he sayd such theues, could not their maker make*] Refers to the doctrine of transubstantiation. See also *A pore helpe* (53–54); *Pathose* (177); *Antipus* (22); *The comparison betwene the Antipus and the Antigraphe* (51); *Doctour doubble ale* (329–330), and *Cauteles preseruatory* (Aiiᵛ).

129 Exodus 4:1–5.

131 John 1:1.

134 *Christe is not made, nor create, but onely was beget*] From the "Athanasian Creed" and incorporated in the Prayer Book (1549).

140–41 Reformist reproach that the word *transubstantiatio* does not occur in the biblical text.

142–54 1 Corinthians 11:17–34.

145 *flesh flies*] Blow-flies that lay their eggs in dead meat. Here used in a figurative and derogatory way against those who believe in the Real Presence, i.e., those who believe they eat the body of Christ in the Eucharist.

146 *Christ the heade*] Ephesians 4:4–5; 5:23.

147 *Prouinge the pore*] 1 Corinthians 11:17–22.

150 *To eate the breade worthely*] 1 Corinthians 11:27–29.

155 *heades*] Headings, topics.

156–57 *To eate christes fleshe & eke to drynke hys bloud / As so to dwel in Christ as he maye dwell in vs*] Echoes the new rite of communion in the *Order of Communion* and also in *The booke of the common prayer* (1549): "so to eat the flesh of thy dear Son Jesus Christ, and to drink his blood, in these holy Mysteries, that we may continually dwell in him, and he in us" (Ketley, *Two Liturgies*, 7; 92).

159 *Beleue and thou hast eaten saynte A[u]gustine sayde thus*] Part of a quotation from St Augustine (based on John 6:35–60): "Ut quid paras dentes et ventrem? Crede et manducasti"; "Why dost thou prepare thy belly and thy teeth? Believe, and thou hast eaten." Shepherd may be quoting Cranmer who uses these exact words (quoting St. Augustine) in his work on the Eucharist (Cox, *Cranmer*, 118; 208 n. 3; Grindal, *Remains*, 44).

160–73 Luke 22:19–20.

175–76 John 6:41; 6:52–53.

177 *pharisey*] Derogatory reference to Mason's Catholicism. For a contemporary visual satire, see illustration in Cranmer's *Catechism* of the parable of the Pharisee and the Publican, where the Pharisee is depicted as a tonsured friar (MacCulloch, *Cranmer*, 387; 389).

181 *Treadinge within the trade*] Habitually following a course or way.

182  *a blind horse in the myl*] Proverbial (Tilley, *Proverbs*, H 697).

193  *some shepebiter*] A dog who bites sheep. A derogatory allusion to Catholics.[21] Shepherd may also pun on his own name as the victim of satiric attack.

195  *full of charitie, ye wishe them in the fire*] Catholics defended the burning of heretics as charitable. See More, *Apology*, 91–92.

201  *gentyll Rope*] The hangman's rope used in executions for treason.

202  *sir hoddy doddy*] Fool.

203  *as crafty*] Ironic; see "As wise as Waltham's calf" (Tilley, *Proverbs*, W 22).

   *as a calf*] A synonym for "papist" (Exodus 32:4–6; 1 Kings 12:28–33). See also "caluish clarke" in *Doctour doubble ale* (333).

208  *a Paynter fyne*] Probably a pun on John Painter, conservative canon of St Paul's (Foxe, *Acts*, 5: 743).

209  *Mugge*] Refers abstrusely to Miles Hogarde. See also line 222. "Mugge" may be a pun on the Latin "mugio" (to bellow or roar), or a deliberate misnaming for alliterative effect. Shepherd puns on his Christian name "myle" in line 226 and in *Phylogamus* (178), and fleetingly refers to "maister huggarde" in *A pore helpe* (311). Bale Latinizes Hogarde's name and calls him "Milo Porcarius, alias Hoggarde" (Bale, *Catalogus*, 2: 111), and Crowley punningly addresses him as "maister Hogherd" in *The Confutation of the mishapen Aunswer to the misnamed, wicked Ballade, called the Abuse of y* blessed sacramen*t of the aultare* (Di; Eiv^v; Fi).

   *Gray*] An unidentified papist.

   *Perkens*] An unidentified papist. See also lines 229–233.

215  *Babilon*] Babylon (Revelation 17).

217  *Nemprothes*] Nemroth [Nimrod], i.e., a tyrant. Refers to Bishop Gardiner. Bale links these names: "The boystuouse tyrauntes of Sodoma wyth their great Nemroth Winchester, and the execrable cytezens of Gomorra w^t their shorne smered captaines," in *The Image Of bothe churches* (preface Bi^v).

   *owne man*] i.e., Mason, who supported Gardiner under Henry VIII.

218  *raineth in Rome*] [Who] reigns in Rome, i.e., Pope Paul III (1534–49).

219  *Thubalkaim*] Tubalcain, Cain's offspring and the first smith (Genesis 4:22–23); an oblique pun on Richard Smith.

224  *my spaniell rugge*] "Spaniel" is a synonym for "papist." James Pilkington links

---

[21] In the Sessions against him in 1543, Anthony Peerson called the Catholic bishops "thieves" and "murderers" leading the laity into "all idolatry, superstition, and hypocrisy . . . through which ye are become rather bite-sheeps than true bishops, biting and devouring the poor sheep of Christ, like ravening wolves" (Foxe, *Acts*, 5: 487–488). John Bale denounces "such cruel biteshepes, as with tirannye maintaine those Idolatries" in *A declaration of Edmonde Bonner's articles, concerning the cleargye of London dyocese whereby that excerable* [sic] *Antychriste, is in his righte colours reueled* (Basle, 1554, *STC* 1289), Hvii.

"papistes" and "spayniels" in *Aggeus and Abdias Prophetes* (Ddiiii^v). See also *Cauteles preseruatory* Avii. "Rugge" may be a misprint for "ruge" (variant of "rouge"), referring to the scarlet color of a cardinal's cassock and alluding to Cardinal Reginald Pole (1500–58). Alternatively, it may refer to William Rugg (Reppes), Bishop of Norwich (d. 1550).[22]

229 *Perkens*] Refers to an unidentified papist with the same name as the earlier traitor, Perkin Warbeck (c. 1474–99).

231 *rowe in the barge*] Probably proverbial.

235 *sword bearer of s. Mildredes*] William Bell, conservative rector of St Mildred's Bread Street (26 October 1536–15 January 1557). In May 1538 three parishioners reported him "for reading at the Easter Mass the forbidden name, 'Saint Gregory Pope'" (Brigden, *London and the Reformation*, 281). Shepherd links both Gardiner and Bell as conservatives. Bell testified on behalf of the bishop before the King's Commissioners in 1551 (Foxe, *Acts*, 6: 201).

235–40 *who knoweth all their mind . . . etcetera*] An ironic reference to auricular confession.

# VII *Phylogamus*

*Phylogamus* is a response to John Mason's non-extant work probably entitled *Heresyes Wylle and Testament*.[23]

title *Phylogamus*] (philogamos) One who loves marriage. See also line 485.

2 Satiric reference to veneration of the eucharistic elements.

5 *Parnase*] Parnassus, sacred to Apollo and the Muses. See also lines 8 and 15.

9 *Hellycons*] Helicon, the source of the fountains of Aganippe and Hippocrene, whose waters conferred poetic inspiration on those who drank them. See also line 13.

11 *Pegase* ] Pegasus.

13 *of one*] i.e., Mason. See also lines 57 and 88.

25–26 *He wrote . . . An Antygraphe*] Mason, author of the *Antigraphium*.

31–32 *yf God were dead . . . raysed in Bread*] Refers disparagingly to the Eucharist.

47–50 *Hys workes . . . be washed away*] A derogatory remark about Mason's writings.

52 *Masonrye*] A pun on Mason's name.

73–78 *them that are bolde . . . takyng to them wyues, / wyth them to leade theyr lyues*] Married priests.

80 *out of towne them dryues*] Refers to Mason's work as royal commissioner (Rochester, 1547). See also lines 415–416.

---

[22] Pole was given a cardinalship by Paul III in 1536 and appointed papal legate to England in November 1554. He was consecrated Archbishop of Canterbury in March 1556. Rugg was given a bishopric in 1536; by 1540 he was a commissioner for dealing with cases of heresy and had gained a reputation for cruelty. He was forced to resign his bishopric in 1549. See Jordan, *Edward VI*, 136.

[23] See Literary Aspects of the Satires (*Phylogamus*).

90 *Of.H. for hys humanitee*] Refers to a collar of state (such as the Collar of "SS" ("S's," "Esses") worn by Chancellor Thomas More). Shepherd satirically imagines Mason wearing a collar comprised of "H" shapes signifying his accomplishments in the humanities (grammar, rhetoric, Latin, and Greek).

91 *Urbanytye*] A pun on Pope Urban IV (d.1264) who established the feast of Corpus Christi.

93 *A double .P.*] Abbreviation of "patrum pater" (father of fathers); the pope. See also line 349.

94 *a traye aboue*] Trey. The triple crown worn by, or carried in front of the pope at important non-liturgical functions.

97 *to Chastenes sweareth*] The Roman Church insisted on a vow of celibacy from its clerics.

103 *latten*] A pun on "Latin" and on "latten" (a blend of metals) and a satirical reference to Mason's "fyne latyn" (see line 137). Also a reference to his Catholicism. Shepherd mixes mock-Latin and English together in his "Latten Clubbe, or Hurle Batte" against Mason (see sub-heading after line 302).

104–06 *oute of Barbarye . . . all hys knowledge gett*] A pun on "barbarous." Shepherd mocks Mason's unclassical Latin and then disparagingly replies to his work in ostentatiously bad Latin (see lines 303–362).

107 *For thys I dare well Sweare*] Above this line is a two-line space. The context suggests that Shepherd accidentally overlooked a space left for the insertion of a quotation from Mason's work.

111 *here it doth succede*] For here it follows (i.e., the subsequent text beginning "O Insensati").

112–31 The Latin words in these lines are printed in smaller type. They may come from Mason's lost work because the next part of Shepherd's poem, "In Praise of the Meter," appears to be a satirical commendation of Mason's skill as a humanist poet. In this case, the interspersed lines in English are either Shepherd's translation of, or a commentary on, Mason's text. These lines display a different, irregular rhyme scheme. The Latin lines appear to have been written originally in couplets, whereas *Phylogamus* is written in a mixture of couplets, tercets, and quatrains. By omitting some lines and inserting others of his own, Shepherd changes the pattern to include six couplets and eight lines of alternating rhymes. A change in type size occurs again in the section entitled "A Latten Club, or Hurle Batte" (303–362), which replies to the Latin in lines 112–131. Shepherd begins with the same words, "O Insensati," but inserts "Uos" [Vos] (You) in order to make a personal attack on Mason and his conservative associates, and to include all conservatives in the insult. The Latin end-words in lines 400–406, all of lines 434–453, the end-words in lines 448–452, and some other individual Latin words (lines 477, 479, 481 and 483), are also printed in this smaller type.

112–31 *O Insensati*] . . . *In sempiterna supplicia*] A translation of these Latin lines follows. The fractured nature of the Latin here and elsewhere necessitates that the translation is only an approximation in some places. Seymour Baker House generously contributed the translation. The interspersed English words are printed here (and in the notes to lines 434–443) within acute brackets for the sake of clarity. Specific references to these lines follow below.

> O irrational ones
> <All marryed preistes that be> veiled (married)
> Disguised with beards
> Called lusty goats
> Whose god is the belly
> <To yᵉ belly they be bound by Indenture>
> Always to obey the belly
> And to serve the womb
> Whose father is Satan
> And (whose) mother is lechery
> <Thys> generation of vipers
> <Runnes> through all the earth
> <O God omnipotent>
> Who reigns and lives
> <Sende shame and punishement
> To all Prestes and theyr wyues
> And let them goo voyde of all grace>
> And punishments of hell
> <Wyth Lucyfer to haue a Place>
> In everlasting pain.

112 *O Insensati*] See also line 303.

114 *Barbis disguisati*] Disguised with beards. The Roman Church forbade priests to wear beards (Foxe, *Acts*, 6: 383).

116 *Quorum deus venter*] Whose god is the belly. A quotation from Philippians 3:19. Compare "your belly god to please" in *The Image of Ypocresye* (335).

122 *Genera Uiperarum*] Generation of vipers (Matthew 3:7; 12:34; 23:33; Luke 3:7). See also line 356.

125 *Qui regnas et viuis*] An inversion of the standard ending to a collect addressed to Christ, "qui vivis et regnas cum Patre et Spiritu Sancto Deus, per omnia saecula saeculorum."

131 *In sempiterna supplicia*] In everlasting pain.

136–37 *from lyn to lygure*] From Lynn (King's Lynn) to Liguria. An alliterative phrase ironically suggesting that these places are important centers of learning and culture. *fyne latyn*] Refers satirically to Mason's writing.

139 *Homer so Heroicall*] Homer (c. 850 BC).

140 *Percius Satyricall*] Aulus Persius Flaccus (AD 34–62).

143 *Urgyll and Ouide*] Virgil, Publius Vergilius Maro (70–19 BC) and Ovid, Publius Ovidius Naso (43 BC–AD 18).

155 *lawrel*] (laurel) Foliage of the laurel or bay tree styled as a wreath and used as an

emblem of distinction in poetry. Shepherd satirically insinuates Mason is without
peer as a poet.

157–59 *oure newe Poete myght / Be crowned . . . Canaby*[n]*e*] Refers to a laurel crown,
Bacchus's vine-leaf crown, and to hanging (the hemp from cannabine was often used
to make ropes for executions).

171 *A Smythe*] A pun on Smith's name. See also line 419.

172–73 *stythe*] Obsolete form of "stithy" (forge, smithy).
*pytthe*] Obsolete form of "pithy" (physical strength).

174 *of lym and lytthe*] Limb and lith, i.e., lith ( joint) and limb.

178–79 *wythin a myle*] A pun on Hogarde's name.
*wyth a fyle*] (one of Smith's tools) A pun.

186 *Smythery*] The art or trade of a smith; another pun.

187 *Uulcanus*] Vulcan, Roman god of fire and a blacksmith. See also line 400.

190–91 *the testymony / And latter wylle of Heresy*] The title of Mason's work to which
Shepherd responds.

203–05 *They be no smalle fooles, / If they be red In scholes / You may syt downe on stooles*]
Compare Skelton's description of Thomas Wolsey in *Collyn Clout*, lines 28–32: "He
is but a foole; / Let hym go to scole! A thre-foted stole / That he may downe sytte, /
For he lacketh wytte" (*Poems*, ed. Scattergood, 247).

209 *By cocke*] An oath — "by God."

211 *kepe the roockes*] Probably proverbial.

214 *For cleane*] Make clean.

215 *on ryght*] Aright, properly.

222 *beare the Bell*] Proverbial (Whiting, *Proverbs*, B 230).

233 *Minerua*] Minerva, Roman goddess of the arts, poetry, science, and wisdom.

234–53 Refers ironically to Mason building a sound, firm foundation for his work;
precisely what Shepherd says Mason does not do in *The comparison betwene the
Antipus and the Antigraphe* (88–95).

256 The only example of a virgule in any of Shepherd's texts.

261–62 *Prest or Curate / Cyuylyan or Rurate*] All those in holy orders.
*Cyuylyan*] Civilian, i.e., those clergy who specialize in civil law rather than canon law.
*Rurate*] Probably a combination of "rural" and "curate" necessitated by the rhyme
scheme.

267 *I sweare by the north doore Rood*] The Rood of Northern; the crucifix near the north
door in St Paul's to which heretics bore their fagots, and where heretical literature was
burned. The Dean of St Paul's, Richard Sampson, had it taken down on 23 August
1538 because it was seen as an object of idolatry (Vallance, *Church Screens*, 76–77).[24]

---

[24] Stephen Cattley mistakenly notes that this rood was removed in 1547 (Foxe, *Acts*, 5: 418
n. 1). It seems certain Cattley is referring to the great rood of Paul's that divided the high altar
from the nave of the church. This rood was removed on 17 November 1547 in such haste that

270 *theyr best blew hood*] Blue-lined academic hoods.

289 *a wand*] A stick to beat them with. Also the "Latin club" Shepherd intends to use on Mason. See sub-heading following line 302.

290 *back and bone*] To the backbone, i.e., through and through.

sub-heading (following line 302) *A Latten Clubbe, or Hurle Batte*] A Latin club or a hurley (hurling) bat. Shepherd's response to Mason's work is to reply to it derisively in barbarous Latin. He begins by requoting one of Mason's lines (see line 112).

303–62 *O UOS Insensati . . . Qui Seruat Millia Mille*] The following is a translation of the Latin lines. Most translation from Seymour Baker House; some translation from King (*Reformation Literature*, 269–270). Specific references to these lines follow below.

> O you irrational ones
> Born of Satan
> And called satyrs
> With shaven beards
> Smooth from bathing
> Marked with little crowns (tonsure)
> By which you might be (are) effeminate
> Soft and ready
> Given to unchastity
> Wanton goats
> Unclean ones and sodomites
> By whom the pious are hurt
> And the innocent are given over
> Certainly it is believable
> Those begetting by a hybrid
> And wearing the Bacchic fawn-skin[.]
> Because you are not married
> This means you are more corrupt
> Professing chastity
> But not keeping it
> Hating truth
> And teaching falsehood
> Not having wives
> Conquering others
> Refusing to marry
> Yielding to unchastity
> Living as wolves
> Following after whore(s)

---

two workmen were killed and others injured. See *Chronicle of the Grey Friars of London*, ed. John Gough Nichols (London, 1852), 55.

Serving Priapus
Erecting [him] as a god
And worshipping him
Seeking out pudenda
Loving enticements
Even as [you are] whoremongers
The wives of others
Daughters and sisters
Servants and handmaids
Seducing them
You ravish everywhere
Living so deviantly[.]
Black necromancers
Wet hydromancers
Stinking pyromancers
Chanting idolaters
Public falsifiers
You have Satan's help
And you keep the pope as your father
You sit in the lap of the mother
And her you may call Gomor(rah)
And you suffer with these punishments[.]
In wolves' clothing
With penises and testicles
Devoted to unchastity
Generation of vipers
Whose deity is Venus
Even to (as far as) hell
She will lead eternally[.]
A sacrifice to Pluto
Since that old man [is the one]
Who maintains innumerable thousands.

331 *Priapo seruientes*] Serving Priapus, the Greek and Roman phallic god and, by extension, the phallus.
349 *Patrem Papamque Tenetis*] (i.e., "patrum pater") And you keep the pope as your father.
351 *Gomor eam Nominetis*] And her you may call Gomor (Hosea 1:3); possibly also refers to Gomorrah (Genesis 19:24–29).
354 Also a sexual pun. See King (270 n. 64).
356 *Uiperarum Genus*] Generation of vipers.
362 *Millia Mille*] See also *Pathose* (705).

# COMMENTARY

sub-heading  *Ecquid Uos Beo?*] A taunt — "Is this enough for you?"

368–69  *my Crowne be not scraped*] The narrator is not a priest, i.e., he does not have a tonsure.

*Nor I in Order mysshaped*] Neither is the narrator a monk wearing a habit.

371  *anoyted Preyste wyth Oyle*] Refers to the Catholic anointing of priests on taking holy orders. Cranmer's 1549 Ordinals replaced the anointing with holy oil by the act of giving the ordinand a Bible and enjoining its reading.

390  *Beades of woodde and Geate*] Rosary beads (fashioned from wood and jet).

392  *our God of wheate*] A derogatory reference to the Eucharist (see John 12:24). See also *Pathose* (153).

398  *a Lyryeum Twynke*] The meaning is unclear.

400–06  Another example of Latinized words:

*Uulcanus*] i.e., Smith.

*Longimanus*] Longarmed, i.e., ascribing characteristics of a blacksmith to Smith.

*Sanus*] Sound, whole.

*Prophanus*] (profanus) Secular.

*Uanus*] Deceitful, foolish, insignificant, useless, vain.

*Alanus*] Alanus ab Insulis (Alain de Lille), rhetorician (c. 1128–1202).

*Nanus*] A dwarf; someone who is very thin.

411  *toppe and towte*] Top and bottom.

415–16  *to dryue oute / The reader in our queare*] Refers to Mason's position as royal commissioner.

422  *dapper as a deare*] Refers to Smith. Probably proverbial. See similar saying, "As dapper as a Crowe, / And perte as any pye" in *The Image of Ypocresye* (95–96).

426  *in text*] In the Scriptures.

*Marge*] Margin. Explanations or glosses written in the margin of a work.

434–43  These lines express the Protestant view about the spiritual way Christ is received in the Eucharist. They echo Cranmer's words "the spiritual eating is with the heart, not with the teeth" (quoted in MacCulloch, *Cranmer*, 464). The last lines also reflect Luther's idea that if we come to the Eucharist expecting to taste Christ then we go away empty. (The words in English are printed within acute brackets for the sake of clarity.)

> <And that> not with teeth
> Piercing bread
> By no means
> Is Christ to be tasted or handed over
> Nor can the senses be deceived
> When the bread will be given to be received
> But barbaric <Smyth>
> Left empty-handed[.]

447  *a tryggum tray*] The exact meaning is unclear. "Tryggum" may be from "trigamy" (married three times); "tray" (trey, three) is necessary for the rhyme. In 1540, as a

153

reward for his services to Henry VIII, Mason was licensed to hold the canonry and prebend of Timsbury, "even if he should marry a second time" (Emden, *Register*, 386); Shepherd may be exaggerating in order to satirize Mason.

448 *Philologus*] A language-lover.

449 *Pantolobus*] Ponce Pantolabus. Pseudonym of John Huntington whose poem, *The genealogye of heresye*, survives only in Bale's *A mysterye of inyquyte contayned within the heretycall Genealogye of Ponce Pantolabus*. Along with Richard Taylor and John Smith, Huntington denounced the Scottish reformer, Alexander Seton in 1541, but he was later converted to Protestantism (Foxe, *Acts*, 5: 449) and became a preacher and a polemical writer.

450 *Spermologus*] (spermologus) Word-sower. A quotation of Acts 17, what Paul on the Areopagus was called by the skeptical Athenians, translated by Tyndale as "babbler."[25] Also a sexual pun.

468 *cowche thy stones*] Refers to Mason; also a sexual pun.

469 *faber*] Smith, another pun on Smith's name.

479 *Misogamus*] Misogamist, i.e., one who hates marriage.

481 *Monogamus*] Monogamist, i.e., one who has married only once.

483 *Apogamus*] Apogamist, i.e., one who believes in celibacy.

# VIII *Doctour doubble ale.*

title *doubble ale*] Strong ale (i.e., twice the strength of regular ale).

12 *dawes*] Fools; also Catholic clergy.

20 *bables*] Foolish things, with a connotation of idolatry or popery as well.

44–48 Another example of Latin and pseudo-Latin words. See also lines 383–390.
*teachis*] Teaches.
*preachis*] Preach.
*lechis*] Physicians.
*dulpatis*] Dull-pates, i.e., stupid persons.
*pratis*] Prate.

49–50 Matthew 7:13.

52–53 Matthew 6:19–20.

54 *papisticall prouisions*] Appointments to a see or benefice not yet vacant, especially those the pope made in derogation of the right of the regular patron.

58 *this good felow stout*] Doctour Doubble Ale; also a pun on "stout" and "ale."

60–61 *olde condicions*] Adherence to the old Catholic ways.
*newe comyssyons*] The new laws. Possibly *The Order of Communion* (8 March 1548) which allowed English to be used for the first time in the sacrament of the Eucharist.

---

[25] I am grateful to Leslie S. B. MacCoull for this information.

64 *syng for dead folkes soules*] Chantry priests earned their living by singing Masses for the souls of the dead. The Dissolution of the Chantries Act (1 Edward VI c. 14) forbade chantry Masses in December 1547.

65 *beade rolles*] (bead-rolls) Bede-rolls. Lists of names of the dead, usually benefactors, kept by every church. The priest read the entire bede-roll at the annual requiem for the benefactors of the parish and a shorter version of it at every Mass on Sunday, so the congregation could pray for those whose names were on it. For discussion, see Duffy, *Stripping of the Altars*, 334–337.

72 *careth not a pyn*] Proverbial (Whiting, *Proverbs*, P 210).

78–79 *And drinke ther of his fyll / Tyll ruddy be his byll*] The Injunctions of 1536–37 forbade clergy to frequent alehouses and taverns, or to spend time drinking or playing cards (Foxe, *Acts*, 5: 167).

83 *a curate*] Harry (Henry) George, curate of St Sepulchre's. See note on *A pore helpe* (382–383).

84 *newgate*] Newgate Street, London.

89 *a*] Reduced form of "at" or "of."

97 *As dronken as a mouse*] Proverbial (Whiting, *Proverbs*, M 731). Skelton has "Dronken as a mouse / At the ale house" in *Collyn Clout*, lines 801–802 (*Poems*, ed. Scattergood, 266).

98 *Mon syre gybet a vous*] (Monsieur gibet a vous) ?"Sir Gallows, to you." The meaning is unclear.

102 *drynke a due taunt*] Drink as much [as possible] (French "autant"). See similar expression in Robert Copland's *The hye way to the Spyttell hous* (Cii^v and Di).

143–50 *head peny*] An individual ecclesiastical payment.
*paskall halpeny*] Paschal half-penny, due to the curate from parishioners at Easter.
*driblars*] These small monetary offerings.

145 *cloth of corpus Christy*] For expenses for this type of decoration, see Rubin, *Corpus Christi*, 252–255.

171 *a cobblers boy*] Someone young, inexperienced, and uneducated.

172 *a wrong gospell*] The curate is a conservative, i.e., he interprets the Scriptures incorrectly; or he was drunk and read the wrong lesson. William Carew Hazlitt suggests he read the wrong Gospel for the day because of ignorance (Hazlitt, *Remains*, 3: 312 n. 1).

176 *chere*] There. For a different meaning, see Glossary.

183 *the pore ladde*] Probably Richard Mekins, who at the age of fifteen was executed as a sacramentarian (30 July 1541) at Bonner's instigation (Foxe, *Acts*, 5: 440–442).

184 *Counter*] The Counter (Compter); the London Guildhall prison located in Bread Street near Coleman Street where Shepherd lived (Foxe, *Acts*, 5: 705).

186 *wranged*] Tortured on the rack (variant of "wrung").

231 *smithfelde*] Smithfield, sixteenth-century execution site, outside London's north west walls.

232–39 *And in my Parysh be some . . . To fynde both wood and timber / To burne them euery member*] Those who support the burning of Protestants, whom they see as heretics.

240–41 *And goth to borde and bed*] Refers to John Twyford of St Sepulchre's parish. A tavern owner and an ardent papist who supplied fagots for the executions of the reformers James Bainham, Richard Bayfield, John Frith, John Lambert, and John Tewkesbury. Twyford was also responsible for the indictment of Thomas Merial, a bricklayer of St Sepulchre's, before Bishop Stokesley in 1535 (Brigden, *London and the Reformation*, 272; Foxe, *Acts*, 5: 601–602).

*At the signe of the kinges head*] A tavern called the King's Head. Probably the public house in Little Old Bailey, in Eliot's Court, close to St Sepulchre's church, and near the premises of the printers, John Day and William Seres, by the Holborn conduit. Very likely owned by Twyford.[26]

248 *the new learning*] Protestantism.

264–67 For a similar topical event which occurred at St Sepulchre's, see Crowley's *An informacion and peticion agaynst the oppressours of the pore commons of this realme, compiled* [for] *the Parliamente* (665–668).

265 *dirige*] Dirge. So called for the first word of the antiphon at Matins in the Office of the Dead that begins: "Dirige, Domine, Deus meus, in conspectu tuo viam meam"; "Direct, O Lord, my God, my way in thy sight" (Psalm 5:9, *Vulgate*). Cranmer's new burial service eliminated all this (MacCulloch, *Cranmer*, 508–510).

267 *Chey*] They.

271 *a gay chering*] A gay cheering. See similar use ("gay chearynge") in *Iohn Bon and Mast person* (79).

279 *set not a rysh*] Proverbial. Whiting has "Not worth a rysh" (Whiting, *Proverbs*, R 250).

280 hary George] Harry (Henry) George.

282 *Dankester Dancastre*] ?Dan Caster/Kester. "Dan" is a variant of "Don" or "Dominus," a fellow of a college or university, and thus the title given to regulars. Henry George appears to address another former friar. Possibly also refers to Doncaster, although George is not listed in the Order of St Austin there.

285 *my speciall frynde*] Most likely John Twyford.[27]

297 *I perse I*] I per se, I. I by myself, I.

299 *chem*] Them.

308 *bisshops visitour*] An official appointed to visit churches in order to prevent, or remove abuses or irregularities.

311 *Care not a fly*] Probably proverbial. Whiting has "Not worth a fly" (Whiting, *Proverbs*, F 345).

---

[26] While the location of the King's Head strongly suggests that it was the tavern owned by John Twyford, it is not possible to establish conclusively Twyford's ownership since the earliest recorded evidence shows the landlord of this tavern as M. Bradwood in 1606 (*STC* 3: 237).

[27] See Brigden, *London and the Reformation*, 421; Janice Devereux, "The Identity of the Curate's Friend in Luke Shepherd's *Doctour doubble ale*," *Notes and Queries* n.s.45 (1998): 295–296.

COMMENTARY

316 *beare them out*] Overcome, withstand.

321 *passe not a fygge*] Proverbial (Whiting, *Proverbs*, F 137).

323 *Away the ma*re] Banish melancholy. Proverbial (Whiting, *Proverbs*, M 375). For similar expression, see Skelton's *Elynour Rummynge*, line 110 and *Magnyfycence*, line 1325 (*Poems*, ed. Scattergood, 217, 177; 443 n. 1325, 450 n. 110–112).
*Away the mare* quod *walis*] Most likely a song refrain.

324 *I set not a whitinge*] Proverbial (Whiting, *Proverbs*, W 317).

327 *The Masses priuat*] Private or privy Masses were held in private chapels, rather than in the chancel. The Privy Council's Proclamation forbade these Masses in February 1548.

329–30 *That I of a cake / My maker may make*] Refers to the sacramental element of bread and to the doctrine of transubstantiation. See also *A pore helpe* (53–54); *Pathose* (177); *Antipus* (22); *The comparison betwene the Antipus and the Antigraphe* (51; 127), and *Cauteles preseruatory* (Aiiᵛ).

333 *caluish*] Papist (Exodus 32:4–7; 1 Kings 12:28–33). Possibly also a pun on clerical tonsure (from Latin "calvus" meaning "bald").

347 *he sayd Messe*] Bale suggests that home visitations by clerics sometimes involved sexual gratification rather than the celebration of the Mass. In *A declaration of Edmonde Bonner's articles, concerning the cleargye of London dyocese whereby that excerable* [sic] *Antychriste, is in his righte colours reueled*, he recounts a story about a Welsh priest visiting a sick parishioner "wyth hys cake God in a boxe." Leaving the sexton outside with his bell and lantern, and "The doore beinge fast barred . . . he put downe his breche, and gotte him to bed to the wyfe" (Miii–Miiiᵛ).

357 *learning olde*] Catholicism.

362–63 *such learning / As now a dayes*] New Protestant beliefs.

383–90 Another example of adapted endings pretending to be Latin:
*wota*] Know.
*nota*] Note.
*idiota*] Silly person.
*pota*] Ale pot.
*grota*] Groat, a thick coin worth 4d.
*rota*] Rote.
*cota*] Coat.
*bota*] Boat. See also note below.

390 *cocke losels bota*] A misprint for "Lorels." Rogue, so-called after a character in the 1518 anonymous verse satire, *Here endeth Cocke Lorelles bote*.

391–92 *the durty doctour / The popes owne proctour*] A proctor collects Church dues, including tithes; the term also describes an agent who collects alms for lepers. Shepherd links his figure of a diseased pope with the contemporary image of the Roman Church as the whore of Babylon.

395 *rutter*] A gallant. Skelton has "Am not I a joly rutter?" in *Magnyfycence*, line 752 (*Poems*, ed. Scattergood, 161).

396 *Hys latin*] The following lines parody Doctour Doubble Ale's very bad Latin. Most translation from Seymour Baker House; some from King, *English Reformation Literature* (264–265).

398–99 *tu non possum / Loquere latinum*] You are not able to speak Latin. Another example of Shepherd playing games with Latin. The line should be "tu non potes." The misquotation gives Shepherd the rhyme he needs.

400–01 *This alum finum / Is bonus then vinum*] This excellent ale is better than wine.

402–04 *Ego volo quare / Cum tu drinkare / Pro tuum caput*] Therefore I wish to drink with you for your health/life. Also an oath, literally "by your head."

405–06 *Quia apud / Te propiciacio*] Because with you is satisfaction. A quotation from the "De profundis"; "Quia apud te propitiatio est: et propter legem tuam sustinui te, Domine"; "For with thee there is merciful forgiveness: and because of thy law, I have waited for thee, O Lord" (Psalm 129:4, *Vulgate*).

407–08 *Tu non potes facio / Tot quam ego*] You cannot do as much as I can, i.e., you cannot consecrate bread and wine into the body and blood of Christ.

409 *Quam librum tu lego*] Whatever book you read.

410 *Caue de me*] Watch out for me.

411 *Apponere te*] Put yourself [in the right place].

412 *Iuro per deum*] I swear by God.

413 *Hoc est lifum meum*] This is my life. A mock-Latin pun on the words of consecration of the host during the Mass: "Hoc est enim corpus meum," "For this is my body."

414 *Quia drinkum stalum*] Therefore, to drink stale [ale], with a pun on "stale," i.e., urine.

415 *Non facere malum*] [Is] to do nothing bad. Doctour Doubble Ale will settle for drinking ale, rather than drink communion wine, i.e., carry out his priestly duty of saying Mass.

416 *dominus dodkin*] Parson Worthless.
*dominus*] Master or parson.
*dodkin*] A small coin of little value.

417 *ita vera bodkin*] Such a true little body. A pun on the communion host.

433–34 *Sed perlagus ista, / Si velis Papista*] But read this if you like, papist.

435 *adewe*] Adieu.

436–37 *whirlary whewe*] Circling, whirling, whistling sound.
*tirlary typpe*] Flighty, whirling. See similar expression line 292 in Skelton's *Elynour Rummynge* (*Poems*, ed. Scattergood, 221; 451 n. 292).

438 *Beware of the whyppe*] Alludes to the Six Articles, "The Whip with Six Strings" (Foxe, *Acts*, 5: 262). The Act of Repeal of 2 December 1547 formally abolished the Six Articles and left the way clear for the introduction of more radical liturgical reforms.

# IX *Cauteles preseruatory concerning the preseruation of the Gods which are kept in the pixe*

title *Cauteles*] Cautels. Traditionally, a written set of rubrical instructions about the proper manner of implementing the sacraments. Shepherd's parody gives ironic directions for the preservation of communion hosts, rather than the correct procedures regarding the administration of the Eucharist itself.

*pixe*] Pyx.

[Sig Aii<sup>v</sup>] *makers of the greate maker whom ye can make & fassion at your owne wyl and pleasures*] Another reference to the doctrine of transubstantiation. See also *A pore helpe* (53–54); *Pathose* (177); *Antipus* (22); *The comparison betwene the Antipus and the Antigraphe* (51; 127), and *Doctour doubble ale* (329–330).

*the workes yͭ ye make*] Communion hosts; also refers to the medieval notion of the Mass as a good work.

*bred wormes*] Breed worms. See also *A pore helpe* (185). Because hosts were in danger of being eaten by weevils, custom limited the time for their reservation to seven days, after which they were burned or buried. For various examples, see Rubin, *Corpus Christi*, 44–45.

*be eaten of a mouse, ratte or munkay*] Hosts were also in danger of being eaten by mice. A contemporary adds bats to this list: "I [the host] breed worms; I am kept in a box for fear of bats. If you leave me out all night, I shall be devoured before morning; for if the mouse get me, I am gone" (Grindal, *Remains*, 61). The threat of destruction by small vermin was one of the main reasons why many churches replaced the wooden box, which traditionally had stored hosts, with a new pyx made of metal (Rubin, *Corpus Christi*, 45–47).

*munkay*] Shepherd may parody a fourteenth-century exemplum which tells the story of a pet monkey who wandered into a church and consumed the host. The monkey's owner, an old woman, burnt the animal and rescued the miraculously unharmed host from its stomach (quoted in Rubin, *Corpus Christi*, 113).

*robin redbrest or philip Sparowe*] Traditionally, robins are friends of humans and frequently carry out good deeds. Literary references to robins can be found in English verses, hymns, and stories from the twelfth-century onwards. Robins living in churches and appearing to take part in the services are well documented in literature from the seventeenth-century onwards, although very likely earlier stories existed in the oral tradition (Lack, *Robin Redbreast*, passim). In lines 399–402 of Skelton's *Phyllyp Sparowe*, a mock elegy on the death of a pet sparrow, the robin redbreast is the "priest" who is to sing the Requiem Mass (*Poems*, ed. Scattergood, 81). The poem reworks the Office of the Dead and begins "Placebo" (*Poems*, ed. Scattergood, 71; 406 n. 1). Philip (Phip, Pip) was a favorite name for a pet sparrow in imitation of its chirping. Sparrows were also often associated with lechery (e.g., Gaius Catullus's "Lugete, O Veneres Cupidinesque," a lament for Lesbia's dead sparrow).

[Sig Aiii^v] *when the olde be rotten and burned or buried*] Unused hosts were generally burned and their ashes flushed down the piscina or buried under the altar (Whitelock, Brett, and Brooke, *English Church*, 1: pt. 1, 326). See also Avii^v and *A pore helpe* (193).

[Sig Aiiii] *I haue composed thys lytell boke for you to beare in youre handes*] Ironic. Shepherd suggests that his irreverent tract should be carried by the priest at Mass as though it were a portable breviary or missal.

*whether the wafer maker be an honest man, & of good conscience, and connyng in the feate*] Shepherd parodies regulations concerning correct manufacture of communion hosts.

[Sig Aiiii^v] *the fairest roundest and whighteste*] Instructions concerning the appearance of the host: "Christ's host should be clean, wheaten, thin, not large, round, unleavened. It is inscribed, not cooked in water but baked in fire" (quoted in Rubin, *Corpus Christi*, 39).

*The clippinge or paringes whereof, maye paruenture be a refreshing to youre clarke or to the boye that healpeth you to saye Masse.*] Only priests and servers consumed consecrated hosts, except on special occasions (e.g., Easter), when the laity received the Eucharist as well (Rubin, *Corpus Christi*, 43).

*irrorate*] Moisten.

*enmyst*] Make misty or wet ("enmyst" not listed in *OED*).

*or pthisic*] Phthisic, a wasting disease of the lungs (tuberculosis).

[Sig Av] *aposteme*] Abscess consisting of pus.

*fautie*] (foughty) Musty.

[Sig Av^v] *pixt*] Pyx. See also Avi and Avii^v.

[Sig Avi] *ye must all wayes haue an od God, for they maye not be euen in numbre*] Exact significance remains unclear. In his translation of an earlier cautels, *The Cavteles, Canon, And Most Blashphemous, abhominable, and monstrous Popish Masse*, Peter Viret suggests that an "od" number is necessary: "one for the vnite of the diuinitie: three, for the personnes in Trinitie: fiue, for the fiuefoulde passion of Iesus Christ, and of his woundes and seauen, for the seuen foulde grace of the holy Ghost" (Viret, *Cavteles*, Biiij^v). For discussion regarding the traditional devotions to the five wounds of Christ and also the seven words on the Cross, see Duffy, *Stripping of the Altars*, 238–256.

*fram*] Frame (mistake, or variant of "frame," not listed in *OED*). Shepherd has "frame" later in the sentence.

*brimstone*] Recalls alchemical procedures for bleaching.

*w^t a lytel wormwode, tansey or rue*] Wormwood (absinthe), tansy, and rue. Bitter-tasting plants used medicinally; wormwood was used to eliminate mites and to protect objects from moths and fleas.

COMMENTARY

[Sig Avi<sup>v</sup>] *coloquintida*] Coloquintida. A bitter tasting drug made from the colocynth (bitter apple) and used as a purgative.

*if ye shall minister them to healthey and well tasting persons it wil be easily espied, and may peraduentre cause them to spit them out agayne*] Refers ironically to the instructions detailed in the Easter Day sermon (*Speculum Sacerdotale*) regarding the care to be taken in receiving communion. "Care when taking the Host, the avoidance of spitting, belching and sneezing afterwards are urged" (quoted in Heath, *Parish Clergy*, 98). Also refers to the procedure priests were meant to follow in the administration of the Eucharist to the sick. For instance, if a sick person vomited up the host then "the vomited host [should] be crumbled into a chalice with wine and be consumed by the priest, or given in communion to a person with a pure conscience" (Rubin, *Corpus Christi*, 81).

*y bitternes & proprietie*] Shepherd satirically suggests that communicants may be healed through the restorative properties of the drugs used to preserve the hosts, rather than by the powers of Christ through the reception of the Eucharist.

*& so become hole*] Refers to the traditional belief that communion hosts could work miracles. For various examples, see Brigden, *London and the Reformation*, 17–18; Duffy, *Stripping of the Altars*, 102–106; Rubin, *Corpus Christi*, 82; 108–147.

[Sig Avii] *benne*] Been (variation of "ben").

*memento*] The prayers for the Commemoration of the Living in the Mass.

*the leuation*] The Levation (elevation) of the host during the Mass.

*whilse ye wincke*] Shepherd satirizes the practice of the priest saying the Secrets or Prayers over the Oblation during the Mass with his eyes closed.

[Sig Avii<sup>v</sup>] *the chauncel*] The chancel. The eastern part of a church used by those officiating in the performance of the services. A lattice screen originally divided the chancel from the nave.

*that dwelleth in the pixt aboue, dayly sensing in & out bi a stryng betwene the altare and the roffe*] Refers to the reserved host in the pyx, suspended above the altar (Rubin, *Corpus Christi*, 46–47). The Eucharist thus suspended was often vulgarly referred to as "round Roben" (Calvin, *Treatyse*, Aii) and "Jacke of the boxe" and "divers other shamfulle names" (*Grey Friars*, 55).

*he defend that dwelleth in the pixt aboue . . . to whom be honoure worship and prayse worthye Amen.*] Traditional doxology, ironically addressed to the host contained in the pyx.

*who sitteth on the right hand of God the father*] Quoting the Nicene Creed.

[Sig Aviii<sup>v</sup>] *their worshippers and makers*] Catholic priests.

*all that beleue only in hym*] Protestants, i.e., those who believe in Christ's redemption and in justification by faith alone, not in wafers of bread.

# Appendix

**John Bale** (1495–1563), bibliographer, dramatist, and reformer. Bale was born at Cove, near Dunwich. He joined the Carmelite Order at Norwich and was educated there and later at Jesus College, Cambridge. By 1530 he was prior at Malden and in 1531 he was licensed to preach in the London diocese. In 1533 he was prior at Ipswich. Through the teaching of Lord Wentworth, Bale became interested in the Protestant cause and was probably converted around 1534, the same year that he became prior at Doncaster. He was licensed to preach (probably in support of the Royal Supremacy) at York on 24 July by Archbishop Lee. By early 1536 Bale was in London again. He renounced his vows, became a secular priest, and held the living of Thorndon in Suffolk. Bale married about this time. In January he was summoned before Bishop Stokesley to answer a charge of heresy. Bale attracted Thomas Cromwell's attention and protection because of his dramas. From 1537 Bale led a troupe of players sponsored by the Lord Privy Seal for propagandist reasons. The plays were acted in monastic and civic halls, as well as in private houses throughout England. However, with Cromwell's downfall in 1540, Bale fled to the Continent, where he worked on his catalogue of English texts and writers. He returned to England in 1548 to the rectory of Bishopstoke in Hampshire. In December 1552 he was recognized by Edward VI and given the bishopric of Ossory, Kilkenny, Ireland. On 2 February 1553, at Dublin, he was consecrated according to the new Anglican ritual that had not yet been sanctioned by the Irish parliament. On Mary I's accession Bale fled to the Continent and remained in Basel until 1558. On 1 January 1560, when he returned to England, Bale accepted a prebend at Canterbury, where he remained for the last years of his life.

**Thomas Becon** (1512–67), English reformer and writer. Educated at St John's College, Cambridge, he became an admirer of Latimer and was ordained in 1538, his first living being the vicarage of Brenzett in Kent. He began writing in favor of the Reformation and in 1541 was ordered to recant for preaching in Suffolk and Norfolk. In 1543, with Robert Singleton and Robert Wisdom, he was forced to recant and destroy his books at Paul's Cross. Retiring to Derbyshire, he continued his writing. Later he joined Wisdom in Staffordshire and then moved to Warwickshire. Reinstated on Edward VI's accession, he was instituted to the rectory of St Stephen, Walbrook. He was chaplain to Cranmer, as well as one of the six preachers in Canterbury Cathedral. He also held the position of chaplain to Somerset. On Mary I's accession Becon was sent to the Tower for being a seditious preacher and was deprived of his living for being a married priest. Released on 22 March 1554, he went to Frankfurt and continued his religious writings, which were denounced as heresies in England. In 1556 he moved to Marburg. On Elizabeth I's accession he returned to England, where he was restored to his London benefice and given supplementary livings.

**Thomas Bilney (1495?–1531)**, Protestant martyr. He was educated at Trinity Hall, Cambridge and ordained in 1519. After hearing Latimer read his thesis against Melanchthon in 1524, Bilney presented a reply which was so convincing that it changed Latimer's ideas. They became friends, met daily, and together carried out works of charity. Though Bilney remained generally orthodox, he was intractable on the question of saint and relic veneration and believed that at least some of the New Testament should be available for the laity in English. He obtained a license to preach throughout the diocese of Ely, but in 1526 Wolsey cautioned him because of his sermons which denounced prayer to the saints. In 1527 he was forced to recant by Bishop Tunstall of London, despite which he was imprisoned in the Tower. Upon his release in 1529 he returned to Cambridge. Overwhelmed with remorse for apostasy, he became increasingly despondent, but eventually he resumed his preaching in Norfolk, teaching privately at first and then preaching in the fields (because churches were closed to him as his license had been revoked). Finally, he was apprehended, degraded of his orders, and burned as a heretic at Norwich in August 1531.

**Edmund Bonner (1500–69)**, Bishop of London. Educated at Oxford, he was chaplain to Cardinal Wolsey by 1529 and in 1532 was sent to Rome by Henry VIII in connection with his divorce case and later rewarded with the benefice of Cherry Burton near Beverley. He returned to England in 1534 and was given the living of East Dereham in Norfolk. He was installed as Archdeacon of Leicester in 1535 and from 1537–39 he was a prebendary of St Paul's. In 1538 he was ambassador to the French king, Francis I. Bonner was elected Bishop of London in 1539 and consecrated in 1540. Over the next several years he actively persecuted Protestants. He opposed even moderate reform such as the removal of images from churches. In 1547 he declared he would accept the Royal Injunctions and the *Book of Homilies* only insofar as they were not contrary to God's laws. He finally retracted his refusal, but failed to convince Edward VI's Council of his sincerity and was sent, like Gardiner, to the Fleet prison. He was soon discharged and over the next two years offered little resistance to the reformation processes. At the end of June 1549 he was commanded to stop the private Masses in St Paul's parish and ordered to preach a prepared text at St Paul's on 1 September. He ignored the instruction regarding the king's authority during his minority, and was later examined over a period of days by Cranmer. He was deprived of his bishopric in October 1549 and imprisoned in the Marshalsea in Southwark, from whence he was released in August 1553 and restored to his see by Mary I. On Elizabeth I's accession he again fell from favor because he refused the oath of supremacy. In 1559 he was returned to the Marshalsea where he died ten years later.

**John Fisher** (1469–1535), Bishop of Rochester. Fisher was born at Beverley in Yorkshire. Educated at Michaelhouse, Cambridge, he became Vice-Chancellor there in 1501 and two years later was appointed to the newly founded chair of Divinity. He was given his bishopric in 1504 and was Chancellor of the University of Cambridge from that year until 1514, when he was re-elected for life. In 1511 he arranged for Erasmus to visit Cambridge and ensured that the teaching of Greek at the university was not hampered by opposition to the new Protestant ideas. However, he was an implacable enemy of the Reformation and of Luther, whose work he refuted in several published discourses. Fisher refused to accept the validity of Henry VIII's divorce and opposed the Royal Supremacy, although he accepted most of the Act of Succession. In 1533 he was placed under house arrest from April until June, and on 16 April 1534 he was committed to the Tower for refusing the oath in its entirety. He was deprived of his bishopric the following January. On 31 May 1535 he was given a cardinalship by Pope Paul III. Still refusing to recognize the king as supreme head of the church in England, Fisher was found guilty of high treason and executed on 22 June 1535.

**Stephen Gardiner** (1483–1555), Bishop of Winchester. Gardiner became Wolsey's secretary after taking doctorates in both canon and civil law at Trinity Hall, Cambridge, and was made the king's principal secretary in 1529 after the Lord Chancellor's dismissal. He argued Henry VIII's case in Rome, was consecrated Bishop of Winchester in 1531, and appointed ambassador to France in 1535. Gardiner supported the Henrician reforms, accepted the Royal Supremacy, and helped to frame the Six Articles. He represented Henry VIII at the Diet of Regensburg, but was not mentioned in Henry's will and was excluded from the regency Council. On Edward VI's accession he was excluded from the Privy Council, as well as from the Chancellorship of the University of Cambridge. Refusing to accept the Royal Injunctions and the *Book of Homilies*, he was committed to the Fleet prison in September 1547 and released in the following January. He continued to resist doctrinal reformation and maintained the doctrine of the Real Presence. Ordered by Somerset to preach the sermon for St Peter's day, Gardiner spoke on most of the topics he had been told to include. However, his statements were questioned by the Privy Councillors, who believed he was a threat to any future reforms, and he was imprisoned in the Tower on the last day of June 1548. He was not deprived of his see until February 1551. On Mary I's accession he was released, restored to power, and made Lord Chancellor. In his sermon at Paul's Cross on 2 December 1554, he celebrated the return of a Catholic monarch who would restore the country to the obedience of Rome, preaching "Now it is time to awake out of sleep" (Redworth, *Gardiner*, 328). Gardiner spent the next few months before his health failed in diplomatic activity, including aiding the papal legate in his work of mediation between the emperor and Henry II of France. He died on 12 November 1555.

**Hugh Latimer** (c.1485–1555), Bishop of Worcester and Protestant martyr. He was born at Thurcaston near Leicester and was educated at Clare College, Cambridge. Latimer took holy orders at Lincoln, and in 1522 was one of twelve preachers licensed by Cambridge University to preach throughout England. Under the influence of Bilney, he became converted to reformist ideas and acquired a reputation as a zealous preacher. One of the Cambridge divines appointed to decide on the lawfulness of Henry VIII's marriage to Katherine of Aragon, Latimer declared for the king. He became chaplain to Anne Boleyn and was given the rectory of West Kington in Wiltshire. He was consecrated Bishop of Worcester in 1535. In his two sermons at the opening of Convocation in June of the following year, he pressed relentlessly for the continuation of the Reformation. His great strength was his ability to deliver powerful sermons. After the passage in parliament of the Act of the Six Articles, he resigned his bishopric and in 1539 he was imprisoned in the Tower. He was released in July 1540, and his next six years are unrecorded. He was committed to the Tower again in 1546, but was released on Edward VI's accession. During Edward's reign he devoted himself to preaching and good works, declining to resume episcopal duties. Soon after Mary I's accession a summons was issued against him. He appeared before the Council and was again consigned to the Tower. Despite illness, Latimer joined Cranmer and Ridley in Oxford in March 1554 to dispute with divines from Cambridge and Oxford about the Eucharist. The proceedings began on 14 April with the reading of a commission from Convocation and continued for several days. When the three prisoners were brought up to hear their sentence on 20 April they were encouraged to recant and when they refused they were formally excommunicated. Re-examined in September 1555, they were found guilty of heresy and burned at the stake on 16 October.

**Sir John Mason (1503–66),** statesman, member of the Edwardian Privy Council, and Chancellor of Oxford. After graduating from All Souls College, Oxford, he was appointed king's scholar in Paris. His first church appointment was as rector of the parish of Kyngeston (Kingston) Bagpuize, Berkshire, in the Diocese of Salisbury. He was instituted through his proctor on 23 February 1531 (see Bishop Campeggio's register, Wiltshire Record Office D1/2/15, fol.25). He was appointed rector of Farthingstone, Northamptonshire, on 30 June 1535; rector of Swerford, Oxfordshire, on 22 June 1536; canon of Crediton, Devon, and prebendary of Crosse, circa July 1536; canon and prebendary of Timsbury, Hampshire, on 28 May 1540; and appointed canon of Lincoln and prebendary of Buckingham cum Sutton on 28 September 1553. Mason was Dean of Winchester from 1549–54. He was acting clerk of the Privy Council in 1541 and appointed clerk on 13 April

1543. Edward VI created him Knight of the Carpet circa February 1547, and in the same year Mason visited Rochester as one of the royal visitors. He was appointed Privy Councillor on 19 April 1550. He was appointed ambassador to Henry II of France on 19 April 1550 and to Emperor Charles V in October 1553. He was elected Chancellor of Oxford on 18 November 1552. Mason was known to be "compliant in matters of religion" (Emden, *Register*, 387). He read the denunciation (at the third Session against Bonner before the king's Commissioners) of Bishop Bonner in 1549. He accepted the proclamation of Lady Jane Grey as queen after Edward's death (1553), and he later held his position on the Privy Council under Elizabeth I. In the days following the proclamation of Lady Jane Grey, he changed sides again and helped arrange for Mary I's proclamation in London (19 July 1553). Thus, when Edward Underhill was being examined for writing a ballad against the papists after Mary I's accession, he taunted Mason by calling him a turncoat. After being asked by Mason to define a papist, Underhill replied: "Why, syr, . . . it is nott lounge syns you could defyne a papist better than I" (Underhill, *Anecdotes*, 140).

**Sir Thomas More (1478–1535)**, humanist, writer, and Lord Chancellor. He was educated at St Anthony's (London) and at Oxford before studying at New Inn and Lincoln's Inn. He contemplated becoming a priest, but returned to secular affairs after spending four years in the Charterhouse (the Carthusian monastery in London). A brilliantly successful lawyer, he was also a Member of Parliament (1504 and 1523) and Undersheriff of London (1510–19). He became a Privy Councillor in 1518 and was knighted in 1521. He was Undertreasurer of the Exchequer in 1521, Speaker of the House of Commons in 1523, and on 25 October 1529 he succeeded Wolsey as Lord Chancellor. On 10 May 1532 the king demanded three articles of submission from Convocation, requiring in effect that the Church surrender its legislative independence. More disagreed with what he saw as the king's usurpation of the pope's authority; he also believed that the heresy laws (which were now officially relaxed) should be enforced. He resigned his position as Lord Chancellor on 16 May 1532. Despite his retirement from political life, he continued to write polemical works in support of the Catholic Church. While willing to swear fidelity to the Act of Succession, More opposed the Royal Supremacy and consequently was named in a Bill of

Attainder and examined by the king's Council. In April 1534 he was committed to the Tower with John Fisher. The following May he was again examined by the Council. In July 1535 he was tried for treason, found guilty, and executed.

**Doctor Richard Smith** (1500–63), an active defender of the Mass who wrote several defenses of the Eucharist. Smith held a Regius Professorship of Divinity at Oxford from 1536. He publicly recanted at Paul's Cross on 15 May 1547 and declared that the pope's authority had been justly abolished in England. He repeated this statement at Oxford in July, but added that he had not earlier recanted, but only retracted. He was, therefore, deprived of his Oxford position and his revocation, *A Godly And Faythfull Retractation made and published at Paules crosse in London, the yeare of oure Lorde God 1547*, was published in order to reach a larger audience. Smith was imprisoned early in 1549 and then released on finding security for good behavior. He fled to Louvain where he was afterwards appointed Professor of Divinity. He continued to publish abroad until Mary I's accession, when he was restored to his position at Oxford. He later lost all preferments under Elizabeth I and again sought shelter in France.

**Rowland Taylor** (d.1555), Protestant martyr. He was born at Rothbury, educated at Cambridge with his friend William Turner, and ordained acolyte in 1528 at Norwich. Influenced by Latimer's preaching, Taylor became a reformer. He was Cranmer's domestic chaplain before 1540 and in that year he was a member of Convocation. In 1543 he was one of two commissioners appointed to inquire into the charges brought against Cranmer by the prebendaries of Canterbury, and in 1544 the Archbishop presented him to the living of Hadleigh. Along with two other reformers, Dr Tonge and John Cardmaker, he gave the Spital sermon on Whitsun in 1548. In 1551 he was appointed secretary to Bishop Ridley of London and made Archdeacon of Exeter in 1552. Six days after Mary I's accession (1553) he was arrested, though it appears that he was later released and allowed to resume his ministry at Hadleigh. However, he was again arrested for opposing the celebration of the Mass. Imprisoned in London in March 1554, he was examined on various occasions by Gardiner and eventually condemned to death, excommunicated, and degraded (by Bonner). He was burned as a heretic in February 1555 on Aldham Common, near Hadleigh.

# Appendix

**William Turner** (c. 1520–68), writer and botanist. He was born at Morpeth and educated at Pembroke College, Cambridge. There he heard Latimer preach, was converted to his ideas, and joined a group of young reformers. His writing at this time was divided between religious and scientific works. He was ordained deacon at Lincoln on 15 April 1536 and received a license to preach in the following year. About this time he was brought before Gardiner, who vilified him as a heretic. So began a long and bitter hostility between the two; Gardiner eventually had Turner's religious books banned as heretical on 8 July 1546. Turner spoke out against clerical celibacy and had married by 1540. That same year he left Cambridge and traveled extensively in Holland and Germany before studying medicine in Bologna and Ferrara. From Italy he went to Zurich, where he met the famous naturalist, Conrad Gesner. He traveled to Basel in 1543 and to Cologne the following year. He collected plant specimens in the Rhineland and composed the first part of *A new Herball, wherin are conteyned the names of Herbes in Greke, Latin, Englysh, Duch Frenche, and in the Potecaries and Herbaries Latin, with the properties degrees and naturall places of the same*. His famous *Herbal* was published (1551) after he returned to England. While he was abroad he was appointed clerk of Prince Edward's chamber at Westminster. On the accession of Edward VI he was summoned back to England and became chaplain and physician to the Duke of Somerset. That same year he won a seat (Ludgershall) in the House of Commons. He received a prebend in York Minster in February 1550, although he was not ordained. Turner continued his botanical studies, kept his own garden at Kew, and in 1551 was appointed Dean of Wells, with a license for non-residence so that he could preach. In December 1552 he was ordained priest by Bishop Ridley. On Mary I's accession he was deprived of his deanery and left England with John á Lasco (Jan Laski), the Polish reformer, spending most of the years of Mary I's reign in various German states. His books were again condemned as heretical in 1555. He returned to England on Elizabeth I's accession, preached at Paul's Cross on 10 September 1559, and was restored Dean of Wells by royal order on 18 June 1560.

# GLOSSARY

This selective glossary explains the words whose form within the works may cause difficulties of recognition, or whose meaning departs from that of modern English. When more than one spelling of a word appears the variants are arranged in alphabetical order. When the same word bears more than one meaning the meanings are listed alphabetically according to the part of speech and alphabetically by definition if the part of speech is the same. Generally all entries from the texts are noted. However, when a word occurs in a particular text four or more times the first example only is given; "etc." is used after the first entry to indicate multiple examples. Within the alphabetical listing each entry is arranged chronologically according to the text in which it occurs and the number of the text is specifically cited, followed by the line number (in the case of the verse satires) or the page signature (in the case of the prose work). The chronology of the texts corresponds exactly with that in the other sections of the edition. Texts are numbered accordingly and listed below. The titles of Shepherd's works have been abbreviated in the Glossary. The following abbreviations are used:

| | |
|---|---|
| *adj* adjective | *p part* past participle |
| *adv* adverb | *phr* phrase |
| *conj* conjunction | *prep* preposition |
| *def art* definite article | *pres part* present participle |
| *fig* figurative | *pro* pronoun |
| *ger* gerund | *sb* substantive |
| *inter* interjection | *v* verb |
| *n* noun | *vbl sb* verbal substantive |

# GLOSSARY

## The Text Key

a slepe *adv* asleep IV 81

a wrye *adj* askew, awry III 635

abel *adj* able III 447

abiecte *p part* cast out, rejected III 228

abhominacion, abomynacions *n* abomination(s) I 380; VI 138

abrode *adv* abroad VIII 346; widely apart IX Av$^v$, Avii

adbettour *n* abetter, instigator VI 223

adiourned *v* adjourned III 391

adred *adj* afraid, frightened I 287; III 491

aduenturinge *pres part* risking II 250

afeard, affraed, afray(e)de *adj* afraid II 2, 241; III 455; VI 120; VII 295; VIII 199

agayne *adv* again I 195 etc.; II 130; 172, 229; III 472, 574; IV 135, 164; VII 200; VIII 250, 367; IX Av$^v$, Avi$^v$

agone *adv* ago VII 14

aide, ayde(r) *n* aid(er), help(er) III 452; VI 119, 223; VII 228, 293; IX Aviii

ake *v* ache IV prefatory verse

al *adj* all, every I prefatory verse etc.; II 100 etc.; III 424 etc.; IV 157; VI 137 etc.; VII 33 etc.; IX Aiii etc.

a lack(e), alacke (a lack) *inter* alack, exclamation of regret I 26; II 280, 350; III 205, 377; VII 183 alewiues, alewyfes *n* alewives, publicans VIII 103, 107

althinges *pro* everything VI 82

alway(e) (s), alwaies *adv* always I 373; VI 110; VII 10, 239; IX Av

alyue *adj* alive III 409

ambre *n* amber VIII 377

amisse, a mysse, amys(se) *adj* amiss, out of order I 146, 220, 237; II 200

an *conj* and IV 7

ancre *n* anchor VII 243

and *conj* if IV 10

anhelation *n* panting IX Aiiii$^v$

anon(e) (a none) *adv* at once, forthwith III 764; VII 16; VIII 344

apeare, apere(th), appayre, appeare, appere(th) *v* appear(s) I 319; II 338; III 36, 415; VI 91, 230; VII 169, 419

appayer *v* apay, please, satisfy VII 70

applie *v* administer a remedy II 54; III 110, 462

appoticaries *n* apothecaries IX Aiii

ar *v* are III 551

arabies *n* Arabians III 75

arantly *adv* abominably IV 81

ascused *p part* excused IV 24

aslake *v* abate, mitigate III 360

assayle, assayll *v* assail, attack III 345; VII 298

auaunce *v* advance II 298

auncient, auncyent *adj* ancient I 133; II 31

auow *v* declare, affirm IV 97; VII 145

auter *n* altar IV 90

axe *v* ask VI 187

ayre *n* air II 337


bables *n* childish, foolish things II 296; VIII 20

barcke *v* cry out aggressively, angrily I 122

bare *v* bear III 322

bassing *ger* kissing III 681

battaile *n* battle III 344

beades *n* originally prayers, now small beads for counting prayers said; a rosary I 369; III 782; VII 390; VIII 374, 376, 381

becone *n* beacon I 34

beddle *n* beadle, overseer VIII 425

befalde *p part* fallen IV 67

beforne *adv* before VII 75

beheste *n* promise III 396

behoue *n* sake I 155

behoue(th) *v* benefit(s) II 102; IX Aiiiᵛ

bel, belles *n* bell(s) I 79, 342; III 419, 782

beleue *v* believe I 236; II 20, 276; IV 75, 131; VI 79 etc.; VII 99, 184; VIII 168; IX Aiiᵛ, Aiiiᵛ, Aviiiᵛ

ben(e) *p part* been I 75 etc.; II 235, 262; III 119, 206; IV 100; VI prefatory verse (ii), 94, 112; VII 175, 264, 269; VIII 370; IX Avii

beneditions (benediccions) *n* benediction IX Aviii

beniuolent *adj* benevolent III 18

benumme *p part* benumbed IV 124

bere *v* bear I 139; VI 110

bestowe *v* store up, stow away IX Avᵛ

besy, bisy *adj* busy II 219; IX Avii, Aviii

betid(e) *p part* befallen, happened to III 29; *v* befall III 583; IX Avii

beyng *pres part* being VII 74; IX Aviᵛ

bi *prep* by II 33; IX Aviiᵛ

bicause *adv* because III 356

bleache *n* disease of the skin II 153

blew *adj* blue VII 270

blisse, blysse(d) *adj* blessed I 58; *v* bless I 51; III 724; gladden VII 364

blooddes, bloods, bloudes *n* (young) men of spirit II 249; VII 79, 278

blot *n* moral stain II 312

blout *adj* unpolished, without refinement IX Aviii

blurre *n* moral stain II 312

blyn *v* leave off, stop I 392

blyndefylde *adj* blindfold I 285

bodyly *adv* bodily I 167

boeth *adj* both II 359; III 678; IV 45, 111; *pro* both VI 191

boke(s) *n* book(s) I 64 etc.; II 197; III 419; VII 11 etc.; VIII 126; IX Aiiii

bolke *v* heave, throb III 327

bon *adj* good IV title etc.; *n* bone III 625

boost *v* boast VIII 393

border *n* district IV 141; VIII 87

boste *ger* boasting III 38

bourned *p part* burned III 393

bouse *v* drink, booze VIII 99

bragge *adj* boastful, bold I 254; *v* boast I 77; VIII 393

brake *v* break III 432

brast *v* burst III 254

brat *n* cloak III 197

breade, bred(eth) *v* breed I 185; IX Aiiᵛ, Aviᵛ

brent(e) *p part* burned I 193, 204

brode *n* brood III 125

brouse *n* fodder VIII 100

builde, buylde(d) *v* build, built VI 93, 221; VII 48

bukler *n* protection, shield I prefatory verse

buriyng *pres part* burying IX Avii<sup>v</sup>

by and by *phr* directly IV 115; VIII 298

byb *v* drink, booze VIII 99

byggely *adv* bigly, with force VII 383

byles *n* boils II 154

bynde *v* bind III 190; VI 81; VII 474


cache *v* catch I 331

cal *v* call II 144, 146; III 135; VI 194, 216

calde *p part* called IV 66

capitall *n* chief, head III 23

carall *n* carol VIII 267

carkas *n* carcass III 198

carke *n* anxious solicitude III 659

celebracion *n* celebration I 161

certes *adv* certainly VII 182, 474

chafid *adj* chafed II 157

chambre *n* chamber, room VIII 378

charge *n* authority to impose spiritual injunction or penance VIII 86

chast, chastenes *adj* chaste VII 75; *n* VII 97

chaunce(d), chaunsed *n* chance VIII 307; *v* chance(d) II 342, 365; IV 53; VI 107; VIII 263; IX Avii

chauntyng *n* chanting, singing II 219

chau[n]geable *adj* changeable VII 421

cheare, chere *n* disposition, mood III 231, 721; VII 421

chearynge *n* entertainment IV 79

checkes *n* cheeks III 631

cheres *n* cherries IX Aiii

cherly *adv* carefully IV 165

chuse *v* choose II 332

citrones *n* fruits of the citron tree IX Aiii

clap *n* mishap III 2

clar(c)k(e)ly *adv* clerkly I 320; VII 413

clarke(s) *n* cleric(s) I 120 etc.; VII 34; VIII 333; IX Aiiii<sup>v</sup>

claymith *v* claims VIII 146

cle(a)ne *adj* clean II 44, 261, 312; VI 76; VIII 361; IX Aiii<sup>v</sup>; *adv* absolutely, wholly I 104, 215; II 207; III 252; VII 19, 153; *v* (make) clean II 4; VII 214; IX Avii

cleargy *n* clergy VII 214

cleauyng *pres part* cleaving IX Av

clere, clerly *adj* clear II 170; III 229; *adv* clearly VII 29

clodde *n* blockhead, clodhopper VI 132

cloute, clowte *v* clout, hit VII 376, 413

coles *n* coals IX Avi

coller *n* collar VII 89

comber *v* harass, trouble VIII 255

comly *adj* pleasing III 750, 762

compasse *n* (within) limits VI 182

compesse *v* compesce, restrain VII 29

condensate *adj* condensate, condensed VII 258

condicion(s) *n* condition(s) II 41; VIII 60, 296

confuse *adj* confused VI 97; VII 235

conning(e), connyng, cunnynge *adj* cunning III 270; *n* III 307; VI 102; VII 41, 251; IX Aii, Aiiii, Av

consciens *n* conscience II 270

consecracion, consecratyng, consecratyon *n* consecration I 160; VII 427; *vbl sb* IX Aiiii<sup>v</sup>

contendyng *adj* struggling VII 258

contrie, contrye, countrey *n* country I 246; II 336, 341

contreiths *n* of a/the country's III 288

conueied *v* conveyed VI 87

conuent *n* company III 731

cooste *n* coast III 41

cootis of maile *n* armor III 343

cornes *n* corn crops II 184

corrage *n* courage VII 460

costome *n* custom VI 94

couetest *v* covets VIII 289

coulde *adj* cold IX Aiiii

cowche *v* couch, lay stones etc. in a wall or a building VII 468

cowcher *n* coucher, one who lays stones etc. VI 88

cowlde *v* could VII 38

coyle *v* beat, coil, thrash VII 376

cra(c)ke *v* boast I 28; VIII 228; make a harsh grating sound I 329

crafty *adj* clever IV 153; VI 203

creame *n* consecrated annointing oil, chrism VII 372

crede *n* the Creed, recited during the Mass I 163; IV 30

croke *n* crook, rogue II 199

cruse *n* drunkard VIII 68

cum(e) *v* come III 69 etc.; IV 165; IX Avi

cumbre *v* destroy, overthrow VII 376

cure *n* care of souls or spiritual charge of parishioners VIII 428
curstly *adv* with curses I 268; VIII 255

damasene prunes *n* Damson plums IX Aiii
darcke *adj* devoid of spiritual light I 123
dath *n* death VI 154
decline *v* incline, lean VIII 32
dede *n* act, deed I 162; III 131
dedecorate *adj* dedecorate, disgraced VII 256
deiect *adj* dejected, downcast VII 460
denaye *v* deny VI 101
denomynacyons *n* denominations VII 85
depnes *n* deepness, depth III 313
depraue *v* deprave, desecrate I 69
depute *n* deputy II 16
derkenes, derknes *n* darkness III 792; VIII 50
despect *v* despise III 224
desyre *n* desire III 313
detter *n* debtor III 573
dettes *n* debts V 27; VI 27, 60, 188
deuast (devast) *v* devastate III 658
deuel(l), deuyll *n* devil IV 108; V 17; VI 17, 46; VIII 14, 55
deuelishnes *n* devilishness III 803
deuise *n* device VI 116; *v* devise IX Aiiii$^v$
deuout *adj* devout, pious II 9; IX Aviii
diuyne *adj* divine I 150
diete *n* way of living, thinking III 432
dyfferyng *adj* different, differing I 102
dight *v* appoint, order III 63
dinumeracion *n* dinumeration, numbering out one by one III 529
dirisions *n* derisions VIII 55
disired *v* desired III 476
dispayre *sb* spoilation IX Aii$^v$
dispight, dispyte *n* malice III 67; VIII 352
dockes *n* rump II 161
doeth, doth, dothe *v* do(es) I 312; II 318, 328; III 36 etc.; V 18, 21; VI 18 etc.; VII 10
    etc.; VIII 76 etc.
domes daye *n* doomsday VI 189
dought *n* doubt VI 199
do(u)ne *adv* down III 656, 657; IV 162; VII 2
dowbtles *adj* doubtless V 8

# GLOSSARY

dowe bake *adj* half-baked I 56
dreede *n* dread III 130
driue, dryue *v* pass I 95; III 407
duely *adv* duly, properly I 353
dum *adj* dumb, meaningless VIII 39
durst(e) *v* dare(d) I 61 etc.; II 105, 111, 121
durty *adj* dirty VIII 391
dyd *v* did I 132 etc.; IV 27, 121, 137; V 3 etc.; VI 3 etc.; VII 40 etc.; VIII 190; IX Aii
dye(d) *v* die(d) I 155; II 342; III 377, 654
dyffuse *adj* confused, diffused VII 234
dyke *n* ditch I 375
dyng *v* reprove, taunt VII 366
dyuerse *adj* diverse I 352

ech(e) *adj* each II 358; III 543, 545, 573; VII 224; IX Avi
edg *n* edge IX Avii^v
eiecte *v* eject IX Avi^v
eke *adv* also VI 156
elde *adj* old IV 25, 113
eles, ell(e)s, els *adv* else I 6 etc.; II 20, 115, 331; III 467 etc.; VII 212; VIII 122, 186, 253; IX Aiiii^v, Avii^v
eluyshe *adj* weird, supernatural IV 105
encreace, encrese *v* increase II 137; III 374
endecent *adj* indecent VII 256
endes *n* deaths III 798
endeuer, endeuouryng *n* endeavor III 449; *pres part* endeavoring VII 415
endight, endyght *v* indict, indite I 171; VIII 351
endue *v* endow III 620
endurate *adj* obstinate VIII 8
endynge *n* death VI 71, 198
engyne *n* engine, genius VII 160
enhaunce *v* exalt, elevate spiritually II 299; VIII 34
enimyes, enymye *n* enemies, enemy II 65; III 379
ensure *v* assure II 45
(th)entent *n* intent II 278, 285; IX Aiiii
entrate, intreate *v* entreat III 542, 769; VII 387
epilence *n* epilepsy II 177
euangelie, euangelium, euangely *n* the Gospels I 14; II 129; VI 141
euel(s), euil(l), euyl(l) *n* evil I 84; II 41; III 132; IV 99; VI 92, 232; VIII 13; IX Avi, Avi^v
euen by and by *phr* instantaneously IV 115
euen, eueninge(s) *n* eve, evening(s) I 346; II 187; IV 8; VI 165

177

euen, euyn *adj* even, divisible by two, not odd IX Avi; *adv* indeed III 242, 288, 358; IV
    40 etc.; VI 111; VII 201; IX Aiiii^v
euer *adv* ever I 244, 367; II 7 etc.; III 258, 450; IV 28 etc.; IX Aviii^v
euerie, euery *adj* every I 91, 306; II 175; III 125 etc.; IV 98, 141; VIII 239; IX Avii
euydently *adv* evidently VII 189
exceadynge, exceding *adj* exceeding VII 60; VIII 169
execration *n* abomination VI 139
exemple *n* example, illustration II 323
exinanicion (exinanition) *n* abasement, humiliation IX Aiiii
exposicion(s) *n* exposition(s) II 42, 115
exprobracyons *n* exprobations, reproaches VII 83


facion(s), faction, fasshyons, fassion, fation *n* behaviour(s), fashion(s), mode(s) of action
    I 198, 379; III 203, 317, 528; IV 21; VII 87; VIII 38; IX Aii, Aii^v, Aiii^v
factes *n* actions, deeds II 32
falshed *n* falsehood V 26; VI 26
fare *adj* far III 376; VI 65
faye(th), fayth *n* faith IV 15, 63, 100; VII 283; IX Aii^v
fayer, fayre *adj* fair I 258; II 180, 336; III 33, 87; IV 157; VII 69; VIII 376; IX Av, Av^v
fayne *adv* gladly I 345; II 63; VII 388; VIII 163, 341
fayne(d) (eth) *adj* feign(ed), pretend(ed) IV 11; VII 30
faynt *v* faint IV 376
feacte *adj* feat, proper VII 380, 384
feased *v* feezed, frightened off, put to flight VII 283
featly *adv* fitly, properly IX Aiiii^v
feche *v* fetch I 334
feele *v* feel VII 277
fele *v* believe IV 119
fell on *v* commenced, fell to VIII 272
fel(l)ow(e) (s) *n* fellows I 3 etc.; III 799; IV 25, 33, 113; VI 187; VIII 58, 228
fendes *n* devils, fiends III 797
fenestre *n* lattice, window VIII 132
fet(e), fett *v* fetch(ed) II 191; III 376, 560; VII 105
fete *n* feet III 778
feuer *n* fever II 177; III 92
fible fables *n* nonsense II 297
fistis, fystes *n* fists III 179; VII 301
flayle *n* flail VII 299
fleshely *adj* fleshly, not spiritual VI 177
fleshelynes *n* fleshiness VI 174
flookes (flukes) *n* flat fish, flounders VII 213
fole(s), foole(s) *n* fool(s) IV prefatory verse, 131, 148; VI 109; VII 203; VIII 368

folish(e) *adj* foolish IV 34; VI 67; VIII 37

foly *n* folly VI 187; IX Aii<sup>v</sup>

fooes *n* enemies VI 210

forbod(e) *adj* forbidden V 2; VI 2, 33; *v* forbid IV 21

fordone *p part* abolished, discontinued IV 72

fote *n* foot IX Avii<sup>v</sup>

fote men *n* footmen III 749

fourth to fare *phr* go on IV 135

foyle *n* dung, manure VII 373

freate *v* fret VII 394

frendes, frynde *n* friend(s) III 353, 799; VIII 285

frendfully *adv* like friends II 67

frenticke *adj* frantic III 610

fretteth *v* consume, devour VIII 94

fridge (frig) *v* move restlessly VII 394

fro *prep* from III 795; VI 121

frothe *v* froth VII 394

frowarde *adj* bad, perverse III 182

fume *n* a fit of anger I 229

furth *adv* forth IV 161

fyersly *adv* fiercely VII 414

fyre *n* fire I 34, 193, 258; III 312


galaunt *adj* fine, grand, splendid II 75

gall *n* bile VIII 94

gaped *v* desirous of, eager for VII 370

gaue *v* gave III 363, 793; VI 39, 160, 173; VII 163

gaulde *adj* galled, rubbed raw II 162

gear(e), geere *n* new, reformist ideas or ways I 137; III 605; IV 20; VII 108

geate, gete *n* black lignite, jet VII 390; VIII 377

gemman *n* gentleman IV 77; VIII 195, 197

gentil(l), gentyll, ientill *adj* noble III 78, 243, 290; VIII 151

gesse *v* guess II 259

gest *n* guest VIII 122

gete *v* get, receive III 375

geue, geuyst, gyue *v* give(s) III 139 etc.; V 8; VI 8, 76; VII 1, 185; VIII 119, 167, 247

geuen, gyuen *p part* given III 59; VI 163

geyst *v* jest VII 208

goddes *n* goddess III 133; VII 232; God's V 18; VI 18, 130; gods III 109, 168, 248; IX Aiii<sup>v</sup> etc.

godhed *n* Godhead IV 41

gon *v* gone III 623

goo(e) *v* go II 345; IV 85, 165; VII 128

gorge *n* violent resentment VIII 281

gose, goth *v* goes IV 92; VIII 214, 240

gost *n* ghost, spirit III 37; IX Aviii[v]

gots *n* goats III 123

gouernaunce *n* governance III 7

gramercy *n* thanks VI 201

grauell *n* gravel VII 287

grauer *n* engraver VI 219

graunt(e) *v* grant II 281; III 192; IV 45; VI 183

grayne *n* grain III 133

grene *adj* green VII 155; IX Avi

greue(th) *v* grieves I 22, 26; II 353; IX Aii[v]

grieffe *n* grief VI 126

grosly *adv* literally, unlearnedly VI 175

grossers *n* grocers IX Aiii


ha *pro* he IV 47, 126; *v* have IV 117, 121

hafter *n* dodger, wrangler VIII 219

halasse *inter* alas III 414

handell *v* handle, deal with I 65

hangle *n* hinge VII 212

hanous *adj* heinous IX Aiiii[v]

hap(pe) *n* chance, lot I 256, 259; III 1

harde, herd(e) *v* heard II 1, 107, 113; IV 55; VIII 161, 274

hart(e) (s), hert(e) *n* heart(s) II 353; III 326 etc.; IV 6, 112; VI 80, 110; VII 274; VIII 271; IX Aii[v]

haue *v* have I 94 etc.; II 41 etc.; III 19 etc.; IV 4 etc.; VI prefatory verse (ii) etc.; VII 6 etc.; VIII 29 etc.; IX Aii etc.

haue *v* heave IV 164

hayle *adj* hale VII 297; *n* hail VII 246

healp(e) (th) *n* aid, help IX Aviii; *v* aid(s), help(s) IX Aiiii[v], Avii[v]

heare *adv* here III 720; *n* hair III 607

hede *n* heed I 23, 248, 260; IX Avi[v], Avii, Avii[v]

here(s), herest, hereth *v* hear(s) I 197, 266, 272; II 225, 237; III 31; IV 52,72, 149

hereticke, heretike(s), heretyke, heritike, heritique *n* heretic(s) II 70; III 524, 612; IV 66; VI 73, 120; VIII 188, 242, 276

hereynge *ger* hearing IV 78

herken *v* harken, hearken I 293

het *adj* hot VIII 370

heuy *n* hay VIII 100
hie *v* hasten III 597
hir *adv* here II 46; *pro* her II 47 etc.; III 59 etc.
hogges *n* castrated swine, hogs II 166
hole *adj* complete, whole III 289, 595; V 121, 223; VIII 114; IX Avi<sup>v</sup>
holi, holyest *adj* holy, holiest II 27; IV 101
holines, holynes *n* holiness I 107; IV 109
holowe *adv* completely II 59
holpe *n* help, succour II 192
hore *n* defilement, foulness IX Aiiii
horson *adj* whoreson, scurvy IV 162
hower, howre *n* hour II 316; VI 225; VII 224
hoyste *v* hoist I 37
hubble shubble *n* commotion VIII 178
hyd *p part* hidden VII 41
hyer *n* hire I 259
hygh(e) (ly) *adj* high VII 134, 177, 225; *adv* highly VII 193
hyght *p part* called VI 222
hym *pro* them I 281
hynderaunce *n* hinderance VIII 306

iaper *n* professional jester I 41
iauel(les) *n* low fellow(s), rascal(s) I 83; III 760
idell, ydle *adj* idle I 93; VIII 133
ielous *adj* jealous IX Aiiii<sup>v</sup>
iest *v* jest I 200; II 89
iet *v* brag, boast VIII 372
illudente *adj* illudent, mocking VII 233
imbute *v* soak, steep VII 62
in hand(e) *phr* to take in hand, to take charge of I 2; in the company or presence of
    someone II 107
incongrue *adj* incongrue, incongruous VII 235
indede (in dede) *adv* indeed I 42 etc.; III 131, 402; IV 29; VII 168; VIII 173
infection *n* communication of harmful opinions or beliefs II 302
inoughe *adv* enough IV 160; IX Aiiii
inquysicion *n* inquisition II 40
insensate *adj* lacking sense VII 257
in stead(e) *adv* instead V 26; VI 26; III 60
insultacions *n* insults VII 84
inter *v* enter VI 125
interpryse *n* enterprise VII 39

# GLOSSARY

intitled *adj* entitled I 321

intituled *v* entitled VI 192

inuented, inuentyng *pres p* inventing VII 239; *v* invented VI 140

iolest (most jolly) *adj* finely dressed, splendid IV 77

iournay *n* journey III 259, 738

isesicles, isickelles, isicles *n* icicles V 19; VI 19, 48

iudge(s) *n* judges VII 100; *v* judge VI 113; IX Aviii, Aviii<sup>v</sup>

iudg(e)ment(e) *n* judgement III 422; VI 178; VIII 202

iuell(es), iwelle *n* jewel(s) II 78; III 666, 783

iuggling *ger* deception, trickery IV 153

iust *adj* just VI 115


kepe(est) (eth) *n* heed, notice IV 80; *v* keep(s) I 366; II 124, 159, 184; III 737; VI 61, 182; VII 75; VIII 60, 88, 117; IX Aiii etc.

kepe (kipe) *v* catch fish with a kipe (osier basket) VII 211

keping *ger* keeping, preservation III 677; VIII 428

ketching *pres part* catching VIII 182

knacke *n* trick II 202; IV 60

knackys *n* trinkets II 84

knaue *n* rascal I 91; VIII 177

kne *n* knee III 148

kowe *n* cow II 156

kyrke *n* church I prefatory verse, 228


labefactiue *adj* impaired, ruined III 408

lad *p part* led III 214

lade *n* load VIII 19; *p part* laden IV prefatory verse

lamentacion *n* lamentation III 319

lapte *v* bound, wrapped VII 137

latine, latten, latyn(e) *adj* Latin I 341; IV 147; VI prefatory verse; VII 103, 137, subtitle (following l.302)

lauacre (lavacre) *n* font VII 227

leache, lechis *n* physician II 152; VIII 46

leades *n* roof (i.e., strips of lead used to cover a roof) IX Av<sup>v</sup>

leasing *n* falsehood, lying VIII 273

leasure *n* convenience, leisure III 31

lerned *v* learned III 267

lese *v* lose VIII 122

let *n* hindrance II 259; III 378

letters missiue *n* a missive, especially from an authority III 406

leue *v* leave III 86; IV 154

leuel *n* level VI 90

leuer *adv* rather IV 48

lewde, lewdly *adj* unlearned, vulgar I 76; *adv* roughly, vulgarly III 207

ley(e) *v* lay I 289; IV prefatory verse; IX Av^v, Avi

lieth, lye(st) (th), lyueth *n* lie VI 225; *v* lie(s) II 64; IV 27; VIII 209; lie(s) (down etc.) I 261, 375; III 286, 410; IV 140; IX Avii^v

lifte *n* crisis, emergency III 246

lightly, lyght(ly) *adv* easily, lightly III 462; IV 131; IX Aii, Aiii^v

lippes, lyppes *n* lips III 629; VII 13

listis, lystes *v* choose(es), please(s), want(s) III 178; VII 302

lit(t)el, littyll, lytyll *adj* little II 50; IV 62; VI 107; IX Avi, Aviii

liyng *pres part* lying VIII 338

loke for *v* look for IX Aii

lokes *n* appearance, looks II 100; VII 209; *v* look(s), see(s) I 119 etc.; II 198, 203, 329; III 305; IV prefatory verse; VII 98; *fig* IX Avii

loke(ing) to *v* look(ing) after IX Aii, Av

longes *n* lungs IX Av

loselles *n* scoundrels I 76

loue *n* love I 154; II 103; III 188; V 17; VI 17, 46; VII 95

loue(d) (th), louyth *v* love(d) (s) I 92, 137; II 313, 315; III 39, 499; IV 20; VIII 90, 206

loulars *n* lollars, heretics I 124

louse *n* louse VIII 96; *v* loose III 646

loute, lowt *n* lout II 205; VII 408

lowde, lowdly *adj* loud II 174; *adv* loudly II 195

lowre *v* abase, humble III 15

lowt *v* lower III 15

lubber *n* lazy, sturdy fellow VII 408

lyke *adv* likely II 273; III 590; *v* lick II 291

lykenes *n* likeness III 48

lykewyse *adv* likewise VII 516

lyue(s) *n* life, lives I 84; IV 77; VII 78; *v* live III 186, 369


maintaine, mayntayne, maynteyn *v* maintain I 133; VI 98, 128; VIII 422

maist *v* may III 725

maister *n* lord, master I 311; II 129; VI 20

mar, marde, marre(th) *v* damage morally, lead astray IV 133; mar(s), marred I 215, 245; II 331; VII 300; VIII 268

marryed *adj* married VII 113, 263

marters *n* martyrs II 27

maruaill, maruail(l)e(s), maruel(l) *adj* marvellous III 281; *n* marvel(s) III 26; IV prefatory verse, 132; VI 218; *v* IX Aii^v

mary *n* Mary (mother of God) IV 137; *phr* by Mary! IV 6, 96

masse, masses, mes(se), messinge(s) *n* celebration of the Eucharist, the Mass (Masses) I
58, 92, 263; II title etc.; III title etc.; IV 47 etc.; VI 181; VIII 195 etc.; IX Aiiii^v

mastres, mestres *n* mistress II 252, 347

matche *n* consort, husband VII 381

matins, mattens *n* matins, one of the canonical hours of the breviary: properly a midnight
office, occasionally recited at daybreak I 345; IV 78, 147; VIII 379

maungye *adj* mangy, scabby II 167

mayne *adv* very well VII 26; *n* strength III 62

mayntainynge *pres p* maintaining I 354

meate(s) *n* food, nourishment III 397; V 11; VI 11, 42; VII 391

medes *n* meadows VIII 373

meede *n* meed, reward III 404

meke *adj* meek VI 49

mell *v* associate, mingle, mix III 280

melles *v* occupy (themselves) I 5

mencion *n* mention, reference II 19

menne(s) *n* men( 's) I 85, 88

ment(est) *v* meant II 282; IV 57, 63

meselde *adj* diseased, leprous II 166

mikle, myckle, mycle *adj* much III 392; VII 55; VIII 86, 106

ministracion *n* ministration III 149

ministre(d) *n* minister VIII 133; *v* ministered VIII 278; IX Avi^v

mintes *n* garden mint IX Avi

mischefe, myscheffe *n* mischief III 28, 362

mo *adj* more I 111; II 346; VIII 113; most III 531

mone *n* moan III 159; moon III 640; *v* moan I 356; II 351; III 310, 349

moneth *n* month VIII 237

morne(s) *n* mornings II 187; *v* mourne III 310

moue *v* move III 193; VI 106; VIII 257

munkay *n* monkey IX Aii^v, Avii

myer *n* mire I 259

myghti(e), myghty(e) *adj* mighty III 6, 391; VII 8, 173

myl *n* mill VI 182

myn(e) *pro* mine III 17, 159, 547; IV 118; my III 32, 473, 790

mys(se) (t) *v* miss I 238; II 39; III 74, 211; VI 214


na *adv* now IV 15

nacion, nacyons *n* nation(s) I 199; III 530; VII 86; VIII 37

natiue *adj* native II 341

ne(a)de(s) (th), nede(s) (th) *n* need I 24; II 68; III 129; IX Aiiii^v; *v* need(s) I 44, 73; II
114 etc.; III 575; V 23; VI 23, 109, 220; IX Aviii

nere *adv* near III 230, 664; never II 259; IV 120

# GLOSSARY

net *adj* neat IX Aiii<sup>v</sup>

net *adj* neat IX Aiii$^v$

nettes *n* nets I 330; VI 28, 61

neybor *n* neighbour IV 19

noddy *n* fool VI 78, 204

nomber, nombre *n* number I 4; VIII 254

nother *adj* neither IV 43, 51; IX Aiii$^v$

noyse *n* noise II 265


obeysaunce *n* submission III 10

obfuscate *adj* obfuscate, obscure VII 236

oblacion *n* oblation, sacrifice III 150

obloquie *adj* abuse, slander IX Aiii$^v$

obturate *adj* impervious, obturate VII 259

obtused *adj* obtuse, dull VII 259

obumbylate *adj* obumbilate, unknown VII 260

of *adv* off IV 165; V 226

omyt *v* omit VI 102

one *prep* on III 581

onely *adj* only VI 134; VII 109, 162; IX Aii

on hie *phr* on high III 109

ons *adv* once VIII 70

or *adv* before, ere II 269, 291; IV 71; VII 444; VIII 4

order *n* prescribed by ecclesiastical authority IV 140; VI 97; IX Aiii$^v$, Avii$^v$

ordinaunce *n* authority III 8; VIII 33

othe *n* oath IV 47

ouer cast *adj* overthrown I 387

ouer *prep* over III 24; IX Aiii$^v$, Avi

ouerhipt *p part* omitted III 271

ouersene *adj* deceived, mistaken III 207; VI 86; impetuous IV 62

ouersight *n* oversight IX Aii$^v$

ouerthrowe *p part* overthrown VI 99


pacience *n* patience IV 50; VIII 256

panyers *n* panniers II 164

papall *adj* papal III 332

papasye *n* papacy III 335

papistrie, papistry *n* papistry, (hostile term for) Roman Catholic religion I 10; VIII 206

paraduenture, peraduentre (paradventure) *adv* perhaps VI 104; IX Avi$^v$

parishons *n* parishioners VIII 295

parrel *n* peril VII 465

partakers *n* partakers VI 152; supporters I 396

parte *n* ability VII 272

parysh *n* parish VIII 85, 232

passeth *v* surpasses II 169; VII 138

paye the skore *v* avenge an injury I 294

payer, payre *n* pair VIII 375; IX Aiiii^v

payn(e) (s), peyne *n* pain(s) I 224, 362; II 228, 350; III 136 etc.; VII 463; IX Aii

peare, peere *n* equal, peer II 11; VIII 18

peason *n* peas IV 49

pens, peny *n* pence, penny VIII 104, 143, 146

perceiue, perceyue *v* perceive III 215; IV 20, 153; VI 2, 193

perchaunce *adv* perchance IV 121

perfyt *adj* perfect III 82

perkynge *v* assuming a lively, self-conceited attitude I 344

perliament *n* parliament III 20

perlowes *adj* dangerous VIII 46

perseuer *v* persevere III 448

perswade *v* persuade VIII 22, 295

pesilence *n* pestilence II 176

peuish *adj* peevish VI 130

phisi(c)ke *n* medicine, physic III 77, 280, 592

phisicians, phisicions *n* physicians III 421, 563

phisnomyes *n* physiognomy III 77

pige *n* pig III 124

piuish *adj* peevish VIII 10

plage *n* plague II 176

plaine, playne *adj* plain I 72 etc.; III 751; IV 23, 52; V 4; VI 4, 35, 68; *adv* III 415, 435; VI 158; VII 25

plannetes *n* planets III 641

poetycale *adj* poetical VII 141

pokkes, pox *n* the pox, syphilis II 160; IX Av

pore *n* power VI 56

portaise(s), portas *n* portable breviary; a book containing the Divine Office (psalms, collects, and readings from the Scriptures and the lives of the saints) for each day, which those in orders are bound to recite I 102, 104; VIII 380

post *prep* behind III 348

pot, pottes *n* vessel(s) for holding ale II 315; VIII 74 etc.

pouder *n* powder IX Av^v, Avi, Avi^v

powre *n* power III 651

poynte *n* point IV 98

prate *v* talk in a long-winded way I 70; II 194; VIII 190

preased *v* pressed VII 282

preistes, prest(es), preyste, priestes, pristes *n* priest(s) I 280, 372; II 186, 320; V 22; VI 22; VII 113 etc.; VIII 291

prelacie *n* prelacy, collective body of bishops or prelates I 8

prelat(t)es *n* high ranking ecclesiastics I 39; V 20; VI 20, 49

presoner *n* prisoner I 183

prest *adj* prepared VIII 123

preuaile *v* prevail III 342

pricke *v* pain III 608

primar *n* primer, a prayer book for the use of the laity VIII 380

pristine *adj* former, original III 431

profe *n* proof VII 168

profyte *n* profit II 249

prosession *n* procession IV 14, 82

proue(d) (eth), prouid *v* prove(d) (s) I 121, 152; II 111, 290; III 191, 497; VI 120, 205; VIII 256; IX Avi$^v$

prouinge *p part* proving VI 147

pytie *n* pity VIII 421

purenes *n* pureness II 306

puysance *n* power, strength III 9


quar(r)el(l) *n* quarrel II 252; VII 466

quauer *v* quaver III 364

queare, quere *n* choir, chancel III 417; VII 416

quiknes *n* life III 49

quite *v* acquit oneself well III 68

quiuer *v* quiver III 366

q[u]o[d] *v* said IV 47, 126; VIII 323


raine, rayne *n* rain I 363; II 173

raineth *v* reigns VI 218

rampinge, rampynge *adj* ranging wildly, ramping V 9; VI 9, 40

ramys *n* rams III 122

ranke *adj* licentious, lustful II 127

rashli *adv* rashly VI 86

raue *v* rave I 90

rayle, railed *v* rail(ed), rant(ed) I 90, 227; III 341; IV 142

rayse(d) *v* raised(d) II 265; VII 32, 58

rechelesnes *n* recklessness IX Aiiii

rechelesse, rechels *adj* reckless IX Aii, Aiii$^v$

recure *n* cure, hope of recovery III 441

red(e), reede *v* read III 405; IV 93; VII 204; VIII 172, 388

redy *adj* ready IV 84; VIII 123

reders *n* readers VII 455

reiect *v* reject III 233

remayn(e) *v* remain I 365; III 555; V 6; VI 6; VII 10, 462

remeued *v* remedied II 277

repayre *v* return II 339

replete *v* fill III 331

reproue(d) *v* reprove(d) VI 88, 105

repyne *v* repine I 83

retayne *v* retain III 235; VII 464

retorne(d) *v* return(ed) III 309, 390

retynue *n* following II 245

retyre *v* retire III 315

reuert *v* revert III 471

reuiue *v* revive III 411

reygne *v* reign I 132

reynes *n* reins, kidneys III 424

roffe *n* roof IX Avii<sup>v</sup>

ron *v* run (*fig*) IX Av

roockes *n* rocks VII 211

roother *n* rudder VII 244

rore *v* roar III 488; VII 197

rotes *n* roots IX Aiii

rougheli *adv* roughly VI 86

rout, rowte *n* a disorderly crowd of people I 271; VII 412; VIII 114

rufflyng *adj* annoying, troublesome VII 412

ruggid *adj* rugged VI 87

sacre *adj* sacred VII 226

sapyence *n* sapience, wisdom VII 61

satyres *n* satires VII 151

sayd(e), sayed *v* said I 290, 340; II 240, 260; IV 56; VI 127 etc.; VIII 187 etc.

sayeinge, sayinge(s) *n* saying(s) IV 87; VI 142; *pres part* I 10, 353

sayest, sayeth, sayste, sayth *v* say(s) IV 27, 95; VI 77, 79; VIII 163

scabes *n* scab, disease of the skin where pustules are formed II 153

scarsly *adv* scarcely III 197

schole(s) *n* school(s) VII 204; VIII 367

scholer *n* scholar VII 88

scoore *n* twenty III 121

sculker *n* skulker I 384

se *v* say VII 145; see I 46 etc.; II 53 etc.; III 51 etc.; IV 23 etc.; VI 74, 158, 183; VII 189; VIII 229; IX Aii, Aiii, Aviii

seaceth, seased *v* cease(d) (s) II 174; VII 280

season *v* seize IX Avii

# GLOSSARY

sede *n* seed, semen I 87

sedicion *n* sedition VI 29, 62

seke *v* seek III 66, 169; VIII 95

sely *adj* ignorant II 236

seme(s) (th) *v* seem(s) II 308; III 624; IV 159; VI 126, 185

sence *v* burn or offer incense I 51

sene (besene, be sene) *v* seen II 106, 257; III, 399, 762; VII 17, 24, 152; VIII 158, 210;
  IX Avii

sens, sins, syns *adv* because, since I 25; II 356; VIII 263

sensers *n* censers for burning incense in II 83

sensing *pres part* censing, offering or burning of incense IX Avii<sup>v</sup>

serch(e) *v* search II 204; VI 141

seue[n] *adj* seven III 641

sey *v* say III 440

shannot *v* shall not IV 65

shew(e) (d) (th) *v* show(ed) (s) I 32, 312; III 436 etc.; VI 114; VII 69 etc.; VIII 197 etc.;
  IX Aviii

shifte *n* expedient, stratagem II 356; VI 135

shittil *adj* fickle, flighty I 109

showre *n* shower I 363

shrewde *adj* wicked VIII 254

shuld(e) *v* should I 63 etc.; II 4; III 46 etc.; VIII 126 etc.

sick(e)nes *n* sickness III 46, 107, 371; IX Avi<sup>v</sup>

sinue *n* sinew II 246

skabed *adj* scabby I 278

skalde *adj* scalded, i.e., hairless I 278

skine *n* skin III 632

skuruy *adj* scurvy I 278

skyll(ed) *n* skill VII 7; VIII 350; *v* to be skilled in the knowledge of I 208; VII 51; VIII
  2, 51

slackenes *n* slackness IX Aiiii

slake (aslake) *v* come to an end, extinguished VIII 229; III 360

sleue *n* sleeve III 187

slouth *n* sloth IX Aii

slyd(e) *v* slid(e) III 329, 352

smal(l) (e) *adj* slight, small I 172; II 369; III 123, 487, 630; IV 18; VII 34, 203; VIII 91;
  IX Av<sup>v</sup>

soddy *adj* sodden IX Av

sodenly *adv* suddenly VII 20; IX Avii<sup>v</sup>

solempnely *adv* solemnly IV 85

son *n* sun III 640

sone(r), soone *adv* soon(er) I 130, 159; III 82 etc.; IV 3 etc.; VI 95 etc.; VII 472; VIII 294, 364; IX Aiii<sup>v</sup> etc.

song *n* song I 346; IV 58; *p part* sung I 340; II 240; *v* sang VIII 267

sorte *n* a considerable number (of people) I 127; IX Aiii<sup>v</sup>

sower *adj* sour VI 226

soyle *n* dung, filth, soil VII 372

sowterly *adj* vulgar IX Aiii<sup>v</sup>

sparyng *pres part* sparing VII 261

sped(e) *n* speed, success I 43; III 403; VII 166; *v* prosper, succeed I 222; III 132, 492; IV 161; IX Aviii

spight *n* spite VIII 281, 317

spightfull *as adv* (obs spiteful), excessively, extremely IV 102

spill *v* destroy III 371

spitfull *adj* spiteful III 517

stacker *v* reel, stagger, totter III 367

starkenes *n* absoluteness, utterness VIII 51

start *v* go forth II 354

stauer *v* stagger III 367

stay . . . vpon *v* attend VIII 141

stayre *n* stair III 35

stife *adj* stiff III 628

stifly *adv* stubbornly I 169

stike *v* stick I 391; III 591

stockes *n* stocks (restraining device) I 181

stode *v* stood I 245

stomake *n* stomach VI 107; IX Av

stoure *adj* warrior-like III 772

stoute, stowte, stowtly *adj* stout VII 268, 407; *adv* stoutly VI 186

straunge *adj* strange I 379; VII 85; IX Avii<sup>v</sup>

striue, stryue(s) *v* strive(s) I 199; III 412; VII 79

strond *n* strand VII 288

studente *n* student VII 231

study *v* understand IV 125, 126

styl(l) *adj* still I 138, 318; *adv* I 366; II 318, 321; III 369; IV 130; VII 462; VIII 21, 258

subtile *adj* subtle III 505

sue *v* ensure II 103

suer(ly) *adj* firm, sure VI 77; *adv* firmly, surely VII 396

sum(e) *adj* some III 56, 493; VIII 105, 131, 140; *pro* II 67; III 492

sumthing, sum thynge *n* something III 464; VIII 4

sumtime *n* sometime VIII 112

sum what *n* somewhat III 497

supersticion(s) *n* superstition(s) II 38; VIII 62
suppresse, supprest *v* suppresse(d) II 91; VII 28
suspection *n* suspection, suspicion II 304
swarue *v* swerve III 365
swauer *v* sway III 365
swelles *adj* pompous I 78
swere *v* swear III 473; IV 9, 47
swete *adj* sweet I 382; II 319; III 779; IX Aiii^v, Aiiii^v
swonne *n* faint, swoon III 638
swynke *v* labor, toil, work VII 399
sycke *adj* sick III 609
syng(e) *v* sing I 205, 350; II 217, 344, 358; VIII 64
sythen *adv* since VI 108

take . . . amys *v* miss its meaning I 237
tantes *n* quips, taunts VII 446
taried, tary(ed) *v* tarried, tarry I 381; II 12, 243; VII 266
tasted *p part* provided with taste IV 118
tauern(e) (s) *n* tavern(s) I 201; VIII 90
taxacions *n* accusations II 81
taxe(d) *v* blame(d), reprove(d) II 30; VI 108
telles *v* tell(s) I 7, 213
tende *v* intend IV 5
the *pro* thee III 89 etc.; IV 1 etc.; VI 178, 179; VIII 286
theare *adv* there VII 109
thee *v* prosper, thrive IV 2
thefe(s), theues *n* thief, thieves V 22, 29; VI 22 etc.
thei *pro* they II 193, 194; III 577; VI 210, 211, 213; IX Aiii
then *conj* than I 60; II 76, 263; III 903; IV 5 etc.; VI 30 etc.; VII 425; VIII 204, 297; IX Av^v, Aviii
thens *adv* thence II 269
ther *adv* there II 131 etc.; III 563; IV 54 etc.; VII 24 etc.; *pro* their III 798; IV 87, 145; VIII 103; IX Avi^v
therbe, ther be *adv* there be II 133; IV 7; VI 106; VIII 73
therby *adv* thereby I 169
therfore *adv* therefore I 23, 293, 395; II 37; III 50, 120, 401; VII 71, 194; VIII 310, 431; IX Aii^v, Aiii
therin *adv* therein I 99, 391; VIII 71; IX Aviii
therof *adv* thereof I 118; VII 168; IX Aiii^v, Avi^v, Avii^v
theron *adv* thereon II 198
therto *adv* thereto VI 106; IX Aviii
therunto *adv* thereunto VI title

# GLOSSARY

thes *adj* these I 164; II 31; 296; III 360; *pro* III 585
thonder *n* thunder II 174
thorowe *prep* through IX Aiii<sup>v</sup>; throughout II 266
thos *pro* those III 363
threashe *v* thrash VII 299
thryue *v* thrive IV 76
thyn(n) (e) *adj* thin III 631; VIII 75; IX Aiiii
thyther *adv* thither II 596
tog, tugge *v* tug VII 374; VIII 148
toke, tokeste *v* took II 200; IV 57; VI 116, 170
(in) tokenynge *n* (in) token VII 95
to(o)les *n* tools VI 221; VII 202
tonge *n* tongue IV 147
torne, tourne(d) *v* change(d), turn(ed) IV 115, 145; VI 52, 75; IX Av, Avi
tost *v* tossed III 42
tothe *n* tooth I 36
touche *v* beat, hit I 42; VII 411
towre *n* tower III 14; VI 216; Tower of London II 317
toy *n* foolish, facetious composition VIII 197
toyle *v* toil VII 374
tradicyons *n* traditions VIII 63
transmutacion *n* transmutation VII 429
transubstanciation *n* transubstantiation VII 428
trauile *v* suffer III 759
treuth, troeth, trueth *n* faith, troth IV 150; truth IV 148; VI 59, 96; VII 182
triste *n* confidence, faith, hope III 208
troble *v* trouble VIII 177
trow(e) *n* truth IV 65; *v* trust I 67, 235, 327; II 182; III 359, 381; IV 108; VII 149, 291, 364
trumpery *n* nonsense; applied contemptuously to religious beliefs or ceremonies VIII 213
tryckys *n* knick-knacks, trinkets II 80
trymmed *v* exhorted VII 445
turmoyle *v* agitate, harass, turmoil VII 375
tush(e) *inter* exclamation of impatient contempt II 296, 355; VIII 93, 225
tut *inter* exclamation of rebuke II 345
twayne *adj* twain III 236; VIII 249
tyer *v* tire I 260
tyl(l) *adv* until I 393; III 399; IV 32, 93; VII 24, 50, 366, 397; VIII 79 etc.
typycal *adj* typical VII 135

ueneracion *n* veneration VII 431
uncowthe *n* uncouth(ness) VII 395

varyed *v* depart from VII 264

vaunt *n* boast, brag VIII 103

vayne *adj* vain I 134; III 135; VII 461

vengaunce *adv* extremely IV 87

ventyng *pres part* venting, detecting a scent, snuffing up the air VII 410

verely, verily *adv* truly V 1 etc.; VI 1 etc.

verie, verye *adj* very IV 40, 159; VI 84

veritie *n* truth III 496; VIII 202

vestures *n* apparel, vestments II 71

vewe *v* see I 166; VII 164

vexacyons *n* vexations VII 82

vexe, vext *v* vex(ed) I 268; VIII 360

vexing *p part* vexing VIII 194

vgly *adj* ugly III 778

vnburned *adj* unburnt II 6; V 6

voiage *n* voyage III 741

voide, voyde *adj* void VI 62; VII 128

volupt *n* sensuous pleasures III 431

voysed *p part* voiced II 266

vp *adv* up I 37, 195, 314; III 574; IV 74, 90; VII 98, 137, 210; IX Av^v

vphale *v* drink up VIII 154

vpreare *v* rears, rises up VIII 17

vprore *n* uproar II 145

vpsnatche *v* snatch up VII 380

vs *pro* us II 235, 348, 358; III 81 etc.; IV 24 etc.; VI 45, 157; VII 388; VIII 56, 226, 290

vse(d) (s) (th) *v* use(d) (s) I 75, 103, 371; III 178; IV 133; VI 94; VII 18, 237; VIII 62, 66; IX Avii^v

vtensile *n* utensil IX Aiiii

vtter, vtterly(e) *adj* complete, utter VIII 50; IX Aiiii; *adv* completely, utterly II 6, 66; *v* utter VIII 396

vyle *adj* vile II 95

vyolent *adj* violent VII 82


wache *v* watch IX Av^v

war *v* were I 244

war(c)k(e) (s), wircke, wyrcke *n* work(s) I 121, 227; III 660; *v* I prefatory verse; IV 5; VIII 334

(be)ware, (be well) ware *v* beware IV 134; IX Avii^v

warely *adv* warily IX Av^v

wast *v* waste III 220, 251

watter *n* water I 71

wauer(ynge) *v* waver(ing) I 117; III 366

# GLOSSARY

wayte(th) *v* wait(s) I 46; III 732; VII 739

waxe(th) *v* grow(s) I 264; III 237

weapen *n* weapon I prefatory verse

welcum *inter* welcome III 386

wel wayde (well-weighed) *p part* duly considered, pondered VIII 188

well willers *n* well-wishers II 383

wene *v* believe I 233; II 260, 346; IV 63; VI 88; VII 154

wepe *v* weep III 340

wer *v* were II 25, 67

werye *adj* weary II 227

wether, whether *n* weather IX Aiiiiᵛ, Av

wext *v* angered, incensed I 269

whan *adv* when II 113, 332; III 619

wher *adv* where II 49, 328; III 479, 535; VI 96; VIII 76

wherby *adv* whereby IX Aiiiᵛ

wherfore *adv* wherefore I 368; II 203 etc.; III 61 etc.; IV 7; VI 91, 124; VII 33 etc.; VIII 119 etc.; IX Aviᵛ

wherin *adv* wherein II 22, 190; VI 119, 182; VIII 5; IX Aiii, Aviiᵛ

wheron *adv* whereon I 145; III 454

wherto *adv* whereto VII 265

wherwith *adv* wherewith VIII 188

whight(este) *adj* white(st) IV 129; IX Aiiiiᵛ

whilse *conj* whiles IX Avii

whistill *v* whistle IV 161

whomwarde *adv* homeward IV 165

whych(e) *pro* which VII 97, 231; IX Aiiiᵛ, Aviᵛ

whyt *n* whit VIII 359

wight *n* being, person III 66

wincke *v* disregard, overlook II 256

wist, wyst *p part* known III 210; *v* knew IV 102; VIII 190

witnes(se) (th) *n* witness II 191; IV 53; VI 172; *v* witnesses III 263

without *prep* outside I 177; VIII 84

wittye *adj* witty II 88

wo, wo(o)ful(l) *n* woe III 50; IV 127; *adj* woeful II 104; III 660

wold(e) *v* would I 61 etc.; II 63, 66, 149; III 86, 118, 318; VI 205; VII 153, 451; VIII 29 etc.

wont *v* accustomed to V prefatory verse; VI prefatory verse etc.

woordes *n* words VII 389

woorshyppe *n* worship VII 370

woorthy *adj* worthy VII 365

wors(se) *adj* worse I 303; III 670; IV 56; IX Aviii

wot(e), wotteth *v* know(s) II 286, 313; III 194; IV 55, 120; VII 151; VIII 109, 159, 161 wright, wryght, wrytest *v* set right I 170; III 548; write(s) VII 216

wroth *adj* angry IV 46, 47

wroughte *p part* wrought II 285; VII 188

wrytynges *ger* works, writings VII 64

wy *adv* why IV 22

wyl(l), wylt *n* will VI 183; VII 6, 191; VIII 349; IX Aii^v; *v* I 1 etc.; II 59 etc.; III 405 etc.;
   IV prefatory verse etc.; V 23; VI 23 etc.; VII 53 etc.; VIII 3 etc.; IX Aiii^v etc.

wylbe *v* will be IV 143

wyle *n* cunning, deceit, wile VII 180; VIII 353

wyn *v* win II 273; VIII 74

wynde(s) *n* wind(s) I 117; II 180; III 98, 383; VII 246; IX Av^v

wyne *n* wine I 158; III 155, 163; IV 115 etc.

wyt(t), wyttes *n* wit(s) I 314, 360; IV 124; VI 100, 124; VII 160, 180, 273

wyth(e) *prep* with II 157, 164; III 163 etc.; IV 48 etc.; V 28; VI 28 etc.; VII 55 etc.; VIII
   20 etc.; IX Aii, Avii, Aviii^v

wyues *n* wives I 85; VII 77 etc.

yche *pro* I IV 113, 153

ye (form of) *def art* the VI 154, 155, 227; VII 117; IX Aii^v etc.

ye, yea *adv* yes I 11, 54; II 13, 209; III 189, 585; IV 29 etc.; IX Aiii etc.

yeares, yere(s) *n* year(s) I 109, 129; II 13, 104, 171; III 284; VII 170; VIII 123; IX Avi

yelde *v* yield I 389

yelding *pres p* yielding III 17

yf *conj* if I 126 etc.; VII 31 etc.

yl *adv* badly, evilly IV 54

ynke *n* ink I 40

yt *pro* it II 37; VII 162 etc.

yockes *n* yokes II 157

yong(e) *adj* young I 343; III 106

yonkers *n* (fashionable) young men I 316

# LIST OF VARIANTS

Abbreviations as used in the *STC:*

| | |
|---|---|
| C: | University Library, Cambridge |
| HN: | Huntington Library, San Marino, California |
| L: | The British Library, London |
| N: | Newberry Library, Chicago |
| NLW: | National Library of Wales, Aberystwyth |
| O: | Bodleian Library, Oxford |
| O⁹: | All Souls College, Oxford |

## *A pore helpe,*

Copies at: C, NLW (imperfect), O (2)

| | |
|---|---|
| heading | bukler O; buklar C |
| | and O; & C |
| | defence O; befence C |
| | kyrke, O; kyrke C |
| | driue hence O; driuehence C |
| | that O; yᵗ C |
| | her O; here C |
| | wircke O; wircke, C |
| 1 | WYll O; WIl C |
| | all O; al C |
| 2 | and O; & C |
| | hande O; hand C |
| 3 | withstande O; wᵗstand C |
| 4 | nombre O; number C |
| | lyke O; like C |
| 5 | with O; wyth C |
| | Gospell O; Gospel C |
| 6 | wyll O; wil C |

196

| | |
|---|---|
| 7 | tratlynge O; tratlinge C |
| 8 | Agaynst O; Agaynste C |
| 9 | dygnitie O; dignitie C |
| 11 | Hipocrisy O; Hypocrisy C |
| 13 | theyr O; theire C |
| | aucthoritie O; authoritye C |
| 14 | Euangelie O; euangelie C |
| 16 | rytes O; rites C |
| | ecclesiasticall O; ecclesiastical C |
| 19 | maye O; may C |
| 20 | alure O; allure C |
| 21 | your O; youre C |
| 22 | wyll O; wil C |
| 26 | greueth O; greuith C |
| 27 | heare O; here C |
| | behynde O; be hind C |
| 30 | Whiche O; With C, Wich NLW |
| 31 | there O; ther C, NLW |
| | be O; by NLW |
| 32 | theyr O; there C, NLW |
| 33 | priest O; preist NLW |
| 34 | wyll O; wyl C, NLW |
| | fyre O; fire C, NLW |
| | becone O; be cone C |
| 35 | Agaynst O; Against C |
| | frayle O; fraile C, NLW |
| 36 | with O; wyth C, NLW |
| 37 | meyne O; mayne C, NLW |
| | sayle O; saile C, NLW |
| 39 | ryght O; right C, NLW |
| 40 | With O; Wyth NLW |
| 41 | lyke O; like C, NLW |
| | triflynge O; trifling C, NLW |
| 42 | touche O; touch C |
| 43 | all O; al NLW |
| 43–44 | *These 2 lines omitted* C |
| 46 | wayteth O; waiteth NLW |
| 50 | some O; sume C, NLW |
| 52 | vndertake O; vnder take C, NLW |
| 53 | Ryght O; Right C |
| | thynges O; thinges C, NLW |
| 54 | God O; god C, NLW |

| | |
|---|---|
| 56 | shall be  O; shalbe  C, NLW |
| 58 | blyssed  O; blissed  C, NLW |
| 60 | fyrst  O; firste  C, NLW |
| 61 | wolde  O; woulde  C, NLW |
| | durst  O; dourst  C; durste  NLW |
| 62 | worst  O; wurst  NLW |
| 63 | shulde  O; should  C, NLW |
| 64 | W ith boke, bell and candell  O; With boke and bell and candel  C, NLW |
| 65 | wolde  O; would  C, NLW |
| | hym  O; him  C, NLW |
| | handell  O; handel  C, NLW |
| 66 | shulde  O; shoulde  C, NLW |
| | ryght  O; right  C, NLW |
| | well  O; wel  C, NLW |
| 67 | trowe  O; trow  C, NLW |
| 68 | heade  O; head  C, NLW |
| 71 | Agaynst  O; Against  C, NLW |
| | our  O; oure  C, NLW |
| 74 | thynges  O; thinges  C, NLW |
| 75 | kynges  O; kinges  C, NLW |
| 77 | theyr  O; ther  C, NLW |
| 80 | at  O; et  NLW |
| | our longe gownes  O; your longe gownes  C, NLW |
| 82 | typttes  O; tipettes  C, NLW |
| 83 | wyll  O; will  C, NLW |
| 84 | leade  O; lead  C, NLW |
| | euyll  O; euil  C, NLW |
| | lyues  O; liues  C, NLW |
| 85 | With  O; Wyth  C, NLW |
| | mennes  O; mens  C, NLW |
| 86 | wyll  O; wil  C, NLW |
| 88 | mennes  O; menns  C |
| 89 | confounde  O; confound  C, NLW |
| 90 | rayle  O; raile  C, NLW |
| | raue  O; Raue  C, NLW |
| 91 | Callynge  O; Calling  C, NLW |
| 93 | ydle  O; Idel  C, NLW |
| | all  O; al  C, NLW |
| | daye  O; day  C, NLW |
| 94 | wolde  O; woulde  C, NLW |
| 95 | dryue  O; driue  C, NLW |

|      | |
|------|---|
|      | tyme  O; time  C, NLW |
|      | awaye  O; a waye  NLW |
| 96   | Byble  O; bybble  C, NLW |
| 97   | vnpossible  O; vn possible  C, NLW |
| 98   | learned  O; lerned  C, NLW |
|      | all  O; al  C, NLW |
|      | lyfe  O; life  C, NLW |
| 99   | ryfe  O; rife  C, NLW |
| 100  | Whiche  O; Which  C, NLW |
|      | all  O; al  C, NLW |
|      | stryfe  O; strife  C, NLW |
| 101  | Paraphrasies  O; paraphrasies  C, NLW |
| 102  | Moche  O; Much  C, NLW |
|      | dyfferyng  O; differeing  C, NLW |
|      | from  O; from  C, NLW |
|      | portaises  O; porteises  C, NLW |
| 103  | wolde  O; woulde  C, NLW |
| 104  | portaise  O; porteise  C, NLW |
| 105  | shall be  O; shalbe  C, NLW |
| 106  | farre  O; far  C, NLW |
| 107  | Theyr  O; Their  C, NLW |
|      | tongues  O; tonges  C, tonges  NLW |
|      | agaynst  O; against  C, NLW |
|      | suche  O; such  C, NLW |
|      | holynes  O; holines  C, NLW |
| 108  | busynes  O; busines  C, NLW |
| 109  | yeares  O; yeres  C, NLW |
| 110  | affyrmeth  O; affirmeth  C, NLW |
| 112  | fro.  O; fro  C |
| 114  | behynde  O; behinde  C, NLW |
| 116  | Amonge  O; A monge  C, NLW |
|      | blynde  O; blind  C, blinde  NLW |
| 117  | wauerynge  O; waueringe  C, wauering  NLW |
| 118  | wrote  O; wrot  NLW |
|      | therof  O; thereof  C, NLW |
|      | suche  O; such  NLW |
| 120  | Shall  O; Shal  C, NLW |
|      | fynde  O; find  C |
| 121  | theyr  O; their  C |
|      | warkes  O; warks  C, NLW |
| 122  | there be  O; therebe  C, ther be  NLW |
|      | barcke  O; barke  C, NLW |

| | |
|---|---|
| 123 | saye O; say C |
| 125 | well O; wel C |
| 126 | yf O; if C, NLW |
| 127 | sorte O; sort C |
| | shall O; shal NLW |
| 128 | well O; wel C |
| 129 | Within O; Wythin C, NLW |
| | two O; tow C |
| | yeares O; yeres C, NLW |
| | daye O; day C |
| 130 | soone O; sone C, NLW |
| | runne O; rune C, NLW |
| | awaye O; a waye C, NLW |
| 131 | suche O; such C, NLW |
| 132 | some O; sume C |
| 133 | thynges O; thinges C, NLW |
| | mayntayne O; maintayne C, NLW |
| 134 | Whiche O; Which C, NLW |
| | vayne O; vaine C, NLW |
| 135 | dysdayne O; disdayne C, NLW |
| 137 | this O; thys C, NLW |
| 138 | styll O; styl C |
| 139 | or O; o NLW |
| 140 | durst O; durste C, NLW |
| | bolde O; blode C |
| 141 | Agaynst O; Against C, Agaynste NLW |
| | learnynges O; lerninges C, NLW |
| 143 | Whiche O; Which C, NLW |
| 144 | laye O; lay C |
| | mannes O; ma*n*nes C |
| 145 | Wheron O; Whereon C, NLW |
| 146 | worde O; word NLW |
| | mysse O; misse C, NLW |
| 147 | saye O; say C |
| | this O; thys NLW |
| 149 | thynge O; thinge C |
| 150 | dyd O; did C |
| | diuyne O; deuyne C, diui[n]e NLW |
| 151 | enclyne O; encline C, NLW |
| 152 | defyne O; define C, NLW |
| 153 | aboue O; a boue NLW |
| 154 | Whiche O; Which NLW |

| | |
|---|---|
| | our O; oure C, NLW |
| 155 | dyed O; died C, NLW |
| | for O; fo NLW |
| | our O; oure C, NLW |
| 157 | bloude O; bloud NLW |
| 158 | breade O; bread NLW |
| | awaye O; a waye C, NLW |
| 161 | tyme O; time C, NLW |
| 163 | Thoughe O; Though C, NLW |
| 164 | these O; thes C, NLW |
| 165 | Wyll O; Wyl C, NLW |
| 167 | With O; Wyth C, NLW |
| | bodyly O; bodely C, NLW |
| 169 | stifly O; stifely C, NLW |
| | stande O; stand C, NLW |
| 170 | enterpryse O; enter prise C, NLW |
| | wryght O; wright C, NLW |
| 171 | endyght O; endight C, NLW |
| 173 | Agaynst O; Agaynste C, NLW |
| | all O; al C, NLW |
| 174 | call O; cal C, NLW |
| 175 | shulde O; should C, NLW |
| | teache O; teach C, NLW |
| 177 | Suche O; Such C, NLW |
| | thynges O; things C, NLW |
| | theyr O; their C, NLW |
| | reache O; reach C, NLW |
| 178 | there O; ther C, NLW |
| | saye O; say C, NLW |
| 179 | all day O; alday C, NLW |
| 181 | stockes O; stokes C |
| 182 | hydden O; hidden C, NLW |
| | lyke O; like C, NLW |
| 184 | with O; w$^t$ C, NLW |
| 185 | stynkynge O; stinking C, NLW |
| | vermyne O; vermine C, NLW |
| 186 | dweleth O; dwelleth C, NLW |
| 188–191 | *These 4 lines omitted* C |
| 188 | rustye O; rustie NLW |
| 189 | moth O; mothe NLW |
| | mustye O; mustie NLW |
| 190 | lyght O; light NLW |

| | |
|---|---|
| 191 | awaye O; a waye NLW |
| 193 | fyre O; fire C, NLW |
| | brente O; brent C, NLW |
| 198 | Agaynst O; Agaynste C, NLW |
| | these O; thes C, NLW |
| | newe O; new C, NLW |
| 199 | stryue O; striue C, NLW |
| | nacion O; nacion C, NLW |
| 200 | playes O; plays C, NLW |
| 202 | dysprayse O; disprayse C, NLW |
| 203 | martyrs O; martirs C, NLW |
| | wolde O; woulde C, NLW |
| 205 | synge O; sing C, NLW |
| | pype O; pipe C, NLW |
| | mery O; meri C, NLW |
| 206 | wyll O; wil C, NLW |
| 207 | wyll O; wil C, NLW |
| 208 | Thoughe O; Though C, NLW |
| | speake O; speke C, NLW |
| | skyll not O; skil (not C, NLW |
| 210 | worthy O; worthie C, NLW |
| 211 | chekmate O; chek mate C, NLW |
| 213 | suche O; such C, NLW |
| 216 | theyr O; their C, NLW |
| | pastyme O; pastime C, NLW |
| 217 | all O; al C, NLW |
| 218 | this O; thys C, NLW |
| 219 | yf O; if C, NLW |
| 220 | Wolde O; Woulde C, NLW |
| | mende O; mend C, NLW |
| | a mysse O; amys C, NLW |
| 221 | meanynge O; meaninge C, NLW |
| 222 | yf O; if C, NLW |
| | well O; wel C, NLW |
| 223 | agayne O; againe C, NLW |
| 224 | shulde O; shoulde C, NLW |
| | theyr O; their C, NLW |
| | payne O; paine C, NLW |
| 225 | thynke O; thinke C, NLW |
| 226 | sturdye O; sturdy C, NLW |
| 227 | agaynst O; agaynste C, NLW |
| | wyrcke O; wircke C, NLW |

| | |
|---|---|
| 229 | there  O; ther  C, NLW |
| 230 | proudly  O; prowdly  C, NLW |
| 231 | this  O; thys  C, NLW |
| 235 | wyll be  O; wilbe  C, NLW |
| 237 | a mys  O; amys  C, NLW |
| 239 | very  O; verie  C, NLW |
| | his  O; hys  C, NLW |
| 240 | Well  O; Wel  C, NLW |
| | yf  O; if  C, NLW |
| 242 | Shall  O; Shal  C, NLW |
| | do  O; doe  C, NLW |
| 244 | there  O; ther  C, NLW |
| 246 | countrey  O; contrey  C, NLW |
| 249 | wyll  O; wyl  C, NLW |
| | with  O; wyth  C, NLW |
| 251 | wyll  O; wyl  C, NLW |
| | knowe  O; know  C, NLW |
| | henne  O; hen  C, NLW |
| 258 | fayre  O; fayer  C, NLW |
| | fyre  O; fyer  C, NLW |
| 259 | happe  O; hap  C, NLW |
| | hyer  O; hier  C, NLW |
| 260 | least  O; lest  C, NLW |
| 264 | Lorde  O; Lord  C, NLW |
| 265 | wyl  O; wyll  C, NLW |
| 266 | heare  O; here  C, NLW |
| | hym  O; him  C, NLW |
| 267 | Marke  O; Marcke  C, NLW |
| | text  O; texte  C, NLW |
| 269 | feare  O; fere  C |
| 272 | hym  O; him  C, NLW |
| 273 | wyll be  O; wylbe  C, NLW |
| 275 | snout  O; snowt  C, NLW |
| 278 | skabed  O; skabbed  C, NLW |
| | skalde  O; skald  C, NLW |
| 279 | balde  O; baule  C |
| 281 | hym  O; him  C, NLW |
| 282 | God  O; god  C, NLW |
| 283 | yf  O; if  C, NLW |
| 284 | maye  O; may  C, NLW |
| 285 | Blyndefylde  O; Blyndefild  C, NLW |
| 288 | hym  O; him  C, NLW |

| | |
|---|---|
| 290 | doctor O; docter C, NLW |
| | fryer O; frier C, NLW |
| | sayde O; saide C, NLW |
| 292 | Well O; Wel C, NLW |
| | shall O; shal C, NLW |
| | knowe more O; knowe ∧ more NLW |
| 293 | therfore O; therefore C, NLW |
| 294 | shall O; shal C, NLW |
| 297 | vytailer O; vitaylar C, NLW |
| 298 | lordly O; Lordly C, NLW |
| | hospytelar O; hospitelar C, NLW |
| 301 | Thoughe O; Though C, NLW |
| | Germyn O; Germin C, NLW |
| 303 | Saye O; Say C |
| 304 | hym O; him C, NLW |
| | alone O; a lone C, NLW |
| 306 | Apostles O; Apostelles C, NLW |
| 307 | gyue O; giue C, NLW |
| | warnynge O; warninge C, NLW |
| 308 | Had neuer suche learnynge O; Had neuer no suche learnyng C, Had neuer suche learnyng NLW |
| 309 | this O; thys C, NLW |
| 310 | learned O; lerned C, NLW |
| 311 | maister O; mayster C, NLW |
| 312 | hym O; him C, NLW |
| | sluggarde O; sluggard C, NLW |
| 313 | dronken O; drunkin C, NLW |
| | druggarde O; drunkarde C |
| 314 | his O; hys C, NLW |
| 316 | hyt O; hit C, NLW |
| 317 | wyll O; wil C, NLW |
| | permyt O; permit C, NLW |
| 318 | styll O; stil C, NLW |
| | syt O; sit C, NLW |
| 319 | maye O; may C, NLW |
| | well O; wel C, NLW |
| 321 | whiche O; which NLW |
| | intitled O; initled C, NLW |
| 322 | Agaynst O; Agaynste C, NLW |
| 324 | wryteth O; writeth C, NLW |
| 325 | earnestly O; ernestly C, NLW |
| 326 | heresy O; herecy NLW |

| | |
|---|---|
| 328 | blowe O; bloude C |
| 329 | they O; the C, NLW |
| 330 | wyll O; wyl C |
| | we O; wee C |
| 331 | yf O; if C, NLW |
| 332 | yf O; if C, NLW |
| | begynne O; beging C, begin NLW |
| 333 | brynge O; bringe C, NLW |
| 334 | cosens O; cosyns C, cosins NLW |
| 338 | spiritu tuo O; spiritutuo C |
| 339 | both O; boeth NLW |
| | duo O; duo. NLW |
| 340 | they O; thei NLW |
| | sayde O; sayed C, sayd NLW |
| 341 | tongue O; tonge C, tong NLW |
| 342 | be ronge O; do ringe C, be rong NLW |
| 344 | Perkynge O; Perkyng C |
| 345 | wolde O; would C, NLW |
| | mattens O; matte*n*s C, NLW |
| 346 | eueinge O; eueninge C |
| | a lso O; also C, NLW |
| 348 | baptysinge O; baptising C, NLW |
| 349 | Buryalles O; Burialles C, NLW |
| | thynge O; thyng C, thinge NLW |
| 350 | tongue O; tonge C, NLW |
| | saye O; say NLW |
| | synge O; sing C, NLW |
| 352 | dyuerse O; diuerse C, NLW |
| 354 | Mayntainynge O; Maynteinyng C, NLW |
| 355 | shulde O; shoulde C, NLW |
| | theyr O; their C, NLW |
| | seruyce O; seruice C, NLW |
| 356 | Alas O; Alasse C, NLW |
| | wolde O; woulde C, would NLW |
| 357 | grunt O; grount C, grant NLW |
| | gro[n]e O; grone C, NLW |
| 358 | seruyce O; seruice C, NLW |
| 360 | deadly O; dedly C, NLW |
| 364 | Well O; Wel C |
| 365 | remayne O; remaine NLW |
| 366 | theyr O; there C, ther NLW |
| | styll O; stil C, NLW |

| | |
|---|---|
| 367 | wyll O; wyl C, NLW |
| 368 | Wherfore O; Wherefore NLW |
| 370 | All O; Al C, NLW |
| | saye O; say NLW |
| 371 | praye. O; praye C |
| 372 | suche O; such C, NLW |
| | maye O; maie C, NLW |
| 373 | Contynue O; Continue C, NLW |
| 374 | els O; eles C, NLW |
| | lyke O; like C, NLW |
| 375 | lyeth O; lieth C, NLW |
| 377 | praye O; pray C, NLW |
| 379 | straunge O; straung C, NLW |
| 380 | great O; greate C |
| | abomynacions, O; abonamacions C, abonamacions. NLW |
| 382 | syr O; Sir C, NLW |
| 385 | kan. O; kna. C, NLW |
| | Sepulchre O; sepulchre C, NLW |
| 386 | stande O; stand C, NLW |
| 388 | els O; eles C, NLW |
| 389 | all O; al C, NLW |
| 390 | cyte O; city C, NLW |
| 391 | yf O; if C, NLW |
| 392 | doubt O; doute C, NLW |
| | shall O; shal C, NLW |
| | blyn O; blin C, NLW |
| 393 | Tyll O; Tyl C, NLW |
| | eternytie O; eternitie C, NLW |
| 394 | all O; al C, NLW |
| | fraternyte O; fraternite C, NLW |
| 397 | me. O; me C, NLW |

| | |
|---|---|
| Catchwords | |
| [Sig A vii] | And O; By C, NLW |

## *The vpcheringe of the messe*:

Copies at : C, HN, NLW (imperfect), O (2)

| | |
|---|---|
| 60 | Wherefore NLW; Wherfor O |
| 82 | Whereat NLW; Wherat O |

| | |
|---|---|
| 90 | thinges NLW; thinge O |
| 95 | Al NLW; All O |
| 97 | tell NLW; tel O |
| 118 | institutions NLW; institucio[n]s O |
| 142 | pore NLW; powre O |
| 147 | manslaughter NLW; manslauhgter HN, O |
| 148 | laughter NLW; laughte[r] HN, O |
| 155 | humbled heles NLW; hum bledheles HN, O |
| 165 | say NLW; saye O |
| 169 | thinge NLW; thing O |
| 171 | ceasonable NLW; seasonable O |
| 175 | scatereth NLW; carieth HN, O |
| 191 | witnes NLW; wittnes O |
| 192 | one NLW; on O |
| 203 | Wherfore NLW; Wherefore O |
| 210 | bacon NLW; baco[n] HN, O |
| 220 | glad NLW; glade O |
| 248 | stockfish NLW; stochfish O |
| 310 | For NLW; Nor C, HN, O |
| 323 | Forget NLW; Forge t HN, O |
| 344 | placebo NLW; place bo C, HN, O |
| 354 | ye NLW; y e HN, O |
| 372 | se NLW; so C, HN, O |
| 382 | pillers NLW; p iller HN, O (Douce) |
| rubric | FINI. NLW; FINIS. C, HN, O |

| | |
|---|---|
| Catchwords | |
| [Sig A vi] | Ye NLW; He HN, O; e O (Tanner) |

## Pathose, or an inward passion of the pope for the losse of hys daughter the Masse.

Copies at: C (imperfect), NLW (imperfect)

| | |
|---|---|
| 437 | hereditari[u]s NLW; hereditarius C |
| 469 | aromatite NLW; amorite C |
| 471 | Oh that she myght reuert NLW; That she myght reuert C |
| 525 | Latymers NLW; laytymers C |
| 533 | Emserus NLW; Euserus C |
| 536 | Bilikius NLW; Bilicius C |
| 538 | Nausea NLW; Naufea C |

| 541 | Sadoletus  NLW; Sandoletus  C |
|---|---|
| 543 | Ech of you is a lim  NLW; To helpe vs interim  C |
| 544 | To helpe vs interim  NLW; Ech of you is a lim  C |
| 655 | ceraunus  NLW; ceranus  C |
| 745 | Aboute ye shal ride  NLW; Aboute ye ride  C |

Catchwords
[Sig B iᵛ]      W hich  NLW; Which  C

## *Iohn Bon and Mast person*

Copies at: L, N

| 51 | treason  L; treas on  N |
|---|---|
| 95 | other  L; oth  N |
| 116 | lo  L; l(o)  N |
| 163 | blake ha  L; blake hab  N |

## *Phylogamus.*
Copies at: L (imperfect), O⁹

| 3 | nyne  O⁹; [n]y[n]e  L |
|---|---|
| 83 | earneste  O⁹; earnest  L |
| 85 | denomynacyons  O⁹; denomynacyo[n]s  L |
| 252 | darke  O⁹; dark e  L |
| 254 | say  O⁹; saye  L |

## *Antipus,*

Below is a collation of the variants found between the original version of *Antipus* (Bodleian Library, Oxford) and its repeated form which is included in *The comparison betwene the Antipus and the Antigraphe or answere thereunto, with. An apologie or defence of the same Antipus. And reprehence of the Antigraphe* (Huntington Library, San Marino).

| heading | such  O; suche  HN |
|---|---|
|  | thinges  O; thynges  HN |
| 1 | God  O; God,  HN |
| 3 | kull  O; kil  HN |
|  | hys  O; his  HN |

| | |
|---|---|
| 4 | shyppe O; shippe HN |
| | Noye O; Noe, HN |
| 5 | hys O; his HN |
| | dyd O; did HN |
| 6 | Sodomytes O; Sodomites HN |
| | remayn O; remayne HN |
| 8 | dyd O; did HN |
| | lawe O; law HN |
| | dowbtles O; doubtles HN |
| 9 | rampynge O; rampinge HN |
| 10 | Goliad O; Goliath HN |
| 12 | dragon O; dragone HN |
| 14 | Aposteles O; Apostles HN |
| | gospell O; Gospel HN |
| 15 | Apostels O; Apostles HN |
| 16 | Apostels O; Apostles HN |
| 17 | deuyll O; deuel HN |
| 18 | doth O; doeth HN |
| 19 | Isesicles O; Isicles HN |
| | wythin O; within HN |
| 20 | oure O; our HN |
| | master O; maister HN |
| 21 | bread O; breade HN |
| 22 | prestes O; priestes HN |
| | maker. O; maker HN |
| 25 | knight O; knyght HN |
| 27 | knowith O; knoweth HN |
| | hys O; his HN |
| 28 | netts O; nettes HN |
| 29 | sedition O; sedicion HN |
| 30 | kings O; kinges HN |
| | commission O; commission HN |

# WORKS CITED

## *Primary Sources*

Arber, Edward, ed. *An English Garner.* 8 vols. Westminster: Archibald Constable, 1877–95. Vol. 4.

Bale, John. *A breue Cronycle of the Bysshope of Romes blessynge, and of his Prelates beneficiall and charitable rewardes, from the tyme of Kynge Heralde vnto this daye.* London, 1548.

_____. *The Complete Plays of John Bale.* Ed. Peter Happé. 2 vols. Woodbridge: D. S. Brewer, 1985.

_____. *A declaration of Edmonde Bonner's articles, concerning the cleargye of London dyocese whereby that excerable* [sic] *Antychriste, is in his righte colours reueled.* Basel, 1554.

_____. *The Image of bothe churches after the moste wonderfull and heauenly Reuelacion of Sainct Iohn the Euangelist, contayning a very frutefull exposicion or paraphrase vpon the same. Wherin it is conferred with the other scripturs,* [sic] *and most auctorised historyes.* London, 1548.

_____. *Index Britanniae Scriptorum.* Ed. Reginald L. Poole and Mary Bateson. Oxford: Clarendon Press, 1902.

_____. *A mysterye of inyquyte contayned within the heretycall Genealogye of Ponce Pantolabus is here both dysclosed & confuted.* London, 1545.

_____. *Scriptorum Illustrium Maioris Brytanniae Catalogus.* 2 vols. Basle: John Oporinus, 1557, 1559. Farnborough: Gregg International, 1971.

Barlowe, Jerome, and William Roye. *Rede me and be nott wrothe,* London, 1528.

_____. *Rede Me and Be Nott Wrothe.* Ed. Douglas H. Parker. Toronto: University of Toronto Press, 1992.

Becon, Thomas. *Works.* Ed. John Ayre. 3 vols. Cambridge: Cambridge University Press, 1843–44.

*The Bible.* New Revised Standard Version with the Apocrypha. Oxford: Oxford University Press, 1989.

*The Bible.* Taverner and Tyndale Version. Ed. Edmond Becke. London, 1551.

*Biblia Sacra Iuxta Vulgatam Versionem.* Stuttgart: Deutsche Bibelgesellschaft, 1969.

Black, William Henry, ed. "Iohn Bon and Mast person." *Early English Poetry, Ballads, and Popular Literature of the Middle Ages. Edited from Original Manuscripts and Scarce Publications.* 30 vols. London: T. Richards, 1840–52 Vol. 30.

*The booke of the common prayer and administracion of the Sacramentes, and other rites and ceremonies of the Churche: after the use of the Churche of England.* London, 1549.

Brewer, J. S., J. Gairdner, and R. H. Brodie, eds. *Letters and Papers, Foreign and Domestic, of the Reign of Henry VIII. Preserved in the Public Record Office, the British Museum, and Elsewhere in England.* 22 vols. London: Longman, Green, Longman & Roberts, 1862–1932. Vaduz: Kraus Reprint, 1965.

Brydges, Samuel Egerton. *Censura Literaria. Containing Titles, Abstracts, and Opinions of Old English Books, with Original Disquisitions, Articles of Biography, and Other Literary Antiquities.* 10 vols. 2nd ed. London: printed for Longman, Hurst, Rees, Orme, and Brown, 1815. Vol. 1.

Calvin, John. *A Faythfvl and most Godly treatyse concernyng the most sacred sacrament of the blessed body and bloud of our sauiour Christ.* Tr. Miles Coverdale. London, 1548.

*Chronicle of the Grey Friars of London.* Ed. John Gough Nichols. London, 1852.

Cope, Anthony. *A godly meditacion vpon .XX. select and chosen Psalmes of the Prophet Dauid, as wel necessary to al them that are desirous to haue y͏ͤ darke wordes of the Prophet declared and made playn: as also fruitfull to suche as delyte in the contemplation of the spiritual meanyng of them.* London, 1547.

Copland, Robert. *The hye way to the Spyttell hous.* London, 1536?

Cranmer, Thomas. *Cathechismvs: That is to say a shorte Instruction into Christian Religion for the synguler commoditie and profyte of children and yong people.* London, 1548.

_____. *Writings and Disputations of Thomas Cranmer, Archbishop of Canterbury, Martyr, 1556, Relative to the Sacrament of the Lord's Supper.* Ed. John Edmund Cox. Cambridge: Cambridge University Press, 1844.

Crowley, Robert. *The Confutation of the mishapen Aunswer to the misnamed, wicked Ballade, called the Abuse of y<sup>e</sup> blessed sacrament of the aultare. Wherin, thou haste (gentele Reader) the ryghte vnderstandynge of al the places of scripture that Myles Hoggard, (wyth his learned counsail) hath wrested to make for the transubstanciacion of the bread and wyne.* London, 1548.

———. *An informacion and peticion agaynst the oppressours of the pore commons of this realme, compiled* [for] *the Parliamente.* London, 1548.

Foxe, John. *The Acts and Monuments.* Ed. Stephen Reed Cattley and George Townsend. 8 vols. London: R. B. Seeley and W. Burnside, 1837–41. Vols. 5–8.

Gardiner, Stephen. *Theyr dedes in effecte, my lyfe wolde haue.* London, 1548.

*A godlye and holesome preseruatyue against desperation at all times necessarye for the soule: but then chiefly to be vsed and ministred when the deuill doth assault vs moost fiersely, and deth approcheth niest.* London, 1548.

Grimald, Nicholas. *Christus Redivivus.* Ed. Kurt Tetzeli von Rosador. Hildesheim: Georg Olms, 1982.

Grindal, Edmund. *Remains.* Ed. William Nicholson. Cambridge: Cambridge University Press, 1843.

Hartshorne, Charles Henry, ed. *Ancient Metrical Tales: Printed Chiefly from Original Sources.* London: William Pickering, 1829.

Hazlitt, William Carew, ed. *Fugitive Tracts Written in Verse Which Illustrate the Condition of Religious and Political Feeling in England and the State of Society there during Two Centuries.* 2 vols. London: Chiswick Press, Printed For Private Circulation, 1875. Vol. 1.

———. *Remains of the Early Popular Poetry of England.* 4 vols. London, 1864–66. Vols. 3–4.

Henson, Hensley, ed. *Selected English Sermons: Sixteenth to Nineteenth Centuries.* London: Oxford University Press, 1939.

*Here begynneth the Rule of seynt Benet.* London, 1517.

*Here endeth Cocke Lorelles bote.* London, 1518.

Hogarde, Miles. *The Abuse of y<sup>e</sup> blessed sacrament of the aultare.* Quoted in Robert Crowley. *The Confutation of the mishapen Aunswer to the misnamed, wicked Ballade, called the Abuse of y<sup>e</sup> blessed sacrament of the aultare. Wherin, thou haste (gentele Reader) the ryghte vnderstandynge of al the places of scripture that Myles Hoggard, (wyth his learned counsail) hath wrested to make for the transubstanciacion of the bread and wyne.* London, 1548.

Holinshed, Raphael. *Chronicles of England, Scotland, and Ireland.* Ed. Henry Ellis. 6 vols. London: J. Johnson, F. C. and J. Rivington, T. Payne et al., 1808. Vol. 4.

House, Seymour Baker, ed. "An Unknown Tudor Propaganda Poem." *Notes and Queries* ns 39 (1992): 282–285.

Hughes, Philip, and James F. Larkin, eds. *Tudor Royal Proclamations.* Vol. 1. New Haven: Yale University Press, 1964–69. 3 vols.

*The Image of Ypocresye.* Lansdowne ms. 794. British Library, London.

Jonas, Justus. *Catechismus pro pueris et juventute* Wittenberg, 1539.

Ketley, Joseph, ed. *The Two Liturgies, A.D. 1549, and A.D. 1552: With Other Documents Set Forth by Authority in the Reign of King Edward VI.* Cambridge: Cambridge University Press, 1844.

King, John N., ed. "Luke Shepherd's *John Bon and Mast Person.*" *ANQ: A Quarterly Journal of Short Articles, Notes, and Reviews* ns 5 (1992): 87–91.

Kirchmeyer, Thomas [Thomas Naogeorgus]. *Tragoedia Nova Pammachius. Thomas Naogeorg Sämtliche Werke.* Ed. Hans-Gert Roloff. 4 vols. Berlin: Walter De Gruyter, 1975. Vol. 1.

Latimer, Hugh. *A notable Sermon of yͤ reuerende father Maister Hughe Latemer, whiche he preached in yͤ Shrouds at paules churche in London, on the .xviii. daye of Ianuary.* London, 1548.

———. *Sermons and Remains.* Ed. George Elwes Corrie. Cambridge: Cambridge University Press, 1845.

Maunsell, Andrew. *The First Part of the Catalogue of English printed Bookes: Which concerneth such matters of Diuinitie, as haue bin either written in our owne Tongue, or translated out of anie other language: And haue bin published, to the glory of God, and edification of the Church of Christ in England.* London, 1595.

*Missa de Potatoribus.* Harley ms. 913. British Library, London.

More, Thomas. *The Apology. The Complete Works of St. Thomas More.* Ed. J. B. Trapp. New Haven: Yale University Press, 1963– . Vol. 9.

Myrc (Mirk), John. *Instructions for Parish Priests.* Ed. Edward Peacock. London: Trübner & Co., 1868.

Packer, J. I., and G. E. Duffield, eds. *The Work of Thomas Cranmer.* Appleford: Sutton Courtenay, 1965.

Pantolabus, Ponce [John Huntington]. *The genealogye of heresye.* Quoted in John Bale. *A mysterye of inyquyte contayned within the heretycall Genealogye of Ponce Pantolabus is here both dysclosed & confuted.* London, 1545.

Percy, Thomas. *Reliques of Ancient English Poetry Consisting of Old Heroic Ballads, Songs, and Other Pieces of Our Earlier Poets, together with Some Few of Later Date*. Ed. Henry B. Wheatley. 3 vols. London: Swan Sonnenschein, 1910.

Pilkington, James. *Aggeus and Abdias Prophetes, the one corrected, the other newly added, and both at large declared*. London, 1562.

Pollard, A. F., ed. *Tudor Tracts 1532–1588*. Westminster: Archibald, Constable and Co., 1903.

Punt, William. *A new Dialoge Called The Endightment agaynste mother Messe*. London, 1548.

Ritson, Joseph. *Bibliographia Poetica: A Catalogue of Engleish* [sic] *Poets, of the Twelfth, Thirteenth, Fourteenth, Fifteenth, and Sixteenth Centurys*, [sic] *with A Short Account of Their Works*. London: C. Roworth, 1802.

Robinson, Hastings, ed. *Original Letters Relative to the English Reformation, Written during the Reigns of King Henry VIII., King Edward VI., and Queen Mary: Chiefly from the Archives of Zurich*. 2 pts. Cambridge: The University Press, 1846–47.

*Saint Bonadventura Speculum vite Christi*. London, 1490.

Selwyn, D. G., ed. *A Catechism set forth by Thomas Cranmer*. Appleford: Sutton Courtenay Press, 1978.

Shepherd, Luke. *Antipus*. London, 1548.

_____. *Cauteles preseruatory concerning the preseruation of the Gods which are kept in the pixe*. London, 1548.

_____. *The comparison betwene the Antipus and the Antigraphe or answere thereunto, with. An apologie or defence of the same Antipus. And reprehence of the Antigraphe*. London, 1548.

_____. *Doctour doubble ale*. London, 1548.

_____. *Iohn Bon and Mast person*. London, 1548.

_____. *Pathose, or an inward passion of the pope for the losse of hys daughter the Masse*. London, 1548.

_____. *Phylogamus*. London, 1548.

_____. *A pore helpe*. London, 1548.

_____. *The vpcheringe of the messe*. London, 1548.

Shipp, G. P., ed. *P. Terenti Afri: Andria*. Oxford: Oxford University Press, 1960.

Skelton, John. *The Complete English Poems*. Ed. John Scattergood. Harmondsworth: Penguin, 1983.

———. *The Poetical Works of John Skelton*. Ed. Alexander Dyce. 2 vols. London: Thomas Rodd, 1843, with addenda 1844; New York: AMS, 1965.

Smith, John Hazel, ed. *Two Latin Comedies by John Foxe the Martyrologist*. Ithaca: Cornell University Press, 1973.

Smith, Richard. *A brief treatyse settynge forth diuers truthes necessary both to be beleued of chrysten people, & kepte also, whiche are not expressed in the scripture* [sic] *but left to y' church by the apostles tradition*. London, 1547.

———. *A Godly and Faythfull Retractation made and published at Paules crosse in London, the yeare of oure Lorde God 1547 the 15 daye of May, by Mayster Richard Smyth Doctor of diuinitye, and reader of the Kynges Maiestyes lecture in Oxford. Reuokyng therin certeyn Errors and faultes by hym committyd in some of hys bookes*. London, 1547.

Spurgeon, Dickie Allen. "An Edition of Three Tudor Dialogues." Ph. D. Diss., University of Illinois, 1967.

———. *Three Tudor Dialogues*. New York: Scholars' Facsimiles & Reprints, 1978.

Strype, John. *Ecclesiastical Memorials, Relating Chiefly to Religion, and the Reformation of It, and the Emergencies of the Church of England, Under King Henry VIII. King Edward VI. and Queen Mary I.* 3 vols. Oxford: The Clarendon Press, 1822.

———. *Memorials of the Most Reverend Father in God Thomas Cranmer*. Ed. Philip Edward Barnes. 2 vols. London, 1853.

Tanner, Thomas. *Bibliotheca Britannico-Hibernica*. Ed. David Wilkins. London: Bowyer, 1748.

Turner, William. *The huntyng & fyndyng out of the Romishe fox whiche more then seuen yeares hath bene hyd among the bisshoppes of Englong after that the Kynges Hyghnes had commanded hym to be dryuen out of hys realme*. London, 1543.

———. *Libellus de Re Herbaria Novvs, in quo herbarum aliquot nomina greca, latina, & Anglica habes, vna cum nominibus officinarum, in gratiam studiose iuuentutis nunc primum in lucem æditus*. London, 1538.

———. *A new Herball, wherin are conteyned the names of Herbes in Greke, Latin, Englysh, Duch Frenche, and in the Potecaries and Herbaries Latin, with the properties degrees and naturall places of the same.* London, 1551.

_____. *The Rescvynge of The Romishe Fox Othervvyse called the examination of the hunter deuised by steuen gardiner.* London, 1545.

Underhill, Edward. "Autobiographical Anecdotes." *Narratives of the Days of the Reformation, Chiefly from the Manuscripts of John Foxe the Martyrologist.* Ed. John Gough Nichols. London, 1859.

Viret, Peter. *The Cavteles, Canon, and Most Blashphemous, abhominable, and monstrous Popish Masse.* London, 1584.

Woudhuysen, H. R., ed. *The Penguin Book of Renaissance Verse, 1509–1659.* Introd. David Norbrook. Harmondsworth: Penguin, 1992.

Wright, Thomas, and James Orchard Halliwell, eds., *Reliquiae Antiquae. Scraps from Ancient Manuscripts Illustrating Chiefly Early English Literature and the English Language* Vol. 2. London: William Pickering, 1841–43. 2 vols.

*The wyll of the Deuyll. And last Testament.* London, 1548.

## Secondary Sources

Aston, Margaret. *England's Iconoclasts: Laws against Images.* Oxford: Clarendon Press, 1988.

Bayle, Pierre. *The Dictionary Historical and Critical of Mr Peter [Pierre] Bayle.* Ed. Des Maizeaux. 2nd ed. 5 vols. London: printed for J. J. and P. Knapton; D. Midwinter, J. Brotherton et al., 1734–38.

Berger, Thomas L., and William C. Bradford, eds. *An Index of Characters in English Printed Drama to the Restoration.* Colorado: Microcard Editions Books, 1975.

Bietenholz, Peter G., ed. *Contemporaries of Erasmus.* 3 vols. Toronto: University of Toronto Press, 1985–87.

Bindoff, S. T. *The House of Commons: 1509–1558.* 3 vols. London: Secker & Warburg, 1982. Vol. 3.

Brigden, Susan. *London and the Reformation.* Oxford: Clarendon Press, 1989.

Burnet, Gilbert. *The History of the Reformation of the Church of England.* 3 vols. 4th ed. London, 1715.

Cardwell, Edward. *Documentary Annals of the Reformed Church of England; being a Collection of Injunctions, Declarations, Orders, Articles of Inquiry,*

*&c. from 1546–1716.* 2 vols. Oxford: The University Press, 1844; New Jersey: Gregg, 1966.

*Chambers Biographical Dictionary.* 2 vols. Edinburgh: W. & R. Chambers Ltd., 1974.

Dasent, John Roche, ed. *Acts of the Privy Council of England.* 4 vols. London: Eyre and Spottiswoode, 1890. Vol. 1.

Devereux, Janice. "An Addition to Luke Shepherd's Canon." *Notes and Queries* n.s. 42 (1995): 279–281.

_____. "Dromo: A Minor Dramatic Character Adopted for Protestant Propaganda." *Notes and Queries* n.s. 44 (1997): 27–29.

_____. "The Identity of the Curate's Friend in Luke Shepherd's *Doctour doubble ale.*" *Notes and Queries* n.s. 45 (1998): 295–296.

_____. "The Missing Pages of Luke Shepherd's *Pathose*: A Hypothesis." *Notes and Queries* n.s. 42 (1995): 281–283.

Dixon, Richard Watson. *History of the Church of England from the Abolition of the Roman Jurisdiction.* 6 vols. London, 1878–1902; Westmead: Gregg International, 1970. Vol. 2.

Duff, E. Gordon. *The English Provincial Printers, Stationers and Bookbinders to 1557.* Cambridge: Cambridge University Press, 1912.

Duffy, Eamon. *The Stripping of the Altars: Traditional Religion in England c.1400–c.1580.* New Haven: Yale University Press, 1992.

Dugdale, William. *Monasticon Anglicanum: A History of the Abbies and Other Monasteries, Hospitals, Frieries,* [sic] *and Cathedral and Collegiate Churches.* Ed. John Caley, Henry Ellis, and Bulkeley Bandinel. 6 vols. London: printed for Joseph Harding; Harding and Lepard et al., 1830.

Dugmore, C. W. *The Mass and the English Reformers.* London: Macmillan, 1958.

Emden, A. B. *A Biographical Register of the University of Oxford A.D. 1501 to 1540.* Oxford: Clarendon Press, 1974.

Fox, Alistair G. *Politics and Literature in the Reigns of Henry VII and Henry VIII.* Oxford: Basil Blackwell, 1989.

Germann, Friedrich. *Luke Shepherd, ein Satirendichter der englischen Reformationszeit.* Augsburg: Theodor Lampart, 1911.

Haigh, Christopher. *English Reformations: Religion, Politics, and Society under the Tudors.* Oxford: Clarendon Press, 1993.

_____, ed. *The English Reformation Revised.* Cambridge: Cambridge University Press, 1987.

Hazlitt, William Carew, ed. *Faiths and Folklore: A Dictionary of National Beliefs, Superstitions and Popular Customs, Past and Current, with Their Classical and Foreign Analogues, Described and Illustrated.* 2 vols. London: Reeves and Turner, 1905.

Heath, Peter. *The English Parish Clergy on the Eve of the Reformation.* London: Routledge & Kegan Paul, 1969.

House, Seymour Baker. "Literature, Drama, and Politics." *The Reign of Henry VIII: Politics, Policy, and Piety.* Ed. Diarmaid MacCulloch. London: Macmillan, 1995.

Hughes, Philip. *The Reformation in England.* 3 vols. London: Hollis and Carter, 1953–54.

Jordan, W. K. *Edward VI: The Young King.* London: George Allen & Unwin, 1968.

King, John N. *English Reformation Literature: The Tudor Origins of the Protestant Tradition.* Princeton: Princeton University Press, 1982.

_____. "Freedom of the Press, Protestant Propaganda, and Protector Somerset." *The Huntington Library Quarterly* 40 (1976): 1–9.

_____. *Tudor Royal Iconography: Literature and Art in an Age of Religious Crisis.* Princeton: Princeton University Press, 1989.

Lack, David. *Robin Redbreast.* Oxford: Clarendon Press, 1950.

Legg, J. Wickham. "The Gift of the Papal Cap and Sword to Henry VII." *Archaeological Journal* 57 (1900): 183–203.

Lenthicum, M. Channing. "*A Pore Helpe* and Its Printers." *The Library* 4th ser. 9 (1929): 169–183.

MacCulloch, Diarmaid. *Thomas Cranmer: A Life.* New Haven: Yale University Press, 1996.

McKerrow, R. B., and F. S. Ferguson. *Title-page Borders used in England & Scotland, 1485–1640.* London: Oxford University Press, 1932.

Martin, J. *Religious Radicals in Tudor England.* London: Hambledon Press, 1989.

*New Catholic Encyclopedia.* 17 vols. New York: McGraw-Hill Book Company, 1967.

Oastler, C. L. *John Day, the Elizabethan Printer.* Oxford: Oxford Bibliographical Society, 1975.

Pollard, A. W., and G. R. Redgrave, eds. *A Short-Title Catalogue of Books Printed in England, Scotland, & Ireland and of English Books Printed*

*Abroad, 1475–1640.* 2nd ed. 3 vols. London: Bibliographical Society, 1976–91.

Redworth, Glyn. *In Defence of the Church Catholic: The Life of Stephen Gardiner.* Oxford: Basil Blackwell, 1990.

Richardson, David, ed. *Dictionary of Literary Biography.* 2nd ser. 136 vols. Columbia: Bruccoli Clark Layman, 1994. Vol. 136.

Rubin, Miri. *Corpus Christi: The Eucharist in Late Medieval Culture.* Cambridge: Cambridge University Press, 1991.

Scribner, R. W. *For The Sake of Simple Folk: Popular Propaganda for the German Reformation.* Cambridge: Cambridge University Press, 1981.

Shullenberger, William. "The Word of Reform and the Poetics of the Eucharist." *George Herbert Journal* 13 (1989): 19–36.

Stephen, Leslie, and Sidney Lee, eds. *The Dictionary of National Biography from the Earliest Times to 1900.* 21 vols. London: Smith Elder, 1908–9.

Tilley, Morris Palmer. *A Dictionary of the Proverbs in England in the Sixteenth and Seventeenth Centuries: A Collection of the Proverbs Found in English Literature and the Dictionaries of the Period.* Ann Arbor: University of Michigan Press, 1966.

Took, Patricia M. "Government and the Printing Trade, 1540–1560." Ph. D. Diss., University of London, 1978.

Vallance, Aymer. *Greater English Church Screens Being Great Roods, Screenwork & Rood-Lofts in Cathedral, Monastic & Collegiate Churches in England & Wales.* London: B. T. Batsford, 1947.

Warton, Thomas. *History of English Poetry.* 4 vols. London, 1774–90. Ed. René Wellek. New York: Johnson Reprint, 1968. Vol. 3.

Watt, Tessa. *Cheap Print and Popular Piety, 1550–1640.* Cambridge: Cambridge University Press, 1991.

Wheat, Cathleen Hayhurst. "Luke Shepherd's *Antipi Amicus.*" *Philological Quarterly* 30 (1951): 58–68.

Whitelock, D., M. Brett, and C. N. L. Brooke, eds. *Councils and Synods with Other Documents Relating to the English Church.* 2 vols. in 4. Oxford: Clarendon Press, 1964–81.

Whiting, B. J., and W. H. Whiting. *Proverbs, Sentences, and Proverbial Phrases from English Writings Mainly before 1500.* Cambridge: Belknap Press, 1968.

Wickham, Glynne, ed. *English Moral Interludes.* London: J. M. Dent & Sons, 1976.

# Renaissance English Text Society

## *Officers and Council*

*President*, Arthur F. Kinney, University of Massachusetts at Amherst
*Vice-President*, A. R. Braunmuller, University of California, Los Angeles
*Secretary*, Carolyn Kent, New York, N.Y.
*Treasurer*, Robert E. Bjork, Arizona Center for Medieval and Renaissance
  Studies
*Membership Secretary*, William Gentrup, Arizona Center for Medieval and
  Renaissance Studies
*Past President*, W. Speed Hill, Lehman College and The Graduate Center,
  City University of New York
*Past Publisher*, Mario A. Di Cesare, Fairview, North Carolina

*Susan Felch*, Calvin College
*Roy Catesby Flannagan*, University of South Carolina, Beaufort
*David Freeman*, Memorial University, Newfoundland
*Suzanne Gossett*, Loyola University of Chicago
*Elizabeth Hageman*, University of New Hampshire
*Margaret Hannay*, Siena College
*David Scott Kastan*, Columbia University
*John King*, Ohio State University
*Noel James Kinnamon*, Mars Hill College
*Arthur F. Marotti*, Wayne State University
*Steven May*, Georgetown College
*G. W. Pigman III*, California Institute of Technology
*Lois Dorais Potter*, University of Delaware
*Germaine Warkentin*, Victoria University in the University of Toronto
*George Walton Williams*, Duke University

## *Liaisons*

*Thomas L. Berger*, St. Lawrence University, The Malone Society
*Laetitia Yeandle*, Folger Shakespeare Library
*Mary L. Robertson*, Huntington Library

The Renaissance English Text Society was established to publish literary texts, chiefly nondramatic, of the period 1475–1660. Dues are $35.00 per annum ($25.00, graduate students; life membership is available at $500.00). Members receive the text published for each year of membership. The Society sponsors panels at such annual meetings as those of the Modern Language Association, the Renaissance Society of America, and the Medieval Congress at Kalamazoo.

General inquiries and proposals for editions should be addressed to the president, Arthur Kinney, Massachusetts Center for Renaissance Studies, PO Box 2300, Amherst, Mass., 01004, USA. Inquiries about membership should be addressed to William Gentrup, Membership Secretary, Arizona Center for Medieval and Renaissance Studies, Arizona State University, Box 872301, Tempe, Ariz., 85287-2301.

Copies of volumes X–XII may be purchased from Associated University Presses, 440 Forsgate Drive, Cranbury, N.J., 08512. Members may order copies of earlier volumes still in print or of later volumes from XIII, at special member prices, from the Treasurer.

FIRST SERIES

VOL. I. *Merie Tales of the Mad Men of Gotam* by A. B., edited by Stanley J. Kahrl, and *The History of Tom Thumbe* by R. I., edited by Curt F. Buhler, 1965. (o.p.)

VOL. II. Thomas Watson's Latin *Amyntas*, edited by Walter F. Staton, Jr., and Abraham Fraunce's translation *The Lamentations of Amyntas*, edited by Franklin M. Dickey, 1967.

# RENAISSANCE ENGLISH TEXT SOCIETY

# RENAISSANCE ENGLISH TEXT SOCIETY